Entrepreneur
MAGAZINE'S

ULTIMATE

GUIDE TO

SEARCH ENGINE

OPTIMIZATION

Drive Traffic, Boost Conversion Rates, M...

JON ROGNERUD

EP
Entrepreneur
Press

Publisher: Jere Calmes
Cover Design: Beth Hansen-Winter
Production and Editorial Services: CWL Publishing Enterprises, Inc., Madison, Wisconsin,
www.cwlpub.com

This publication is designed to provide accurate and authoritative information in regard to the subject matter covered. It is sold with the understanding that the publisher is not engaged in rendering
legal, accounting, or other professional services. If legal advice or other expert assistance is
required, the services of a competent professional person should be sought.

—From a Declaration of Principles jointly adopted by a
Committee of the American Bar Association and
a Committee of Publishers and Associations

ISBN 978-1-59918-169-1

Library of Congress Cataloging-in-Publication Data

Rognerud, Jon.
  Ultimate guide to search engine optimization / by Jon Rognerud.
    p. cm. -- (Ultimate guide)
  Includes bibliographical references and index.
  ISBN-13: 978-1-59918-169-1 (alk. paper)
   1. Internet marketing. 2. Internet advertising. 3. Search engines. 4. Web sites—Design. I. Title.
  HF5415.1265.R64 2008
  658.8'72—dc22

                                                                    2007050562

12 11 10 09 08   10 9 8 7 6 5 4 3 2 1

Contents

Gosh! Another Book about SEO

When I was approached about writing a book on a topic like search engine optimization (SEO), I got really amped up. While I was excited at the prospect of writing my first book, I was also enthusiastic about the opportunity to pass on what I have learned thus far. Writing a book would allow me to share with an expanded audience what I've seen in the last 20 years in technology, business, search, and internet marketing, including software architecture, process, application and web design, development, and overall technology solutions and deployments. And, I got really fired up when I started thinking about the umber of opportunities that exist for generating business and income online using search and other online marketing techniques to build it out.

The "build out" goes way beyond the book and will be referenced via an online lifetime membership. The membership site will enable you to watch my own progress, but also that of others as the community grows. It's all about crushing down the walls and black-box secrets of search engine optimization and learning new tools, processes, and techniques to help you drive traffic to your site and convert visitors to customers.

I came to this country over 20 years ago as a recent graduate in business and computers. From that time until now, I've learned a fair share of things that work and don't work in business. The United States provided fertile ground for entrepreneurial ideas and activities. I began developing my business, and I can tell you I've really had such a ride—and it just keeps going and going.

I dedicate this book to others who want to make money online. I started online in 1996, but it really wasn't until 2003 when I began working at Overture Services that I realized the power of all the knowledge and tools and personal friends and networks and how they could help me. Friends asked me, "Is it possible to make money online?" or "How fast can you get rich on the Internet?" or "I don't think I can do it—it's too technical." I wanted to find a way to break answer these questions for myself, but I also felt a deep and growing need to teach and develop programs to show others how they could do it as well. My approaches and results from the many programs I tested provide the foundation for this book. I tell my friends and others, and most all to internet newbies who want to make money online, that it's hard work to create and launch your own business. And, depending on the market niche you're in, it may require more than your full-time attention. This is not just a 40-hour work week undertaking.

The power of the "automation" that an auto-responder e-mail list-building system along with selling "information products" (ebooks, DVDs, etc.) can bring is beyond exciting. However, many get caught up in the simplicity and promises of quick wealth, and buy courses from people who may con you into thinking it's easy and that by buying their ebook or DVD, you can become an "insider." This is not true. As with anything in life, you need to spend time and energy to succeed. Doing something you are passionate and knowledgeable about helps (a lot!)—and so does trying to make a difference.

It's fine to start out with pushing other people's products as an affiliate marketer, for example, but you need to create your own products and differentiation to take it to the mountain tops. In my business, we created a blueprint service that uses tools found in this book, plus some of my own designs and technology, and we now sell this for anywhere from $2,500 to $3,500 one-time. Imagine two years ago, I would create and sell paper forms of these products for only $500. However, the technology and value of these products are significant. And it's a living product and service for companies that choose a full-featured search engine management campaign. Some say another business model might offer it for free (to up-sell other services along the way for much bigger gains)—or, sell it for $6,000 to $8,000 and promise more beyond that. I believe in more value upfront and presenting opportunities to the "lifetime visitor" to grow a sustainable business.

Reading the materials in the book will help you with SEO and teach you how to drive traffic to your site and convert that traffic to sales. It is search marketing, internet marketing, and the "business of …"—teaching you the fundamentals for not only business planning, but execution.

Did you know that many who sell information products online offer guarantee periods ("90-day guarantee and a 100% refund if not satisfied"). This seems to make it an irresistible offer for potential customers—knowing that more than half of them will never pick up the book or ever complete the exercises? Health and fitness clubs are an example of this business model. The health clubs know that many will pay for the membership, but only a small percentage of buyers will ever show up. The same is true of internet marketing.

I don't like that approach (even though it makes money for the internet marketer) since it's aimed more at exploiting potential customers than helping them. I wrote this book and the supportive member site so you could learn and do. I also created a place where you can keep coming back and learn from other like-minded people. There are many people who have tried to build internet businesses and failed but then found that the successful methods were more available than they thought. I hope to help you avoid the failure cycle by providing a continuous learning community that will offer support to help you execute your plan and achieve success.

You will see references to Janet and Bob in this book—people (names have been changed) I have met and dealt with in the field of search marketing. Their thoughts, questions, and issues are raised as you read. Perhaps you will identify with them.

Another thing that has worked well for many before me—and a model I have adapted is—"help others get what they want, and you will have *anything* you want." This model was adapted from a Zig Ziglar quote, "You can have everything in life that you want if you will just help enough other people get what they want." It makes a world of sense—and you must know that I'm here to help you. Please send information directly to me at memyselfandi@jonrognerud.com, and I will answer your questions. And I look forward to learning from you as well.

I believe that succeeding on the web is about attitude, the right attitude, and not whining about where you are failing. Get the information, apply it, and you are 99 percent ahead. Focus on the things you are doing right, believe in yourself, read voraciously, and have fun—it will happen for you too. I got a book deal! On that fateful day in 1996 when I first started in this business, I could never have anticipated the wonderful, fulfilling journey that laid ahead. What's ahead for you? Whatever it is, enjoy the adventure on the road to your own personal best.

This book will cover SEO "expanded," which includes all things related to bringing business online, and effectively using search engine optimization tactics. You will see references to Web 2.0, PPC, paid advertising, paid links, landing page conversions, and much, much more. It's all inclusive to the SEO term—the web optimized!

Lastly, keep this in mind. It's a simple, but effective trick. When dealing with the search engines, write for users first, search engines second. What's good for a user is good for search engines. You'll easily create stickiness and bookmarking, and visitors will tell their friends. If you do that, you're well on your way. Ask someone else—do they think your site or page has value. It's amazing how this simple secret can work in your favor. Also, if you pretend you are a competitor, would you still say it provides good value?

You'll find that chapters reference areas of the online membership portal. This area is always under development, and you can access it at www.jonrognerud.com/amember.

The accompanying CD will have more reading materials, free software (and some you may have to pay for), PDF files, and last minute details not available not available as the book was completed. Have fun, and remember: "life is short, make good use of it!"

—Jon Rognerud
The World's #1 SEO Business Expert

ACKNOWLEDGEMENTS

This book is dedicated to Eilif (Dad) and Patricia (Mum) for bringing me into this wondrous world and my wife, Ana, for being the most loving, patient, and strongest person I've ever known. When I met her, my search (no pun intended) stopped. She brought me three incredible offspring: Victoria Maria and twin brothers Jon-Phillip and Jon-Anthony. I thank God every day for sharing them with me. Of course, without my brothers Nils and Per and my younger sister Anne-Karin, life would not have meant or been the same.

People I Want to Thank

The following were involved in getting the content from my business life to you: Brad Fallon, Bruce Clay, Karen Swim, Jerry Glynn, Brad Kuhlin, Bob Clancy, Sean Allen, Scott Sullivan, Matt Wilson, Lars Rabbe, Mike Filsaime, *Entrepreneur* Magazine, Jere Calmes, Dave Pomijie, Jack Silver, Kevin McCann, Vitor Passos, Dave Nash, Lance Rosenzweig, Steve Kowalski, Klas Back, Rich Jerk, Jill Whalen, Joel Comm, Abby Hossein, Jim Rohn, Perry Marshall, Brian Russell, Leslie Rhode, Matt Cutts, AM Khan, Dan Thies, Aaron Wall, Danny Sullivan, Vanessa Fox, Tim Phillips and many more. Thank you all.

CHAPTER 1

The History of Search

In the beginning there was cyberspace and it was good. It was a land of infinite possibility–a land of untouched beauty, a brave new frontier. The first cyber-settlers beyond the scientific community were appropriately named "Early Adopters." This tribe of netizens with a thirst for adventure set sail in this new land of connectivity to explore its vast frontier. The Early Adopters explored the new land and came home to tell others about the land of plenty. Soon the land gave rise to communication systems allowing people across the vast universe of cyberspace to talk with each other and share ideas.

The land grew and prospered. Businesses were created and some of the early adopters seized the early opportunities and became millionaires. But soon the land became overrun with information and cyberspace became the land of the lost. There was information in every niche but there was no logical way to find what was needed. From the mass of confusion and multiple languages arose The Search Engine. The

Search Engine organized the bits and bytes of information and order was once again restored to the universe known as the internet.

THE SEARCH ENGINE

In reality the search engine technology concept has been around since 1945. MIT professor Vannevar Bush set forth the concept of computers as a flexible storage and retrieval system. Bush's essay "As We May Think" (*Atlantic Monthly,* July 1945) described his ideas on hypertext and memory. He wrote, "A record, if it is to be useful to science, must be continuously extended, it must be stored, and above all it must be consulted."

Years later, Gerard Salton, professor of computer science at Cornell University, led the teams at Harvard and Cornell that developed the information retrieval system, Salton's Magic Automatic Retriever of Text (SMART). Salton, considered the father of modern-day search, authored a book, *A Theory of Indexing* (Society for Industrial Mathematics, 1987), which offers definitive explanations of many of the tests on which search continues to be based.

The first search engine was introduced in 1993 by creator Matthew Gray. Aptly named the World Wide Web Wanderer, it evolved from counting active web servers to capturing active URLs. According to Wikipedia (http://en.wikipedia.org/wiki/World_Wide_Web_Wanderer) it was initially deployed to measure the size of the world wide web. Later in 1993, it was used to generate an index called the "Wandex," which effectively provided the first search engine on the web. It should come as no surprise that Matthew Gray joined the Google team as a software engineer in 2007.

Search engine technology has grown significantly since the days of the Wanderer. With each addition—Excite, LookSmart, Ask Jeeves, Yahoo!—an increasingly competitive market drove improvements in automated search algorithms.

The Google Influence

A discussion of search would not be complete without Google. Google dominates the search market. In many statistical analyses of the market, Google is individually categorized, as no other engine comes close to its market share. Today, the "Big Four" in search (Google, Microsoft, Ask, Yahoo!) dominate 90 percent of the search market.

In 1998 when Google founders Larry Page and Sergey Brin were searching for buyers for their new search technology, one

> ## ▼ Small Goal, Big Results
>
> Our main goal is to improve the quality of web search engines," wrote Sergey Brin and Lawrence Page in the paper that first presented Google. (*The Anatomy of a Large Scale Hypertextual Search Engine*)

portal CEO told them, "As long as we're 80 percent as good as our competitors, that's good enough. Our users don't really care about search."

Either the CEO was wrong or Page and Brin foresaw a need that had not yet manifested in the market. Google officially opened its door in September 1998, and while still in beta, they were answering 10,000 search queries each day. In fact, by the time the beta label came off in September 1999, Google had been named one of the Top 100 Web Sites and Search Engines for 1998 by *PC Magazine*. The accolades continued, and today Google employs more than 10,000 people around the globe and is one of the five most popular sites on the internet. According to comScore, a company that "measures the digital world," in May 2007 Google's web sites had 50.7 percent of the United States search market (comScore, qSearch Analysis, May 2007). The report also noted that Americans conducted 7.6 billion searches in May 2007. Google led in search queries with 3.9 billion. Yahoo! followed with 2.0 billion, Microsoft web sites had 782 million searches, and Ask Network and Time Warner each had 348 million during the month. With 112 international domains and a global audience, Google will certainly continue to be a major influence in search technology.

Search and Marketing

Today 70 percent of adults use the internet.[1] Internet users no longer search, they "Google" even when they "Yahoo." Yet users don't really understand the technology that drives search and neither do most advertisers.

As search technology evolved, savvy marketers sought ways to improve their search engine position. After all, users typically only view the first page of returned results, viewing those as most relevant. If

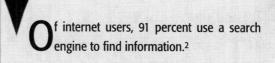

Of internet users, 91 percent use a search engine to find information.[2]

your site is on page two or beyond of returned results, chances are consumers will never find your product or service. Rather than scroll through pages of returned results, if the first page doesn't deliver what they were looking for, users refine their search phrase and search again.

In 2006 ZDNet reporting on a Yahoo! Analyst presentation (*Yahoo!: Searches More Sophisticated and Specific*, Bogatin, Donna, May 2006) indicated that the average search query length was 1.2 words in 1998, 2.5 words in 2004, and in 2006, 3.3 words.

The battle to win the top ten forced search companies and marketers to come

TIP: Being in the first five listings on page one of search engines is considered the hot zone for traffic. Most searchers will click in this area, considered to be the most relevant and trusted of all results.

up with innovative ways to satisfy an insatiable market. Pay per click (PPC) advertising was created as a way to monetize search engines. While search was becoming an integral part of the internet experience, it wasn't generating revenues for the search engine. Instead, it was considered cool technology, but it was difficult to figure how to make money from it. PPC helped the search engines become revenue powerhouses and became a way for companies to buy their way into high-visibility spots. Google, as of this writing, reported gross earnings (Q3, 2007) of $6.3 billion and recently traded over the $700 per share mark.

PPC is also an advancement credited to a start-up company. It was introduced by Jeffrey Brewer of GoTo.com (which later became Overture and now is part of Yahoo!). Brewer presented a PPC search engine proof-of-concept to the TED8 conference in February 1998. According to the investment firm Piper Jaffray, in 2006, it was estimated that the United States spent more than $14 billion on paid search with an expected growth rate of 37 percent each year.

Today we have keyword and content PPC advertising. We are standing at the dawn of "universal search," which will provide integrated search results from all content sources including web sites, video and news—all on one page.

Personalized search is certain to become more intelligent, especially in light of the dynamics of the new market where all media (music, video, television, news) seem to intersect online. Where personalized search was once limited to an integration of your search history and preferences, a new wave of personalized search is likely to be more intelligent, combining some form of universal search into personalized options.

▼ Technological Shift

"The idea that the world is in transition is not new, but in 2007 we can see much more clearly the dimensions of change in technology, society, geopolitics and economics, and the consequences for business." Ged Davis, managing director and head of the Centre for Strategic Insight at the World Economic Forum.

Search technology and search marketing continue to evolve. As new technologies emerge, search experts seek ways to incorporate those elements into a comprehensive user experience. And as competition for those users increases, search marketers continue to innovate ways to dominate the race for space.

Yet with all the advancements and competition, the majority of web site owners remain clueless about search engine technology, optimization, and marketing! They put up a cyber-storefront and have no idea how to tell people they exist.

It's not surprising that internet users and businesses are confused. The industry itself cannot agree on terms, often using *SEO*, *SEM*, or just *search marketing* interchangeably.

Some would argue the technical differences while consumers who fancy themselves experts simply refer to this art/science as SEO/SEM in an attempt to demonstrate their above-average knowledge of technology.

An entire industry has been created around search optimization and search marketing, and with good reason—the effort is well worth the payback. The internet is a key step in the buying process for consumers. In a survey that asked users about their internet activities, 78 percent responded that they use the internet to research a product or service before buying it, and 70 percent use the internet to buy a product. According to Marketing Sherpa, marketers who optimize their web sites using inhouse staff see a 38 percent jump in overall traffic. Marketers who hire outside experts experience a 110 percent jump in site traffic.[3]

THE IMPORTANCE OF SEO AND SEM

If you have a web presence it's worth the effort to learn and implement SEO techniques. Failing to invest time and effort in SEO is a bit like throwing a party, but rather than send invitations, you cross your fingers and hope that people will hear about it and decide to come!

Janet spent six months having her new web site designed for an online coaching service. She spent $20,000 on web design, custom photos, web hosting, and copywriting. Her plan was to offer professional coaching services via telephone and the web but also sell her books and CDs on the site. When she first started she thought the web site would be done in a couple of weeks, but was increasingly frustrated by the delays and amount of money she had to spend to get things right. Finally, Janet's new web site launched. She e-mailed everyone in her address book. Many of her friends and colleagues commented on the beauty of the site. One month later, Janet had not processed a single order!

Throughout the book we'll take the journey with Janet as she works to drive traffic to her site.

Janet's story is a perfect example of what happens to many web site owners, which is why throughout the book we'll follow her search journey. We tend to make the web more complicated than necessary. Whether online or offline, without marketing, people won't know about your product or service. Search marketing employs different technology and tools but at the center of it all is good old-fashioned marketing.

Last month, I visited a neighborhood

▼ Do You Believe?

Marketing begins with a belief in your own product or service. If you have something great to offer—tell people! You may gain a few customers who happen on your site, but accidental marketing only leads to accidental profits.

pizza place. The pizzeria is in a strip mall with a nail salon, surf shop, and dry cleaners. My first visit was a delight. The restaurant was decorated to look like New York, complete with the Brooklyn Bridge extending over the ceiling. Every wall had black and white prints of old New York and enough memorabilia on the walls and ceiling to keep you occupied for hours. The service and food were excellent. The place had been open for several months, but I never knew it existed. By contrast a restaurant across the street had remodeled, put up new signage, and advertised in the local paper. The food was okay but not spectacular, but the lot was filled from opening to closing.

The pizzeria offered great atmosphere and excellent service and food, but it had fewer customers because no one knew it was there. Are you making the same mistake with your web site?

Janet had talked with three web design firms before making her decision. She reviewed their portfolios and met with the firms by phone, going over a list of questions she had prepared. She asked about cost, timelines, design concepts, and service. She even asked specific questions about CSS, HTML, and Flash animation. Janet believed she had done her due diligence with the web site designers. Her selection was a well-regarded firm that had done work for many top corporations. The design firm's typical client was a high-end corporate firm with brick and mortar offices or stores. These clients didn't use their web sites for lead generation but to serve existing customers. Janet didn't ask a single question about site design as it relates to marketing. In fact, she didn't have a marketing plan, believing that "if you build it they will come."

A successful SEM strategy begins with a successful marketing strategy. Technology is a tool, not a replacement for a marketing strategy. The basic principles of marketing apply to both online and offline efforts. While there may be specific tactics that differ with the marketing channel, the underlying principles of the marketing discipline don't change.

The first component critical to success is to have a plan! Part of the planning phase is researching the competitive landscape, your existing market, and your target market. Once you've identified your strengths, weaknesses, opportunities, and threats (known as a SWOT analysis) and know your target, you can develop a well-thought-out plan.

Knowing your target enables you to tailor your plan to capture your desired market. Your marketing message should address the needs and preferences of your target market. All too often SEM efforts fail because the message was targeted at "everyone." You can hire the best copywriters, web designers, and SEM firms but their efforts will be in vain if you're not clear about whom you want to reach. SEM is only as good as the plan that drives it!

WHERE WE ARE TODAY

Now that we understand the importance of SEM, what are our options? Online advertising has come a long way from banner and pop-up advertising. As search technology improved, consumers used search engines to find products and services. This, in turn, led to search engine listings driving significant volumes of targeted traffic to web sites. In response, Search Engine Optimization became a bona fide marketing strategy. This is not to say that SEO should replace all other efforts, but it should be integrated into a comprehensive marketing strategy. The success of page ranking and driving site traffic is still largely dependent on targeted messaging, and that should be consistent across all media.

Search Engine Results Page (SERP) listings have become the new battleground for domination. Reminiscent of traditional Yellow Pages®, businesses seek to be in the top listings. The answer lies in a combination of optimization and marketing. We discuss the specifics later in the book.

Bob is a webmaster and site designer and has been running his own business for 15 years, initially offering graphic design. At the nexus of the online movement he began offering services to internet startups and later moved into web design, hosting, and maintenance. His business has been solid and he has many long-term clients. However, in the past two years he has seen a slowdown in growth and the loss of a few long-term clients. His site designs are top-notch and clients appreciate the responsive service, but Bob isn't an expert in driving site traffic. Bob has decided to take some time to become more proficient at offering his customers full service. In the past he couldn't seem to find the time, but it has now become a business necessity. Bob is tech-savvy but even he needs help with SEO and SEM. Follow Bob's journey throughout the book.

There are many ways to take advantage of search traffic, both direct and indirect. For example, you may choose to advertise on a high-ranking site. This option is similar to traditional advertising. In traditional advertising you would place an ad in a publication that's read by your target audience. The publication could be a magazine, newspaper, trade journal, or even a newsletter, but your goal is to meet your audience where they gather. In this same way, you would choose an online site that matches you to your audience. Not all sites offer advertising opportunities, but for those that do, they will provide you with a media kit that details their demographics and success rates.

The indirect method allows you to catch a ride on someone else's traffic. It isn't exclusive and can be used in conjunction with direct SEM. AdSense, which is a Google program, is another indirect method. You're paying to have your ad run on contextually comparable sites. Your ad runs on a site that targets your audience, providing you visibility via another site's traffic. Later in the book we'll examine in greater detail some strategies to drive traffic.

TRENDS AND THE MARKETPLACE

It's an exciting time in search! As the internet has become an accepted standard, big business and traditional media are seeking ways to keep pace with their market. The increased competition has created many innovations that mirror the way we live.

Social Search

Social search is a relatively new term although the concept has existed since the early 1990s. Social search is powered by human judgment rather than computer-matched results. This taps into the very old but once again very hot trend of "viral marketing," or word-of-mouth marketing. In 1990 the first "social" guide was created by Tim Berners-Lee, who created a page with links to his favorite sites (to date it's still online). Many people relied on these types of pages to find things on the internet in the pre-search-engine days. Yahoo! was one of the first to have a directory of web sites. Those sites were created not by computers but a real live team of human editors who surfed the web and then wrote descriptions of the web sites. Many other directory sites were created by people, including The Open Directory Project (DMOZ) and the Librarians' Index of the Internet.

The social search movement's latest evolution can be traced to social networking. As social sites such as MySpace, Facebook, and LinkedIn have revolutionized the web, we realized that in spite of our tech-savvy society we still like communicating with people! This "revelation" caused yet another evolution in which people became a key element in web marketing. The new buzzwords were *viral marketing, user-generated content,* and *folksonomy* (sites are collaboratively categorized using freely chosen keywords, referred to as *tags*).

In the new era of social networking, people vote for, or tag, sites, articles, blogs, or other web content. For example, you may be reading a *USA Today* news article online and

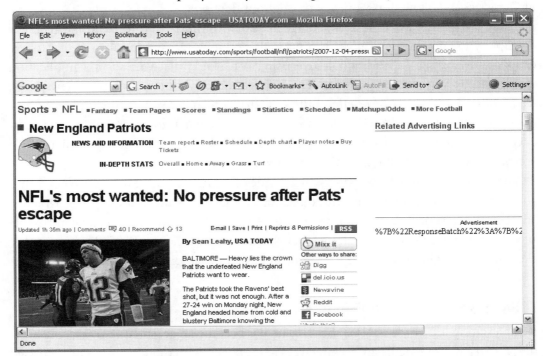

Figure 1-1. Page with Tags—Digg, del.icio.us, Newsvine, Reddit, Facebook

at the bottom you'll see items such as Digg It, Reddit, and del.icio.us. Using these tools you are tagging, or recommending, the article to other web visitors. You can digg, sphinn, blinklist, and more to your heart's content.

The tags concept is not new. Meta tags were standard in 1996 and were used to describe web pages and what the search engines thought that they were about. As with all good things, spammers got into it and started tweaking. It became a disaster. As we'll see in the world of search, when something is overused or overdone, the search engines catch on and simply change the rules. Search engines work hard to keep the competitive landscape fair, and webmasters are busy trying to compete. Overuse diminished the importance of meta tags. They were once a key consideration but today they're largely ignored.

While many debate social search, the trend toward personalized search results continues. Google is adding new personalization to the search results, and it's an important element to look at for optimization techniques. Personalization is increasing in popularity and usefulness.

Why now? Algorithms have reached a plateau, and at the end of the day, humans are still better than computers. A new generation of web users is doing things that are more dynamic than any computer. Leveraging the work of volunteers, there's an infusion of talent to make content powered by people. An example of this is Wikipedia and other wikis, which are user-generated content.

What are these services? I've mentioned a few, but social search is a broad category that includes:

- Shared bookmarks and web pages: del.icio.us, shadows, MyWeb (Yahoo!), Furl, Diigo
- Tag engines, blogs, and RSS: blog content and seed content, Technorati, Bloglines
- Collaborative directories (volunteers): ODP, Prefound, Zimbio, Wikipedia
- Personalized vertical search: Google custom search engine (www.google.com/coop/cse), Eurekster, Rollyo (roll your own search engine)
- Social Q&A sites: Yahoo! Answers, Answerbag
- Collaborative harvesters: Digg, Netscape, Reddit, popurls (aggregator)

Added to all of this you have a hybrid of computer algorithm and human content. Examples of these hybrid social sites are:

- Craigslist
- Judy's Book
- Insider Pages
- Yelp

The social sites like those listed above focus on local events and services, relying on the user community for fresh content. These sites are not only a source of social interaction but can be another opportunity for traffic, which has attracted a lot of interest and opportunity for search marketers. All social search shares the element of human involvement. People contribute to the content, drive content, or share content.

Social search is not without its challenges. Unlike algorithmic search engines, social search can't keep up with the sheer volume of information. Additionally, while traditional search has uniformity built in, social search does not. With social search there's no controlled language or standard, so tags can be inappropriately applied. Reliance on people also opens social search to human laziness, misinformation, and abuse. Spammers or those engaging in unethical SEO (black hat SEO) manipulate and abuse social search to their advantage. For example, a Wikipedia entry for presidential candidate Senator Barack Obama contained nude photos of African Americans. The photos were removed two minutes later by a Wikipedia editor. As Wikipedia depends on users, people can spin information to suit their perspective or personal agenda.

The solution may lie in a combination of algorithms and people-mediated search. A good example of this is Yahoo! Answers. Questions are posted and answered by real people but the categorization and management of the data are handled by algorithms.

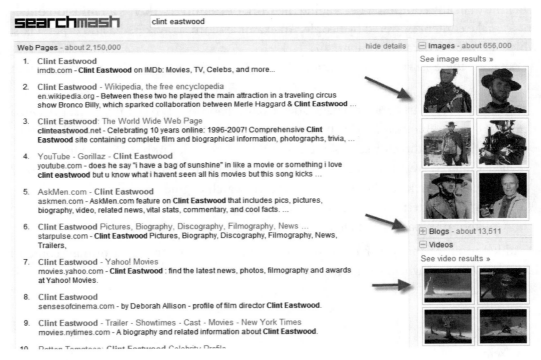

Figure 1-2. Clint Eastwood Universal Search

Figure 1-3. Clint Eastwood Alpha Yahoo!

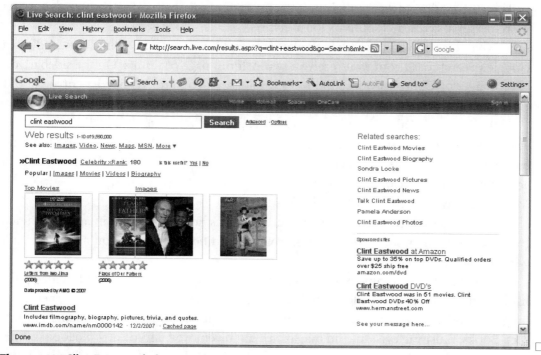

Figure 1-4. Clint Eastwood Live Search

Universal Search

Universal search is one of the latest innovations in search. *Universal search* is the attempt to unite all search results (web pages, video or images, news, etc.) on a single platform. In a May 16, 2007 press release concerning Google's move to universal search, it's explained this way: "Google's vision for universal search is to ultimately search across all its content sources, compare and rank all the information in real time, and deliver a single, integrated set of search results that offers users precisely what they are looking for." Google has updated its toolbar to include navigation tools for images, videos, maps, and Gmail. When you enter your search term you get the traditional results in the body. Then you can click on the toolbar for other types of content related to your search. Google also is testing universal search via Google Experimental™, available on Google Labs™ and with Google-owned Web 2.0 playground Searchmash.com (in beta testing).

> ▼ **Will Computers Replace TV?**
>
> According to eMarketer.com, in 2008 "more than 50% of the US population—155.2 million people—will watch video online."

As of this writing Google, Yahoo!, Ask, and Microsoft all have universal search engines available to some degree, with some in beta testing but available for public use. While each of the engines delivers slightly different results, all share a trend toward creating more personalized search options for users.

So what does universal search look like for users? If you entered "Clint Eastwood" into Google's Searchmash.com, you receive a two-column page of results. On the sidebar you have images of Clint Eastwood and links to blogs, videos, and Wikipedia entries about Clint Eastwood. In the main body of the page are the traditional search results.

Alpha Yahoo! is Yahoo!'s universal search engine. If you enter "Clint Eastwood" you also get a two-column page of results. The main body is the traditional view and the sidebar incorporates results from across Yahoo!-Flickr, and Yahoo! News, Yahoo! Answers, in addition to Videos (Google's YouTube), Wikipedia, and Opensearch. Ask's Ask X and Microsoft's Live Search provide similar results.

Microsoft has added a few unique features, such as hover effects for images and news. By hovering your mouse over the link, you get additional information about the link without having to click on it.

But let's break down some of the components included in universal search. Video publishing, distribution, and video search are fast-rising sectors. Today, the internet is no longer a separate medium but a platform where print, technology, and broadcast intersect. Books, music, television, and magazines can be enjoyed and/or downloaded online. You can watch rebroadcasts of your favorite television shows, blog about it, read blogs from the show's writers, watch music videos that were part of the show, and order products associated with the show from one web site. It's only natural that search technology would evolve to integrate the multitude of offerings. User-generated video à la YouTube initially emerged as entertainment but is quickly gaining popularity as a marketing vehicle for businesses. YouTube and the power of viral marketing made businesses and marketers take note as they began to integrate video marketing into blogs and web pages.

Piper Jaffray conducted a survey that specifically asked U.S. adult internet users if they were willing to watch advertising before a free online video: 30 percent weren't willing, 30 percent were willing depending on the length of the ad, and 31 percent responded that it depended on the content of the ad (Piper Jaffray & Co., "Silk Road: Online Video Usage Increasing as TV Viewing Declines," January 2007). Of those who watched the video, 31 percent checked out the company's web site in response to video.

The ability to convert 31 percent of viewers to take the action by visiting the web site makes video an exciting opportunity for search marketers. eMarketer also reports that in 2007, U.S. marketers will spend $775 million to reach the online video audience. That figure is projected to rise to an astounding $4.3 billion by 2011.

While all the trends in search drive a more dynamic experience for users, it also delivers challenges for search marketing. Search marketing will have to take a broader perspective than it does today to consider the broader platform. We'll also be challenged to discover the right blend of creative media to deliver the highest return on investment (ROI) for our investment dollars and to figure out accurate ways to track and measure those results.

Bob began his search marketing education in earnest. He now realized that his site designs were largely dependent on the client's perspective and not the end users', and this was a mistake. He had lots of questions. How do you leverage social search? What structural changes would make the biggest difference in search and traffic conversion? Could videos be optimized and then have spiders read the text? What tools are available for the new media? What APIs (Application Programming

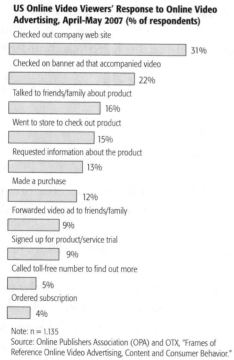

US Online Video Viewers' Response to Online Video Advertising, April-May 2007 (% of respondents)

Checked out company web site — 31%
Checked on banner ad that accompanied video — 22%
Talked to friends/family about product — 16%
Went to store to check out product — 15%
Requested information about the product — 13%
Made a purchase — 12%
Forwarded video ad to friends/family — 9%
Signed up for product/service trial — 9%
Called toll-free number to find out more — 5%
Ordered subscription — 4%

Note: n = 1.135
Source: Online Publishers Association (OPA) and OTX, "Frames of Reference Online Video Advertising, Content and Consumer Behavior."

Figure 1-5. Viewer Response to Online Video

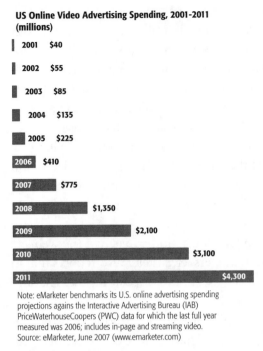

US Online Video Advertising Spending, 2001-2011 (millions)

2001	$40
2002	$55
2003	$85
2004	$135
2005	$225
2006	$410
2007	$775
2008	$1,350
2009	$2,100
2010	$3,100
2011	$4,300

Note: eMarketer benchmarks its U.S. online advertising spending projections agains the Interactive Advertising Bureau (IAB) PriceWaterhouseCoopers (PWC) data for which the last full year measured was 2006; includes in-page and streaming video.
Source: eMarketer, June 2007 (www.emarketer.com)

Figure 1-6. Online Video Advertising Spending

Interfaces) are available to developers? How could somebody start their own YouTube? Bob's excitement grew as he embraced search marketing. But he realized there was a lot to learn.

Video Search

Video search, according to various layperson statistics, is driving up to 30 percent of the growth in total search. With Good Morning America and other major news outlets featuring YouTube videos, this statistic is entirely believable. Yet, opinions are mixed as to how well video search actually works. Voice-to-text technology has not yet matured, which limits some of the functionality. This limitation is one of the reasons Google and others have been unable to include podcasts in their universal search algorithms. Certainly as technology advances we'll see the video search engine market grow significantly.

While the Big Four control 90 percent of the traditional search market, there are several players in the video search engine market.

- **AltaVista Video Search.** Long before Google, AltaVista was a major player in the search market. Once again leading the way, it was one of the first video search engines that were accessible and easy to use.
- **Blinx.** This engine was launched in 2004 and spiders video using speech recognition and visual analysis along with metadata. It claims to have 14 million hours of content in its collection.
- **Dabble.** Launched in 2006, this human-powered search engine indexes 29 million videos across hundreds of sites.
- **Everyzing (formerly Podzinger).** This search engine sees a bright future for search and paints an optimistic picture of present day results. It has invested $50 million in building speech-to-text video search. Everyzing offers a unique twist, enabling users to search not only for the video but an actual point in the video. Its engine takes the user within the actual video content using speech recognition.

AOL Video, Google Video, Yahoo! Video Search, and YouTube all boast large hosted videos. Their hosted content is obviously given preferential treatment in their search results.

Video lends itself especially well to the concept of viral marketing. People tag, share, rate, and comment on videos. Good news for users, not so great for paparazzi-stalked celebrities. As a result of the popularity of user-generated video, news organizations now invite viewers to submit "news" via video. This has opened up the market to new businesses seeking to compete in the news market with their own "from the street" brand of journalism.

Notes

1. Pew Internet & American Life Project Tracking Surveys
2. Pew Internet & American Life Project Tracking Surveys
3. Buyer's Guide to Search Engine Optimization (SEO) Firms 2007

CHAPTER 2

Search Technology

B y now you understand the importance of search marketing, but how in the world does the technology work? In this book we won't get into a deep technical discussion (since this isn't a science book), but rather I give you a broad understanding of the basics so that you can apply this knowledge in your online business.

Now, let's begin this discussion with a basic definition of search engine. A *search engine* is defined as an information retrieval system. In this book we limit our discussion to internet search engines but there are search engines for desktops, mobile applications, intranets, and more. Think of a search engine as your personal electronic detective—you tell it what you're looking for and it finds the information that you're seeking. Of course, the more information you provide, the more refined your results are. For example, if you searched for "Clinton" your search might return Clinton, CT; Bill Clinton; Hillary Clinton; or Oklahoma Clinton. However, a more specific search of "Clinton CT" would return the official home page for the town, hotels in Clinton, and the *Clinton News* (Figure 2-1).

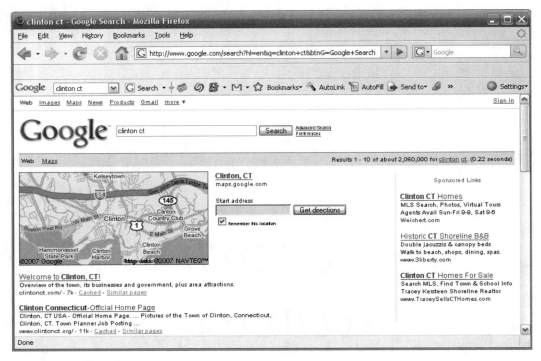

Figure 2-1. Clinton Search

There are various search engines on the web that range from general to specialized. General search engines include:

- Alexa (Amazon company)
- Ask
- Exalead
- Gigablast
- Google
- Live Search (formerly MSN)
- MozDex
- Yahoo! Search

Many users may also use AOL, Netscape, and others. However, these search functions are powered by other search engines such as Google, MSN, and Yahoo.

These general search engines are used to search for—well—everything. There are other types of search engines, such as job search engines (e.g., Indeed.com, Monster.com, Craigslist.org), answer-based engines (e.g., Yahoo! Answers, Answers.com, ehow, open source engines Swish-E, Dataparksearch, Lucene), blog search engines (e.g., Technorati, Bloglines and more). Metasearch engines are search engines that search and collect data across multiple search engines. Dogpile, Metacrawler, and the core data used in Wordtracker keyword research are examples of metasearch engines. Rather than creating a catalog, a metasearch engine creates a virtual database (http://en.wikipedia.org/wiki/Metassearch_engine).

You type your search term into the meta engine and it searches several search engines to compile results. Similar to search engines, metasearch engines differ in their results. No two give you the exact same results. Some metasearch engines look at only major search engines; others query lesser-known engines, newsgroups, and other databases. Metasearch engines include:

Search Underground

Metasearch engines are sometimes called "alternative" search engines. They are typically not as broadly used as Google or the other general search engines but there are hundreds with really nice features such as ChaCha which will "chat" with you until you find what you need.

- Bioinformatic Harvester
- Brainboost (answers.com/bb)
- Clusty
- Dogpile
- Excite
- HotBot
- Info.com
- Ixquick
- Mamma
- Metacrawler
- MetaLib
- Myriad Search
- PolyMeta
- SideStep (travel)
- Turbo10
- WebCrawler

You can search for people rather than web pages using people search engines:

- Ex.plode.us
- InfoSpace
- Spock
- YellowPages.com
- Zabasearch.com
- ZoomInfo

Answer-based search engines answer questions and include:

- Answers.com
- AskMe Now
- BrainBoost
- eHow
- Lexxe
- LycosiQ
- Windows Live QnA
- Yahoo! Answers

Search engines may be broadly grouped into three categories: crawlers, human-powered, and hybrid. Crawler-based search engines are so named because one of the major elements is a "crawler," or "spider" (also called a robot or bot), that reads web pages via links. This is what's meant by your site being "spidered," or "crawled." The crawler reads the web page, and follows links within that page to other pages. The web page is crawled on a regular basis to look for changes. When the crawler reads the site, the information is indexed. (The index is also referred to as a catalog.) There can be delays between your site being crawled and indexed. Indexing is what makes the pages available to search engine users. Thus, search engines are not really searching the entire web as it exists at the point of your search. Rather, they are searching through what has already been crawled and indexed.

To understand this, let's use the analogy of the library. When you go to the library you can use the card catalog (now computerized) to search through the library's collection of books. All the books in the catalog have been processed and entered by the library staff. While you are there performing your search, a new shipment of books arrives. The books are physically present in the library but not yet cataloged and processed for your use. Spiders may have crawled the site, but like the new shipment of books, until they are processed (indexed) the information is not available to you.

The three components of crawler search engines are the spider (bot, robot, crawler), the index, and the software. The software is a key component, as it's the differentiator of

Older than Google

The Dewey Decimal system was created by Melville Louis Kossuth Dewey when he was 21 years old, working as a student assistant in a college library. It's now used in more than 135 countries.

Same Results?

According to the USC Beaufort Library (www.sc.edu/beaufort/library/pages/bones/lesson1.shtml) recent estimates put search engine overlap at approximately 60 percent and unique content at around 40 percent.

each engine. The software program sorts through the millions of indexed pages to match and rank searches based on relevancy. The software scouts the location and frequency of your requested keywords and phrases, and returns results in order of relevancy. While all crawler-based engines have the same components, they all work a bit differently. For example, Google allegedly has 100+ factors that support the core search algorithm and the complex crawlers, including links factors that count into the ranking. For these reasons you may get slightly different results from Google and Yahoo! although both are crawler-based engines.

Of course, search engine ranking is at the heart of search optimization and marketing efforts, which is why search experts spend so much time trying to analyze how the engines rank sites.

Human-powered search engines depends on human beings for their "catalog." The Open Directory (dmoz.org) is an example of a human-powered search engine. Users submit web sites with a short description of each site. When a user types in a search term, the engine searches for matches in the descriptions that have been submitted.

Hybrid search engines give you crawler and human-powered search results. A good example of a hybrid engine is LiveSearch—although, to be fair, Google also uses human editors and doesn't rely solely on algorithms. This is not a widely known fact, so for the purpose of our discussion, we'll continue to classify Google as a crawler-based engine.

Most technical professionals are interested in crawler-based search engines as a comprehensive understanding helps them to be more efficient at optimization.

NO SUGAR, NO FAT, ALL NATURAL

Natural or organic search (also referenced as algorithmic search) results are unpaid or non-sponsored links. Achieving a high position in search results "organically" can't be bought and has become the new "holy grail" for search professionals. Search engines use an algorithm (and many other factors) to rank the importance and relevance of sites as they pertain to search terms. Higher aggregate scores result in higher ranking positions. For example, the search term "job search" on Google will show first page results that include Monster, CareerBuilder, and HotJobs in the natural results. Monster also shows up as a paid listing. These sites are heavily trafficked and have a continuous inflow of new content, so are likely to always show up high in natural results.

Paid or sponsored search listings are the result of web owners paying to have their "ads" shown (Figure 2-2).

WHAT IS OPTIMIZATION?

Now that we understand a little more about search engines, what on earth is optimization? Search engine *optimization* is the process of making your web site more accessible

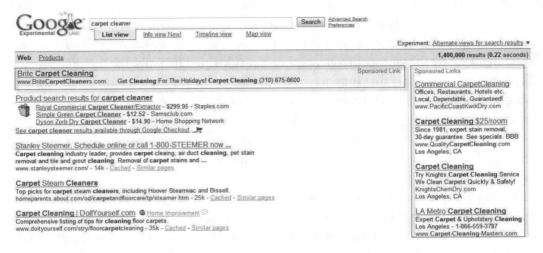

Figure 2-2. Paid Search Listing w/local ads ("Los Angeles")

or visible to search engines. The goal of optimization is to have the spiders not only find your site but rank the relevance so that it appears at the top of the search engine results.

$$\| x - x^* \| \leq \delta$$

In mathematics, *optimization* refers to the study of problems in which one seeks to minimize or maximize a real function by systematically choosing the values of real or integer variables from within an allowed set.

The practice of optimization started in the mid-1990s. Initially the webmaster simply submitted the site URL or page to the search engine. The spiders would then crawl and index the page.

As search caught on, it became clear that being listed was not enough. When users typed in search terms, they weren't going to continue to scroll through page after page to find what they wanted. So the race for ranking dominance began in earnest.

Today the process of optimization requires a holistic approach to the site architecture and content. It's not a one-time process but requires maintenance, tuning, and continuous testing and monitoring.

Much of this book is devoted to the process of optimization and its overall role in the search engine marketing process. Listed below is a broad four-step process for a strategy for search engine optimization. Use this as your checklist. We cover each step in more detail, along with tips and tricks, in the following chapters.

Step 1: Target Market Business Analysis

- **Web Site Analysis.** Analysis of meta sets/keywords, visible text, and code to determine how well you are positioned for search engines.

- **Competitive Analysis.** Examination of content keywords and present engine rankings of competitive web sites to determine an effective engine positioning strategy.
- **Initial Keyword Nomination.** Development of a prioritized list of targeted search terms related to your customer base and market segment.

Step 2: Keyword Research and Development

- **Keyword Analysis.** From nomination, further identify targeted list of keywords and phrases. Review competitive lists and other pertinent industry sources. Use your preliminary list to determine an indicative number of recent search engine queries and how many web sites are competing for each keyword. Prioritize keywords and phrases, plurals, singulars, and misspellings. (Misspelled words may be overlooked by many in their keyword strategy, but if search users commonly misspell a keyword, you should identify and use it). You can also organize keywords into logical thematic groups for SEO content and advertising campaigns. We'll discuss keywords in depth in Chapter 5.
- **Baseline Ranking Assessment.** You need to understand where you are now in order to accurately assess your future rankings.
- **Goals and Objectives.** Clearly define your objectives in advance so that you can truly measure your ROI from any programs that you implement. Start simple, but don't skip this step.

Step 3: Content Optimization and Submission

- **Create Page Titles.** Keyword-based titles help establish page theme.
- **Create Meta Tags.** Metadata (especially descriptions) influence rankings.
- **Place Strategic Search Phrases on Pages.** Integrate selected keywords into your web site source code and existing content on designated pages. Make sure to apply a maximum of one or two keywords/phrases per content page, adding more pages to complete the list.
- **Develop New Sitemaps for Google and Yahoo!** Make it easier for search engines to index your web site. Create both XML and HTML.
- **Submit Web Site to Directories.** Professional search marketers don't submit the URL to the major search engines. Links get your site indexed by the search engines. However, you should submit your URL to directories such as Yahoo! (paid) and DMOZ (free).

Step 4: Continuous Testing and Measuring

- **Test and Measure.** Analyze search engine rankings to determine the effectiveness of the programs you've implemented, including assessment of individual keyword performance. Test the results of changes.

- **Maintenance.** Ongoing addition and modification of keywords and web site content are necessary to continually improve search engine rankings so growth doesn't stall or decline from neglect. You also want to review your link strategy and ensure that your inbound and outbound links are relevant to your business.

Bob thought that he understood the basics of search optimization and was confident he just needed to learn the tips and tricks of the trade. After a visit to a search discussion forum, Bob realized that he had an intensive learning curve. He thought optimization was being overhyped. After all, he had been putting keywords in meta tags and titles for years. He knew very little about keywords and keyword phrases, links, directories, or even how each of the search engines ranked pages. Determined to turn things around, Bob began his journey in earnest to get educated and renew his credibility with his customers.

OVERVIEW OF SEARCH STRATEGIES

The reason for search optimization and search marketing is simple: to drive traffic to your web site. There are a number of strategies that you can employ to improve your rankings and generate traffic. The search strategies fall into several broad categories: paid search, organic, paid inclusion, direct marketing, and link building.

Organic search strategies refer to natural results without the use of fee-based programs. This strategy relies on organic search traffic. For example, say that you own the one and only feed store in Petaluma, California. Your URL is petalumafeedstore.com, and your home page has content that uses "Petaluma" and "feed store". Users who type "feed, petaluma" get results that have your site listed at the top. This is an organic result.

Directory Listings

Directory listings are a good strategy for driving traffic. Some directories require a submission fee while others are free.

Needless to say, this isn't the optimal or final search strategy. Search engine algorithms (and your competition!) change frequently so your ranking results are uncertain. As such, organic search strategy could also be called the "hope and pray" strategy.

Paid inclusion means that you pay a fee to be included in search results. Paid inclusion includes annual fee directories (such as Yahoo!) and cost-per-click directories. LookSmart is the major player in the cost-per-click directory market. You can work with them directly or through agencies. LookSmart is important because its directory is syndicated to Live Search.

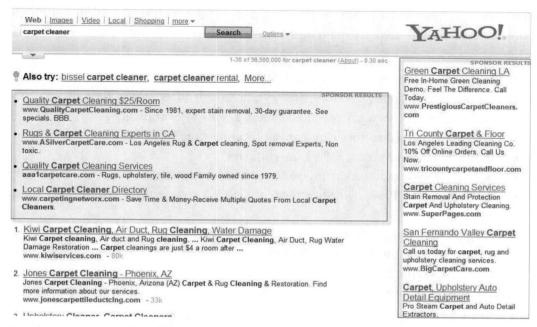

Figure 2-3. Yahoo! Paid Search

Yahoo! Search Directory (https://ecom. yahoo.com/dir/submit/intro) is one of the most important directories for submission. Yahoo! charges $299 annually (non-adult content) but is worth the price if your budget can accommodate it. You submit your site along with billing information and the site is reviewed within seven days by human editors. Your submission should be concise and free of marketing "fluff." The human editors delete any marketing spin and may make other edits. It's wise to wait until your site is completely ready for marketing before submission so that it won't be rejected. The $299 fee is non-refundable so rejection can be costly. It's important to note that although you're paying to be included in the directory you aren't paying for top positioning. In addition to the directory listing, you can pay for higher positioning with Yahoo!'s paid search programs, Sponsored Search (Figure 2-3).

The Open Directory Project (www.dmoz.org) is a free key directory. This directory feeds a number of other search directories, so inclusion is important (the ODP powers AOL Search, Netscape Search, Google, Lycos, DirectHit, and HotBot).

Directory submissions are reviewed by volunteer editors. The submission process isn't very fast and if you're rejected, your resubmission may put you back in the regular waiting queue. In fact, as of this writing, I'm waiting for one of my sites to be included—it's already been more than four weeks.

There are countless other directories available, paid and free. Many of the free directories also offer a fee option (with faster review times). There are industry-specific directories and general directories. If we tried to list them all it would fill ten phone books! However, here are a few paid directories (some have free options) worth considering:

- Business.com (www.business.com, $199 per year)*
- Best of the Web (www.botw.org, $69.95 annually or $199.95 one-time fee)
- UncoverTheNet (www.uncoverthenet.com, $59 to $199 annually)
- Directory @ v7n (directory.v7n.com, $49.95 one-time fee)
- JoeAnt (www.joeant.com, $39.95 one-time fee)
- ExactSeek (www.exactseek.com, free or $12 for top listing)
- WoW Directory (www.wowdirectory.com, $43 for an express review, $65 sponsored)
- Gimpsy (www.gimpsy.com, free to $40 one-time fee)
- InCrawler (www.incrawler.com, $24.95 one-time fee)
- Jayde (www.jayde.com, free)

*Also has paid advertising

There are also programs that allow you to bulk submit to directories. One such program is SubmitWolf 7.0. SubmitWolf costs $169 per year. You may want to use this initially to launch your new or redesigned site, but likely won't need it in subsequent years.

There are still directories to which you would manually submit (like Yahoo and Open Directory) but it can certainly help you with other listings. Just make sure to manage it naturally, and don't spam.

Link building is another important part of your search strategy but can be a bit tricky. Link building is the process of creating inbound and outbound links. To do it well, be sure to work with other relevant sites. Today, link relevancy (think "themes" or "topics") is more important than ever. For example, a resume writer might link out to job search sites and would receive inbound links from those same sites.

The tricky part is determining the quantity and quality of the links. For example: if you get one link from an authority site like CNN or BBC (UK), its value would be more important than dozens (perhaps hundreds) of other links. Since these sites are considered an authority, it may not matter as much if it isn't relevant, but even better if it is! If you use unethical practices to trick the search engines, your site can be downgraded, or worse, banned.

However, legitimate and relevant inbound and outbound links are a valuable way to generate traffic. We'll discuss this in depth in Chapter 8 on link building.

▼ Link Police

As of this writing a number of popular sites had their PageRank downgraded by Google for link farming (selling links on their sites). Some engines prefer a limit on the use of links per page.

When most people think of search marketing they think of the paid search strategies. Specifically, they may think of Google AdWords or pay-per-click campaigns. Paid online advertising is similar to paid offline advertising. In traditional media you pay to have your ad listed. You have a choice of size, location, and advertising channel. In popular publications a full-page ad may cost hundreds of dollars, while a smaller publication may charge far less.

As with traditional media, you must identify your target audience, develop creative content that captures their attention, and place it where they will see it. Paid online advertising has all the same basic elements. Your two primary media channels for online advertising are web sites and search engines. One of the many benefits of working online is the immediacy of results and the ability to make changes quickly. Online, you see results in hours whereas in traditional media it may take months to see results. With online campaigns you can test your messages more frequently, allowing you to fine-tune messaging to maximize results.

> **eM**arketer released a study in 2007 that revealed results of a 2006 year-end survey conducted by ad:tech and Marketing Sherpa. According to survey respondents in 2006, the top performing online ad tactics were paid search ads, e-mail house lists, and search engine optimization.

Paid Advertising. Traditional paid ads are based on cost per thousand impressions (CPM— *M* is the roman numeral for thousand). The ad industry group FAST defines an impression as "the count of a delivered basic advertising unit from an ad distribution point." What that means in plain English is that an impression is eyeballs on the advertisement. CPM is used in online and offline media and is helpful to understand in comparing various media buy options.

The following terms are helpful to understand in a discussion of paid advertising:

Ad Click. As defined by the Interactive Advertising Bureau, it's "a measurement of the user-initiated action of responding to (such as clicking on) an ad element causing a re-direct to another web location or another frame or page within the advertisement." The three types of ad clicks are click-throughs (clicking the ad takes user to a different site or frame), in unit clicks (user stays in the same site, sometimes called click-downs, click-withins, or click-ups), and mouseovers (user holds mouse over ad but doesn't click).

> **TIP:** If you can document that you are a victim of click fraud through Google AdWords, Google will refund your money. (Clickforensics.com has popular programs to assist you.)

Click-Through Rate or Ratio (CTR). CTR is the number of clicks an ad receives divided

> **TIP:** Google rewards relevancy here—the Google AdsBot checks pages for content and relevancy, and the "Quality Score" (Poor, OK, Great) metrics in their PPC engine can help lower CPC charges if done right and help with AdRank (http://blog.searchenginewatch.com/blog/060526-072126).

by the number of times the ad, ad unit or page is viewed. The higher the CTR, the better the performance of the advertisement.

Click Fraud. Fraudulent or invalid clicks generated manually or using automatic tools. Fraudulent clicks generate an improper per-click charge that increases a site owner's profits.

Conversion. A conversion is when a user takes a specific defined action. For example, if you ran an ad to have people sign up for a webinar, those who signed up converted. Your conversion rate measures the unique number of actions from unique exposures.

Pay-per-Click Advertising PPC. This is an online advertising model in which you pay only for the clicks on your ad rather than a set fee for the ad itself. With PPC you develop an ad that links back to a specific page on your site. This page is called a landing page. Many site owners create specific landing pages for different ads. This is a smart strategy because people who click the ad are taken right to the content they need.

The major players in the PPC market are Google, Yahoo and MSN's AdCenter. Other options include Miva, Ask ABCSearch, GoClick, Searchfeed, Findology, Copernic Media Solutions, and 7Search. The per-ad click-through rate is impacted by competitive bids for keywords and the proprietary quality measures of ad and landing page content used by search engines.

Pay-per-action advertising (PPA) is a new advertising and pricing model. In this model you pay when users complete a specific action on your site. For example you may run an ad and predefine signing up for a newsletter as the specific action. If 2,000 visitors click the ad but only 500 sign up for the newsletter, you pay for the 500 users who completed the action.

Pay-per-call advertising works like the PPC model except, rather than clicking on the ad, the visitors call a unique number for the advertiser. The call redirects to the actual business. Pay-per-call targets local, service-based businesses or companies that may only have brochure web sites or aren't online at all. Some of the firms offering pay-per-call advertising include:

> At the 2007 Search Marketing Expo, panelists indicated that pay-per-call may convert ten times higher than PPC and can have conversion rates of up to 45 percent.[1]

- Ingenio
- Marchex (formerly VoiceStar)

- eStara
- ZiffLeads
- UPayPerCall.com

Click to Call is a pay-per-call-type product, but users click the ad or button on your site to be immediately connected.

Pay-per-call users have already made the decision to speak with someone rather than continue to surf for information. Hence, it makes sense that an interactive phone call would have a fairly high conversion rate. Pay-per-call is still a fairly new model but worth considering as part of a search campaign.

This is a broad overview of the search landscape and strategies to be considered. I provide in-depth information in later sections as we delve into the mechanics of driving traffic to your web site.

Janet learned from others in the coaching community that she should do a Google AdWords campaign to promote her site. She created an account and chose the keyword phrase "entrepreneur coaching." She chose the keyword phrase because it was close to what she was doing and at the time it was pretty affordable. Janet didn't have a separate landing page for the campaign: the ad simply clicked through to her home page, which said nothing about entrepreneur coaching. Further, the home page didn't offer any action for visitors to take. She spent $2,000 in her first month and didn't get a single sale. She also didn't perform the proper keyword research and analysis. We'll learn later in the book how to avoid making the same mistake!

Note

1. Janssen, Hallie, "Pay Per Call Ads: Living Up to the Promise? Report from SMXLoMo," *SearchMarketingStandard.com*, October 3, 2007.

CHAPTER 3

The Web Site

R ob and Joe had been friends since third grade. Now both in their 30s, they felt the time was right to start their organic dog food business. They conceived of the idea years ago, but the internet made it easy to start and sustain a business while continuing to work at their full-time jobs.

Rob was the artistic visionary and Joe was the analytical numbers guy, so they perfectly complemented. Rob and Joe wrote and rewrote business and marketing plans, worked through financing, and came up with a solid five-year plan.

Since they had opted to self-finance their venture, they wanted to keep the startup costs at a minimum so that they could heavily invest in marketing and supplies once the business launched. Looking at the to-dos, they decided that building the web site was something they could tackle.

Rob had web design software and Joe opted to learn the basic technical details to help out with programming. They had to pull information from about 25 sources but together they came up with a plan. Rob purchased a template and Joe made a few modifications.

It took them six weeks of effort but finally the site was launched. Looking back on the experience, they don't regret being do-it-yourselfers but they did miss a few key steps. While they were able to write and develop the site, they didn't know about how to optimize the site layout and content for search engines, how to use keywords to maximize their marketing, or even the right elements to include in the site. The missteps cost them time, money, and opportunity.

In this next section we begin digging into the mechanics of optimizing your site, starting with building it. We revisit the topics in the first section in greater depth and provide practical how-to information that you can begin using. In this section you will learn:

- How to create a web site with SEO-enriched content
- The best strategies to use for finding the right keywords for search engine submission
- How to determine what market you need to advertise to
- Natural link-building methods
- White hat versus black hat SEO
- Marketing methods to turn search engine clicks into sales
- And more!

We also check in on Janet and Bob as they progress through their Search Marketing journey.

So, what are you waiting for? Go on and get reading, so you can hurry up and get your site listed as high as it can go.

Web Site Types. There are different types of web sites based mainly on the purpose for their existence. This is an incomplete list because human imagination is continually spawning new uses for the internet.

- affiliate sites
- archive sites
- auction sites
- blogs
- business or brochure web sites
- community web sites
- contest web sites
- corporate sites
- data collection web sites
- dating web sites
- directory or search sites

- e-commerce web sites
- entertainment sites
- game web sites
- government sites
- Java applet sites
- hosting sites
- magazine or ezine sites
- news sites
- personal sites or home pages
- political sites
- polling or survey sites
- portal sites
- rating sites
- review sites
- traffic web sites for advertising
- web site products and support web sites

CHOOSING A DOMAIN NAME

Choosing a domain name is an extremely important part of designing your web site, as that becomes the name of your web site. Your domain name is the first part of the Uniform Resource Locator, or "URL." There are many things to keep in mind while choosing a suitable domain name.

If you haven't already done so, give some thought as to what your domain name is going to be. For those who are new to the internet, the domain name, also known as a web site address, is a word or phrase that a web site visitor has to type in to visit your site. It's preceded by http://www, although for modern-day browsers typing this portion in is optional. It ends with .com, .net, .biz, or a host of other extensions that you'll be exposed to when you're ready to sign up for your domain name.

Stuffing your domain name with keywords isn't going to help much, if at all, unless those keywords naturally make sense. For example, don't pick "peanutbutterandjelly.com" if you're planning to launch a site for fishing supplies. Also, avoid abbreviations. Using your whole site name will make your domain name easier to remember. Try to get a ".com" name,

A Domain by Any Other Name

The Domain Name System was introduced in 1984. The U.S. Department of Defense oversaw the system until 1993. Some of the earliest domain names in the system were symbolics.com, mit.edu, think.com, css.gov, and mitre.org.

as those are the most popular and easiest for most users to remember. However, if this is impossible, don't use .com anywhere in the name if your site is under ".net". Doing so is tacky, and will only cause confusion to potential visitors. Remember to display your site name—prominently. Multiple domains can be a good idea but only when built as a complete strategy. Each domain also requires different content to avoid being penalized by search engines for duplicate content.

> **TIP:** Buying and building several domains within niches in your marketplace is a smart strategy. Don't build them all on a shared IP—use dedicated IPs and different Class C IP ranges.

To buy a domain name, you can do so directly from your web hosting provider (which we focus on in the next section), or through a separate domain name service (a recommended option for those who are using their own servers). If you're using a separate domain name service for your server, make sure you choose one such as no-IP.com, which assigns you a static IP address, the numerical address that identifies your computer. If this address is ever-changing (as it is with some internet service providers), you won't be able to successfully assign a domain name to your server. I personally use register.com and godaddy.com. I like the independence that register.com or similar services provide. Another good strategy is to choose and register your domain in advance of building your site. You then have the comfort of knowing that the name belongs to you. When you register a domain without having a site, typing the name into the browser will bring up a page indicating that it's parked. This means the name is owned by someone but a web site has not yet been launched.

The process for signing up for a domain name works the same way whether it's through a hosting provider or through a separate domain name service. You'll be asked to enter into a text box the domain name you want to register. The service shows you the extensions you can choose. Generally, you always want to go with .com, since this is the most popular domain name extension. In terms of what domain name to use, this is where keyword optimization comes into play. That's right—even your domain name should be keyword optimized. Don't fall into the temptation that many webmasters do and use something catchy and creative for your web site. It might be more memorable to potential visitors, especially if you use a lot of offline marketing, but it won't get your site ranked high in search engines. Ultimately, you will want to use keywords to create a domain name that is both memorable and likely to be ranked in the first ten listings of search engine results.

However, keywords in the domain are useful for reasons outside of just ranking by its words. How people link to you and what the description reads in the incoming "backlink," or anchor text, plays a key role. So if you have realestate-mortgage-loans.com it's better than simply remloans.com. The latter is shorter, but the former yields a better link popularity strategy.

If your desired domain name is taken, the domain name service recommends other selections you could use. This can be helpful, since sometimes they can come up with suggestions that might rank better than your original choice. Or, they could be terrible, especially in terms of their length. Generally, the best domain names are short, contain no hyphens, and offer an excellent one-, two-, or three-word summary of what the site is about. An example of an excellent domain name could be

> **TIP:** Nameboy.com helps by offering more combinations of words to review, and providers such as godaddy.com and namecheap.com have advanced search options.

cheapknives.com. It's short, contains no hyphens, and, if it's pointing to a web site selling affordable knives, perfectly summarizes the main point of the site.

Another alternative when it comes to domain names is buying one that's already established or expiring. This is a popular tactic used by internet marketers to generate traffic for their web sites. You can find these types of domain names anywhere, from eBay to specialized services selling them (they can be found through a general Google search). You could use snapnames.com to bid on a name that's already taken. On this site you enter your contact and billing information, the domain name of interest, and your bid price. When the name becomes available snapnames.com will purchase it for you. This eliminates watching and waiting for the name. This is also helpful after you launch your business if you want to snap up similar domain names.

There are auctions specifically for expired domain names. To find the best deals on expired domain names, don't be afraid to use a shopping comparison site, such as froogle.com. I've purchased domains both on eBay and the SitePoint Marketplace. If you get an admin e-mail account and read on the membership site SitePoint—you can transfer a domain over without losing pagerank and traffic!

Most folks who sell a web site/domain will show you traffic charts and money charts (example: AdSense). Make sure that it's not inflated, and that you can look at it over time. One month is simply not good enough. Make sure you also ask about how traffic has been coming to the site, and ask to see server logs.

Once you've selected your domain name, you need to register it. Be careful of whom you select to handle your domain registrations, as losing your domain name could put you out of business. You may want to choose a hosting company before registering your domain name. Many hosting companies will register the name for you when you set up your hosting account.

A little over a decade ago, Network Solutions dominated the domain registration field, charging $100 annually for service. Today, hundreds of registrars exist, which can cause difficulty in choosing one. Use a tool such as RegSelect, which can help you compare

Figure 3-1. Screenshot of Register.com and GoDaddy.com

prices and options of domain registration companies. All registrars require the name of the company or individual who owns the domain (the registrant), the individual authorized to handle daily matters (the administrative contact), and the person who handles all things technical (the technical contact).

Most registrars have rules against using false names, and you'll run the risk of not receiving important notices if you do so. Whoever possesses the registrar username and password is essentially in control of the domain, despite the fact that the legal owner is the registrant, so be careful. Choose a complex password, as this could protect you from being hacked. Hackers could have the opportunity to change ownership or servers associated with your account. Try to find a registrar that allows you to "lock" your accounts. Finally, avoid registering your domain name with your web hosting service. This could complicate a domain transfer, should you decide to change hosting companies later.

> **TIP:** Register your own name as a domain. For example, jonrognerud.com is one of my web sites. You may later want to launch a member site, speaking service, or other personal business at "yourname.com" and it would be terrible if it was unavailable. Remember, you don't have to build a site for years if you choose not to, and domain name registration is inexpen-

WHO SPEAKS HYPERTEXT MARKUP?

Only computers speak HTML (hypertext markup language), which is a kind of text document that web browsers use to show text and graphics, and is the dominant markup language for web pages. HTML text includes tags to create specific formats for the web page represented. You can use Dreamweaver or GoLive, web page editors that are made to automatically generate the code. Whichever method you use, test your site on different platforms and browsers before you launch it. Avoid tags, plug-ins, and other features that are only available on one type of browser. Remember, you'll want as many people as possible to be able to access your site. Excluding certain users because of exclusive content only available to certain browsers won't help you, it will hurt you.

WordPress is a blog publishing system written in PHP and backed by a MySQL

> According to blogworldexpo.com, 51 percent of blog readers shop online.

database. The system has full World Wide Web Consortium (W3C) standards compliance, which is important for interoperability with other systems and forward compatibility.

WordPress has other advantages, as well, such as the ability to easily manage nonblog content. Any changes you make to your templates or entries are immediately reflected on your site. Finally, WordPress comes with a full theme system, which simplifies the design process. Thus, if you want a different theme every day, you could do it. WordPress is also very search-engine-friendly "out of the box," and I recommend setting up a WordPress blog.

QUICKIE WIKI

A wiki (from the Hawaiian word for quick) site is a web site whose content is almost completely created by users. Contributions can be organized easily, in addition to the actual content you provide. Wikis can easily be tampered with, however, unless the community of users catch false or malicious content and correct it. Vandalism can be a major problem, and intentional disruption by users (trolling) can go unnoticed for quite awhile. In this vein, wikis are generally designed to be easy to create and correct.

Limiting HTML and Cascading Style Sheets (CSS) can promote consistency, while disabling JavaScript prevents users from implementing code. Most wikis keep records of changes made to pages, and often store all versions of that page. That way, authors can revert to an older version of a page, if necessary.

You have many options when considering your web host and technology. Keep your web site in mind when researching, and find out which services you need. Use only what will work best for you, your company, and your web site.

THE INS AND OUTS OF WEB SITE CREATION SOFTWARE

To start your journey into SEO optimization, you must first create a web site. This step is as intimidating as it is obvious. Do not think that impressive graphics and animation equate to a well designed site. While an elegant graphical layout and Flash animations are visually appealing, they won't win over the heart of the web site visitor—content is what does it. As long as you create engaging content, it won't matter as much how your site looks. Of course, this doesn't mean you have a license to produce something tacky. A site that shows no professionalism will drive away traffic, even if the content is good. This is usually the case with layouts with color schemes so awful visitors can't read the content. Ultimately, you want a balance of well-written content and decent layout design.

> **TIP:** To get color scheme ideas, visit colourlovers.com. This site displays color trends and palettes that can be helpful in choosing the right color mix. The site also has a blog and discussion forum.

Fortunately, with word processing programs, HTML editors, and web hosting templates, people with any level of web design background can create professional-looking web sites. Even if you hire someone to design your site, templates can significantly cut the development cost and save time. The upcoming sections will explain in detail how to use each of these programs, along with determining which one is best for your situation.

Word Processing Programs

If you're low on money, look no further than the word processing program that came with your computer to solve your web site creation dilemma. Most current word processors, including Microsoft Word, WordPerfect and Open Office (a free word processor that can be downloaded from the internet), can create web sites because of their "Save As HTML" or "Save As Web Page" option. HTML is the programming format needed to create a web page, so this feature is invaluable to webmasters.

However, one caution in creating pages with these programs: they contain hidden or "junk" HTML code. The hidden code often causes the page to transfer differently from its word processing format. It also adds a lot of other Office code and XML that can be extra overhead to the page. If you've ever copied and pasted from Word to a blog or an online article directory, you're familiar with these quirks. Your perfectly formatted page suddenly has strange breaks in the middle of paragraphs. You may even have to retype the whole thing from scratch because you couldn't fix it. You could teach yourself to do everything in a text editor such as Notepad or WordPad, and copy and paste from that rather than the word processing program.

That said, if it's all you have to use, then by all means use it for a simple web site and check it in various browsers to make sure that what you see is truly what others will see. It may not always provide the cleanest code, but the upside is it makes a site super easy to build!

Ultimately, as long as you remember to save your work in HTML format, you can go about making a web page in the same way you would any other type of document. The what-you-see-is-what-you-get (WYSIWYG) principle most of today's word processing programs observe also applies for web pages, at least to a point. This is because browsers display content differently from other browsers. What looks good in Internet Explorer may look horrible in Firefox. Don't think any knowledge you have of HTML can help fix this problem either, since this is often the result of the junk HTML. You'll have to edit your web page in the word processor, possibly having to take out some of the more advanced features.

For this reason, word processors aren't your answer if you need a more complex web site. However, if a site is simple, a word processor should be okay. There are also web site templates you can download to use with your word processing program (especially with Microsoft Word). The downside to templates is that some of them are overused, so your site won't be unique, but don't worry about this. Remember, in the overall scheme of things the content matters more.

Wondering what's the best way to go about creating a web site in a word processor? First, make sure to use "Web View" if it's available on your word processor. Microsoft Word has an additional "Web Page Preview" that shows you what your web page will look like in Internet Explorer. This is a great resource, because it allows you to know as you design your document how it's going to turn out. The navigation is different in Word 2007, but the options still apply.

Your next step is to put all your files in the same folder. Your web site is essentially a collection of information and the web site looks in that collection for information to load pages. You can't have your home page in one location and About Us in a different location. Name your first file "index.html" because this is how servers identify your default page (something that will be of importance later when you submit your files to a web hosting service). When you need to make connections between web pages, you can use the hyperlink feature in your word processing program. For Word, you only need to select "Insert" then "Hyperlink." If you select "Target Frame" within the Hyperlink menu, then select "New Window." The web page you're linking to will display in a new window. Make sure that when you use the hyperlink feature that your web pages already exist, as you will get an error message if you try to link to pages you have not yet created.

Another thing to keep in mind when creating web sites in a word processor is the use of tables for layout design. With Microsoft Word you can draw a table or insert a table with predefined parameters. But for web page design, you'll want to draw your table. You can create tables within tables for more complex designs. However, the more complex your layout is, the more likely you are to encounter problems when it's time for the web site to display in a browser. This is why you'll want to constantly check your work in different browsers as you're doing it, so you can make the necessary changes right then and there.

HTML Editors

If you're looking to build more complicated sites, consider using an HTML editor. The HTML code they produce is cleaner than word processors', and you can do a lot more with HTML. When using HTML editors, you have three types to choose from: text-based, object-based, and WYSIWYG.

If you're a webmaster and you want to incorporate advanced script programming into your web site, then you use text-based or object-based HTML editors. Both of these work through HTML code only, so if your HTML background is not advanced, they won't be a good choice. On the other hand, if your HTML code is up to par, you are at an advantage using these types of software. How much cleaner can code be if you're doing it yourself? If you're familiar with the concept of objects (which in programming refers to segments of code that can serve as an individual unit, which can be used with other units throughout the coding process), object-based HTML editors might make things easier for you. Examples of object-based and text-based editors include MacroMedia HomeSite and Adobe GoLive.

HomeSite also offers a text editor, TopStylePro, which works with both HTML and CSS. CSS stands for Cascading Style Sheets and is used to style web pages. It's worthwhile to become familiar with both HTML and CSS. You can lay out web pages with style sheets, which saves you coding time and enables you to create faster-loading pages. You'll find many free online tutorials for HTML and CSS. For example, csstutorial.com is an easy-to-follow step-by-step guide to CSS.

If you don't have advanced HTML knowledge, you can still use an HTML editor. You would simply have to use the WYSIWYG form of HTML editors. They are similar to word processors, in that you get a clear picture of how your web site is going to look when it's uploaded into a browser. To use them you type in your text and insert various HTML elements, which can be selected from menus and toolbars. Some examples of popular WYSIWYG HTML editors include FrontPage and Dreamweaver.

Web Hosting Templates

Many web hosting companies (something that I expand on in upcoming sections) offer templates to help webmasters create their web sites. Just as with templates designed for word processing programs, all you have to do is enter the information in the appropriate spots. Granted, the template option isn't an attractive option for advanced webmasters who want more sophisticated features on their web site, but for the average people who may not have an HTML and web design background, the work is pretty much taken care of.

Generalized templates not associated with a web hosting account can also be used in WYSIWYG HTML editors or (as already mentioned) in word processing programs. There are hundreds available for download on the internet. Some are free; others can be purchased. Sites such as templatemonster.com offer a variety of templates, including e-commerce, blog, and web. You can pay a lower fee to purchase nonexclusive use or a higher fee to retire the template (it's removed from the gallery and no one else can purchase it). Both free and paid templates are high-quality when it comes to design, but the free ones tend to be harder to find. Regardless, either can be a suitable option if you don't like the templates available through your web hosting service.

Keep in mind that at some point you will redesign your site. First-generation web sites tend to be simpler with fewer pages because you're just starting out. As your business grows or as you become more knowledgeable about the online marketplace, you will probably design a whole new site. So for your first effort, don't worry if it isn't absolutely everything you want—you can upgrade later.

Bob began reviewing sites of online businesses that were doing well. A friend pointed Bob to a site that sold leather goods. The site was black text on a plain white background with no graphics. In fact, it was borderline terrible! The content was also simple and in many places not even grammatically correct. However, it was honest, and it presented the information that buyers wanted. The owner of the business wrote the About Us section and told visitors about himself. Even with its lack of Flash and its grammatical errors, the business was doing over $1 million in sales annually. Bob learned that day the value of knowing your audience. You don't have to have a perfectly designed site, but you do need a perfectly targeted site. Give people what matters most to them and you'll be successful.

Templates are a better option than word processing software. In fact, many web designers routinely use templates to expedite their design time and help them lower their costs. They can quickly customize elements without having to create a custom site from scratch.

The best place to find general templates is on eBay. I see purchases from people buying over 100 templates for only $9.99. Considering that one template could cost $100 or more, this is an incredible deal. You may not get the flashy graphics and animations you could find with more expensive web site templates, but it's still a good buy. If you have some web site design experience, you can easily customize a template so that it's not so canned.

Keep in mind, however, the more graphics and animations your site has, the longer it takes to load on the computers of your visitors. You have to remember that a lot of people may still be connecting through dial-up and/or slower computers (yes, some people still use dial-up!). A fancier site creates a definitive presence, but if your site is slow to load, the site loses its impact. When it comes to web site creation, simpler is always better unless you're promoting a service or product where you need a more complex design. If you're promoting and generating business, and clients are happy with your site, you're winning!

CREATING THE WEB SITE CONTENT

Once you decide which web site creation software you're going to use, it's time to create the content. You have three options: write it yourself, hire a ghostwriter, or buy private-label content. This section explains each option in detail.

Writing the Content Yourself

Obviously, the cheapest option when it comes to content creation is writing it yourself. Don't get scared at the thought of writing, like many people do. The type of writing you do for web site is different than the formal writing required for academia. It's a little bit more restrictive than creative writing but only in the sense that you have to write with keyword optimization in mind.

Okay… if you're a newbie to internet marketing you might be wondering, "What the heck is keyword optimization?" It sounds more complex than it is. Basically, keyword optimization is making sure your content contains enough instances of your keywords, which are words or phrases commonly used in search engines to find what you offer. For example, if you're selling real estate in Florida, your keywords may be "florida real estate," "jacksonville florida real estate," etc.

You can find keywords by using keyword analyzers. This is software that tells you each of the combinations used with a particular keyword, along with how many times the original keyword and its combinations have been used. Indeed, keyword analyzers are so important in the SEO process that they by themselves are discussed in detail in the following chapters. If you want information on the specific types of keyword analyzers you should use, go immediately to Chapter 5. This is particularly the case if you want to invest in paid keyword analyzers, which offer significant advantages over free ones. Otherwise, you can use Overture's free keyword analyzer tool, which is found at http://inventory.overture.com/d/searchinventory/suggestion/. (It's not always available, so be patient.)

How do you use a keyword analyzer tool? They're all the same: you enter in the desired keyword and you are given a list of results. Paid keyword analyzers return more specific results, while free ones return more basic information. If you find that your keyword receives a lot of visitors, this is the one you'll want to concentrate on when writing your content. However, keep in mind that extremely general keywords may be more competitive than those that are more specific. For example, the term "mortgage" returns over 1.5 million hits, but if you can use paid keyword analyzers, this expanded research capability may reveal that there are too many web sites competing with it. Therefore, you might want to use a more specific keyword relating to mortgages, such as "arizona mortgage loans." It may not have as many hits, but if there are fewer sites using the keyword, you increase your chances of getting a higher ranking on search engines.

When you have selected your keywords, you're ready to write your content. Here is where the keyword optimization takes shape. What you need to do is repeat your keyword several times throughout your content. Generally, you want your keyword to appear 2–5 percent of the time. For example, if you're writing an article of 500 words, you'll want your keyword to appear at least ten times and no more than 30 times. If you don't optimize your keyword enough, search engine bots won't be able to pick up your web page. However, optimizing it too many times actually penalizes you because it is seen as a spamming technique. You'll learn more about this as you progress through this book.

You might be wondering, "What if the nature of my web site can't be optimized 2–5 percent of the time?" This could be the case for web sites with a community theme or those promoting more creative content. You'll have to include separate sections that contain optimized content that still relates to your site. For example, if you're running a site

> **TIP:** Make sure you write for your users first, search engines second. Write naturally!

related to "fan fiction," you could create articles that talk about how to create fan fiction (with "fan fiction" being the optimized keyword). You could also include articles that, while not relating to fan fiction, could still be of interest to your audience. Example keywords could be writing novels, writing movie scripts, and self-publishing.

By including optimized content on a web site that would otherwise not contain such content, you get the advantage of self-expression while making sure your site gets seen by search engine bots.

As you write your content, make sure that it sounds natural and is an enjoyable read for visitors. Although the goal is to include your desired keyword 2–5 percent of the time, if you use it in a context that is inappropriate, you turn away visitors. In situations where using your desired keyword would make the read a chore for visitors, you need to substitute it with another keyword that makes more sense.

Copywriting Tips: Good Copywriting versus Keyword Stuffing

Purpose. Quality keyword writing is a multipurpose exercise. You're serving the search engines and the readers, but write for the readers first!

The Search Engines. The obvious choice is to rank at the top of the relevant organic listings and avoid being banned.

Your Reader. What is the purpose of your writing for the reader? Do you want your reader to act, such as clicking on a link, visiting your site, submitting an e-mail address, or purchasing a product?

Now re-examine your subject. Are your subject and purpose well aligned? You might need to adjust or narrow your subject.

Total Quantity. What is the total number of words or pages you expect in your final project?

Total Keywords and Phrases. What are the keywords and phrases you'll incorporate in your project?

Density. Be careful of the keyword lists you take on. Generally speaking, if you have a long keyword list and require many keywords in your text, most search engines will rank the web page low and you therefore may be unable to achieve the results you want. Keyword density at this writing should be about 2–5 percent. (You should always test this on the various search engines. Don't place too much focus on it, but think/write naturally and continue testing.)

Format. In what format will you create the project and what formats will you use for the final version?

Advertising, Ad Copy, and Copywriting

Writing for the purpose of selling a product or service is advertising copy, also referred to as ad copy or copywriting. Much of web content and SEO writing uses the principles of this type of writing. Articles, blogs, newsletters, and press releases are usually written to elicit an action from the reader. The action might be to return to a web site, click on a link to another web site, or promote or buy a product or service.

When you understand the laws of copywriting, you'll be able to use them in the other types of writing.

The Laws of Copywriting

There is an abundance of data collected and psychological tactics for copywriting, yet by following a few basic principles, you can be successful.

No matter how many millions of dollars are spent and how sophisticated the advertising or web site might seem, I have seen few advertisements and pieces of web copy that succeed without adhering to these basic rules. The first rule of copywriting is AIDA (Attention, Interest, Desire, Action).

Figure 3-2. AIDA

Always follow this age-old principle for successful results. Keep this in mind whenever you write. Bookmark this page or copy it and tape it up where you can see it while you work. Yes, it's that important. Contrary to the infinite variables of successful business, such as the timing, target, media, content, colors, offer, sense of urgency, ad position, etc., the basic principle of AIDA works. By the way, an often overlooked step is the call to action. Once you've gotten their attention, kindled their interest and enthusiasm for your offer, tell them what to do next! This last step is the call to action. Tell your clients what they need to do, as well as where and when to do it.

When your content is finished, figure out your keyword density. To do this, use a text analyzer tool.

To use this you need to copy and paste your content into the text box. Alternatively, if your content is short, you could use the Find feature of your word processor to see how many times your keyword appears. To access this feature in Word, press the F5 key. Count each time your keyword is found. Divide this number by the number of words in your content (which can be found by using the word count feature of your word processor), and you have your keyword density percentage. Granted, this method is more involved than using a keyword density tool, but you should have other ways of figuring out your keyword density, just in case.

Hiring a Ghostwriter

If you don't feel like going through the process of writing your web site content yourself, you can hire an SEO ghostwriter. The keyword is "SEO," because ghostwriters used to writing more creative content may not know the importance of keyword density when writing web content. SEO ghostwriters tend to be a lot cheaper than ghostwriters who specialize in creative writing.

Will They Strike?

The average rate internationally for writers is $1 per word and up. The internet has created opportunities for writers to enter at lower price points while building a portfolio. Internet marketers have the benefit of being able to hire talent at a lower rate. How long will it last? Time will tell.

What can you expect to pay when hiring an SEO ghostwriter? This depends on the ghostwriter and what you can negotiate. If you find SEO ghostwriters on freelancing sites such as elance.com, guru.com, or getafreelancer.com, you might be able to negotiate as low as $1.50 per 350–500 words of content. Remember, though, that you get what you pay for, so for that price don't expect customized, original, perfect content. That being said, "average" SEO ghostwriters will expect payment of at least $20 per 500 words of content. A note of caution here: the SEO ghostwriting market is filled with many low-cost providers. If your goal is average content, then paying the average price is fine. If your business requires highly professional content, expect to pay more. Copywriting can range from $0.25 to $4 per word, depending on the type of content.

When using an SEO ghostwriter, make sure you check it using copyscape.com. This is a service that helps webmasters determine if the content on their web sites has been plagiarized. If there are matches, don't be alarmed—the ghostwriter may have plagiarized accidentally, or it may be a common phrase such as "Christmas Day." Still, make sure he or she makes the necessary changes to ensure that your content is 100 percent original.

Private Label Content

For individuals who don't want to write their content from scratch or hire a ghostwriter, there is the option of buying private label content. What is private label content? It's prewritten content that allows you the same rights as if you bought it yourself. These rights can range from branding it with your own name or company logo to altering it, selling it, or giving it away for free. You can buy private label content as individual articles or books, or you can buy it from membership sites.

In terms of what you can expect to pay, private label articles or books individually can range from $0.01 (especially if you buy them from eBay) to as high as $200. More expensive private label content is usually sold exclusively to you, so you won't need to alter it. On the other hand, if you buy private label content from membership sites, you won't have to pay as much. In fact most membership sites of this nature charge less than $50 for access to their content. There is a major disadvantage to this method, as you aren't the only one buying the content. The unaltered content loses its uniqueness once it's submitted to search engines. In fact, if other people have already posted the content online, the duplicate content filter of search engines will pick this up and penalize your web site. Your web site will be filtered out of search engine results, making even the best SEO attempts futile.

To prevent this problem, you need to alter private label content bought from membership programs. You may think that rewriting the content defeats the purpose of buying it, but even in rewriting, you save a lot of time. When writing web site content yourself, you have to do the keyword research on your own—a step that can take too much time, especially if you want to design a large web site. Most private label content is already optimized, so you have a general idea of what you should write about. While you won't be able to use private label content from membership programs word for word, you can use it as a source of research, using their ideas, rather than their words.

> **TIP:** You can drive traffic to a private label content page/site with pay-per-click programs, and where text and onpage factors matters for AdWords Google Quality Scoring, and you will not be penalized for duplication of content, since these pages are not affected by natural search rankings. Remember that PPC traffic is completely different from SEO/natural search; many are confused about this.

Duplicate Content Horror Stories. Janet wanted to have articles written for her site but had neither the desire nor time to write them herself. On the advice of a colleague she posted a project in an online marketplace. Her colleague advised her to pay $2–5 per one-page article and to commission 10–20 at one time. She followed his advice and posted a project for 20 articles, adding the words "easy project for someone who knows what they are doing." The first day, she received bids from 15 writers. She selected a writer for the project who agreed to write the 20 articles for $50. Janet received the articles one week later. Some were written poorly and she put those aside believing that she could correct them herself later. She posted three articles to test the response. Days later she received a note from the real author politely asking her to remove them. The writer was nice and shared with Janet how to check for duplicate content using Copyscape. Janet took the articles down from her site and was horrified to find that none of the articles were original! Although she had only spent $50, she had risked her own reputation and could have potentially been sued by the woman whose articles she had inadvertently stolen.

This action is more typical of lower-cost ghostwriters. This is not intended to steer you away from ghostwriters but to caution you to choose wisely. In fact, use them if you don't have enough background knowledge to create the content on your own.

Just make sure you check their work for duplicate content before you post it on your site. Also make sure that the ghostwriter includes confidentiality agreements stating that their work is exclusively yours, and won't be shown anywhere else. There are many ghostwriters who are highly professional and well worth using.

WEB SITE GRAPHICS

If you want to include graphics in your web site content, such as photos, clip art, or animations, you need to create the graphics yourself, buy them, or use free graphics.

Creating Web Site Graphics Yourself

You can create graphics yourself by using Adobe's Photoshop, Fireworks, Windows Paint (low-end tool), or other graphic-manipulation software. You still need an image that you legally own as a "base" for your artwork, but with the current technology of most graphic software, you can let your imagination run wild when creating your images. For example, with Photoshop, there's an option to turn an average photo into a drawing or a painting. You can also use Photoshop's pen tool to outline parts of a photo to create a new image. Doing this well takes practice but it lets you create professional-looking images without advanced drawing or art skills.

If you have no original photos or other types of images to work with, you can always use graphic software to create very fancy text and borders. You can also use text to create .GIF images that incorporate animated effects. Additionally, by using a .GIF image, you don't have to worry about how long it takes to load on your visitors' computers, since the images tend to be smaller in size.

Buying Web Site Graphics

If you decide to buy web site graphics, you can purchase them individually, in bundles or through subscription sites. If you buy individually, expect to pay from $1–50. Bundles can be as low as $9.99 to hundreds of dollars. Subscription sites also vary in price, ranging from $20–199. A few low-cost sites are Dreamstime and iStockPhotos. You can buy images for web or print. Most are only $1 per image and there is no subscription

> **TIP:** Log on to my member portal at www.jonrognerud.com/amember and see the "bookmarks" section (check also "Resources" at the end of this book). It has links to some great free sites and paid graphics that you can use.

fee. Other sites, such as Comstock Photos, are more expensive but have higher-quality images with and without royalty fees. Rights-protected images can cost $5,500 per photo for limited use (i.e., for one year). Unless you have a business need for exclusive photos, stock photos are a better option.

Using Free Web Site Graphics

You can get attractive web site graphics for free, but there is a cost. This cost is not money, but advertising space. In order to use free web site graphics, you have to provide a link to the site offering them somewhere on your site. This has an advantage and a disadvantage. The advantage: when it comes to SEO, this creates a backlink if using an associated text link (since graphic links are not read by search engines), increasing the chances that search engine bots will notice your site. The disadvantage: the presence of another site on your web site could divert traffic away from you. However, unless your content relates to selling web site graphics, the average visitor won't have be interested in free web site graphics.

As you determine whether to write your own content or design your own graphics, you must consider the cost factor. How much is your time worth per hour? Is doing it yourself the highest and best use of your time? Sometimes doing it yourself can cost you more than outsourcing the task to a specialist. It's easy to believe that "not spending money" is the cheapest option, but this isn't true. For example, assume your time is worth $100 per hour and it takes you 20 hours to design your site. Your just spent $2,000 for the site. Now, let's say that you could have found a web designer to do the site for $50 an hour and it would have taken 10 hours for a total of $500. Did you really save money? You're faced with this cost-benefit analysis every day in business, so why not here as well?

A Word about Web Structure

Content is important. Just as key is your navigational structure and page access for users and search engines. Users and search engines get to pages via links, and this layout of information is often called information architecture. Building this correctly should be of primary concern (Figure 3-3).

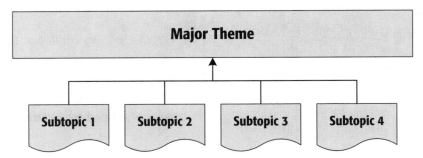

Figure 3-3. The Silo Approach to Web Sites

The easiest way to think about this is as "silos" of information. This forms a logical structure of your site, and creates related and supporting pages of your site. In this approach related information is grouped into distinct sections within your site.

Not only will users enjoy it, but as you build link profiles on your site using keywords in your links (anchor text), you can do the same externally, and build back links to the pages deeper in your site—to build strength and authority to your site—over time.

DEVELOPMENT TIPS

Cartoons. Animation is annoying on your home or landing pages and should only be used under specific circumstances. For instance, if you're a graphic designer selling animation, you would display samples.

Movement on the page is distracting. You either have a media site or a content site—don't mix them on the same page. Leave the animation to Looney Tunes. Here, less is more.

Sound. Auto start sound is annoying and deadly. Many people are surfing in the office or in a public environment, and the surprise of a sudden sound track often makes them panic and hit the button to close your site. While sound is a great addition for selling, be sure you point out the "turn sound off" option.

Pop-Ups. While most people dislike them, pop-ups on exit to collect e-mail addresses have been shown to increase e-mail lists. This is about the only time pop-ups should be used, and even in this case sparingly.

Background Images. Background images are cheesy and amateurish. Review some of the major sites such as Google, Yahoo!, eBay, Amazon, and Monster. You won't see background images. Also, background images slow down load time, as they can easily be 144k.

Organize Your Site. Content should be organized for:

- Relevance –SEO
- Eye appeal
- Navigation

Navigation. Make sure your site is easy to navigate by having a navigational bar at the top of each page. Keep the look consistent on each page.

If pages require scrolling, a side navigational bar and links at the bottom of the page are useful. Remember that every page on your site is a hair trigger (click) away from execution (visitor leaving).

Splash Pages Are All Wet. A splash page (entry or welcome page) is like someone driving by and hitting a puddle while you are walking along the road. You just want to scream. Why would anyone work so hard to attract web site traffic and then make visitors choose whether to enter when they get there? Avoid placing roadblocks on your web site.

Click and Scroll and Rock and Roll. People dance to rock and roll, and that means they keep moving. Imagine every click of a mouse as a roadblock between you and your prospects. Every time you make a visitor click, scroll, or move the mouse, you risk losing that visitor! While you can't eliminate the mouse, you must minimize the number of times a visitor must click and scroll. The last thing you want people to do is rock and roll off your site. Keep mouse clicks from getting between the visitor and your message.

Limit scrolling to article pages and sales pitches. Keep the scrolling on those pages to under eight screens.

There's No Place like Home. An absolute must for every web site is having a "Home" link on every page. Visitors often want to return to the home page, and depending on the depth of your web site and how they arrived there, the back button in their browser might not take them to your home page. Make sure your button or link says "Home Page" or "Back to Home Page." If it makes sense and you have space, maximize your Home button by adding a keyword. For example, if you have a computer supplies business, you could use "Computer Supplies Home."

Include your menu bar on every page. Make navigation as easy as changing channels on the television remote control. Your menu choice should appear at the top and bottom of every page.

Don't Get Framed. Some frames are user-friendly, though they come at a hefty sacrifice: First, the name remains the same. The address bar never changes as visitors travel between your pages. This means no one can bookmark or link to any specific page or share a page by e-mailing the link. Also, when a page in your site other than the frameset appears in search results, visitors will only see the sub-page and not the surrounding frame.

Yes, there are clumsy JavaScript tricks to sidestep this issue, but you're defeating the purpose of using frames in the first place. You can maintain the same elements on your pages with headings and server-side includes.

A Picture's Worth a Thousand Kilobytes (or so). Don't make your visitors wait! A 200k graphic should be compressed to 20k. Use graphics software to compress your pictures to use less disk space and download faster. People don't like to wait. They will leave. Imagine going to the grocery store and finding a 20-minute line just to get inside. Would you even park? Compress your files. There are several inexpensive software programs to do this for you.

Unless you're selling your graphic capabilities, keep the multimedia off your site.

Serve Your Text on the Table. Put text in a fixed-width table in the center of the page. Don't make content too wide for viewers with small screens. Content is fluid and expands as window size increases. A way around that is to fix the width of the content, but that poses another problem. Maximum page size should be 770 pixels wide to account for scrollbars. A percentage width or fluid content is usually the best choice.

Make your text large enough and easy to read. Backgrounds should contrast with text color. Avoid placing text over images. Use space between lines to make text easier to read. Visit web sites and note those you find appealing and easy to read. Mock up the space, background colors, and font colors and sizes.

- Use short bulleted lists.
- Make points in bold.
- Use CAPITAL LETTERS appropriately and exclamation points sparingly!
- Underlining any text other than links only irritates your visitors and makes the text harder to read. Instead, use italics, bold, or color to emphasize.
- Web surfers have come to expect all links in content copy to be underlined and blue. Stay consistent within your site.

Links. Place your links in relevant locations. Keep in mind that when a link is incorporated in text, this can cause your reader to leave and possibly not come back. For this reason, use embedded links only when they invoke the action of your content or web page's purpose. While links are important and convenient, be sure you're not placing an exit door right in front of your cash register.

Clearly Identify All Links. If your links aren't self-explanatory (to your visitor), include a brief description.

Open a Window—Just Don't Close the Door. Make your links open in a new window when people are leaving your site. This gives them the opportunity to revisit your site and keep you in front of them a bit longer. While closing out windows can be a bit of annoyance, the cost here is minimal compared to the benefit of staying power.

> ### Plain and Simple
>
> Maximize your site experience by using descriptive words and keywords for your links rather than obscure URLs or "Click Heres."

Your visitors might have forgotten your URL or failed to bookmark your site, and in these cases you've done them a favor. Remember, sometimes people may be in research mode and have surfed through a few sites or search terms. (Since you have a link to your home page from every page on your site, your site will be easy to navigate; make internal links (to pages within your site) open in the same window.)

Be Easily Locatable–Be Incognito. Make sure your contact information or contact link is on every page of your site and easily found. If you're only reachable by e-mail, let visitors know that. Make sure you encrypt your e-mail address to stay hidden from the spam bots.

Be Original or Get Punished. As tempting as it might be, don't copy content from other sites.

Copyright infringement is serious and if the owner or a client doesn't catch you, the search engines could deal with you harshly. Content must be relevant and original to do you any good with organic rankings and prevent identification as a spam site.

Test-Drive Your Site. Broken links and off images make your site look shoddy and appear untrustworthy. Test your site by loading from the internet and test every image and link. View your site from several browsers. Recruit friends and family to help you identify and resolve any problems before you launch.

Content Management Systems

Consider a Content Management System. This allows you to easily maintain your web site. Any staff member—with or without an IT background—can use a content management system without a webmaster's help. Make sure your content management system is search engine–friendly, with smart navigation, architecture, and file naming conventions. Look for pages on the company's web site that discuss their SEO-compliancy policy to be sure you're making a good choice of companies.

There are two elements to a content management system: the front end and the back end. The front end of a content management system represents the web site as it appears when accessed by a user. The back end is the control panel, or the interface with the system's databases and templates that define the look and feel of your web site. Access to the back end is password-restricted, and you can provide different levels of authority for those restrictions.

If you have a small web site that doesn't need frequent updating, you may not need a content management system. However, rather than relying on external web developers, a content management system could save you money. The system can also reduce the amount of work required from some of your highly trained staff members.

To put your web site on the Internet, you need to acquire web hosting. Specifically, web hosting is the process that puts web sites on the web; it usually works by storing sites on a

TIP: CMS systems to review are Joomla, Drupal, Crownpeak, and HotBanana, GoDaddy Hosting includes optional CMS packages.

server, which is a large computer that houses web sites and their data. You can buy web hosting or try to establish the service yourself. This section talks about the features you should look for when buying web hosting, why you should avoid free web hosting services, server configurations and setup (if you decide to do web hosting yourself), and finally, how to move your files into your web hosting account.

WEB HOSTING

A web host is a company that can provide you with server space for your web site, including pages, graphics, scripts, and files. This is where you'll upload your web site. You should keep certain things in mind when selecting a web host. How many customers do they have? What is their percentage of "uptime"? Your site won't help you at all if your web host's servers are frequently down. Does this web host require advance payment, or do they charge setup fees? Test the web host's customer support, and see how well it fits with your plans. Do they offer fast connections? Your site's visitors will want the fastest connection available. How much daily transfer is allowed? Will you be charged for exceeding their transfer limit? Does the web host offer shopping cart software for your customers, secure servers, and a CGI (Common Gateway Interface) bin? Can you upgrade for free?

There are many basic features you should expect when you look for a suitable web host. You should receive 24/7, reliable support and your own domain name. You'll need at least 10GB of monthly transfer, and a minimum of 20–50MB of server space, depending on the size of your site and data acquisition expectations. You'll want unlimited true POP e-mail accounts, unlimited e-mail aliases, and e-mail forwarding; also "htaccess" password protection, SSI (Server Side Includes) support, FrontPage server extensions, and the ability to design and upload to your site using HTML editing software. You'll want unlimited access to your server through FTP/Telnet, easy access to log files, and statistics on all visits to your site.

You will also want to make sure that the account manager employed by your web hosting provider has an easy-to-use control panel. A good control panel should give you the ability to manage your e-mail addresses, including adding addresses and deleting old ones—generally you will want to avoid web hosting providers that require you to do these things through their technical support. You'll also want the ability to modify passwords associated with your account. Both Unix- and Windows-hosted accounts provide good access panels, and cPanel is popular and effective.

Make sure the web hosting provider can make allowances for complex web site features, if this applies for your web site. This could include making allowances for advanced scripting, such as PHP or CGI. It could include SSL (secure sockets layer), a protocol that sends data in an encrypted format. It might also have MySQL, a database management program. It may even include a shopping cart, a feature that's important for e-commerce web sites.

> **TIP:** You may have heard of the "LAMP stack," a popular term for technology representing Linux, Apache, MySQL, and Python/Perl/PHP.

Finally, you should investigate the operating system used by the servers of your web hosting provider. If you want to use ASP (Active Server Pages, Microsoft scripting language), you'll need to use Windows NT, 2000, or XP. If this is not the case, you can choose setups using Unix and Apache servers.

With so many options, you'll have to decide which ones are right for you. Will you need an unrestricted CGI bin for dynamic content? Do you plan to do any server-side programming with PHP or Perl? You'll want to make sure support for that is available. Do you need MySQL databases? If so, be careful to make sure you have a backup procedure in place and know what you are doing.

Many web hosts charge extra for additional databases past the first. Do some research, and find which web host will serve your web site the most.

> ### Reaching the World
>
> MySQL is one of the most popular open-source databases in the world. It's even used in Antarctica.

Why You Should Avoid Free Hosting Services

After evaluating some of the features offered by paid web hosting services, you may feel that they are excessive for you. Therefore, it might be tempting to sign up for a free web hosting service, especially if your site is small and uncomplicated. Resist the temptation. Why? Well, web sites that use free hosting tend to not get high rankings from search engines. Search engines want what they perceive to be unique sites with separate domain names. Most free hosting services give you a very long and complicated subdomain name. If you use a redirect URL service you could try to circumvent this problem, as you would be purchasing a legitimate domain name that would "point" to the long subdomain. But even with this feature, free hosting services aren't worth your while.

Free sites also tend to offer low bandwidth. It's recommended that you allow 1–3 gigabytes of bandwidth. Most free hosting providers only provide you bandwidth with numbers in the low megabytes. If your traffic goes higher than this number, you will be forced to upgrade to a paid package anyway. So better to go ahead and start with one. Not only will lower-priced web hosting packages provide you with a suitable level of bandwidth, but they will also not put ads on your site, the last major disadvantage to free hosting services. Since you're getting free hosting, free web hosting companies have to get their revenue from other sources, which are advertisers. These ads create more potential for a web site visitor to click away from your site, something that you don't want to happen. Further, you can't assume that these ads will offer backlinks for your site, since most search engines ignore free web hosting sites anyway.

> **TIP:** Google incorporates "age of domain" as a metric of trust and authority, including a number of other factors.

Server Configurations and Setup

If you're technically inclined, have aspirations of starting your own web hosting business, need insane amounts of bandwidth, and feel limited by the current choices available for web hosting providers, you may want to use a server of your own. You can even use your own desktop computer for this purpose, though it's not recommended for two reasons. (1) You won't get as much processing power. (2) You don't want your working computer to be exposed to the risks possible when using your own server as a web host. Thus, you may want to buy a professional-grade server. Be prepared to pay a lot of money, though. The minimum cost for servers tends to be a few thousand, while the most elaborate models can be hundreds of thousands. In fact, if you search froogle.com you'll find out about servers that cost $200,000 and more. Of course, more than likely you won't need this, but even the so-called "cheaper" servers may be out of an ordinary person's budget. However, if you're starting a business you can use your server expense as a deduction on your taxes.

Once you've selected your server, you need to configure it to put your web sites on the internet. To do this you have to use a server configuration program. Apache is one of the most popular because it is easy to use and free to download. To download the software, visit apache.org. After the program is downloaded, you have to use an installer to put Apache on your server.

You should know your network domain, server name, and administration e-mail during the course of installation. Some experts recommend that you say "local host" for network domain and server name, and list your e-mail address for the administration e-mail. The exception would be if you have a network administrator you work with; if so, list their e-mail.

If you want your server to be viewed by other people, right-click "Network Connections" and select "Properties." From there select the "Advanced" tab and press the button on the page. A pop-up containing a list of ports appears. Select "Port 80, HTTP" and check the checkbox by clicking on it.

Now you need to set up your web site files. Look for the folder HTDOCs (depending on setup) in the Apache folder. Put your web site files in this folder. Now your server can place these files onto the internet.

When the configuration and setup of your server are complete, you need to assign it to a domain name. If you've already bought a domain name, then all you have to do is log into your account. You now have to configure the DNS A and CNAME with your server settings; usually this involves just entering in your IP address.

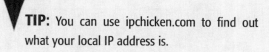

TIP: You can use ipchicken.com to find out what your local IP address is.

Moving Your Files into Your Web Hosting Account

If you're using web hosting through your own server, obviously you don't have to worry about this step. However, if you use the services of a web hosting company, you will. Depending on the host that you use, they may already have made this process easier through file managers found in the control panel of your account. If not, you need to use an FTP program.

FTP programs use FTP (file transfer protocol) to transfer files from your computer to your web host server. FTP programs can be free or paid. Some of the most commonly used FTP programs include SmartFTP, a free FTP program, and WS_FTP (my personal favorite), a paid FTP program.

When you begin using an FTP program, you need: a host name or IP address, a username, and a password. Your web host provides you with this information. In fact, your username and password may even be the same as that initially used for your account. Check your web hosting company's welcome documentation to make sure. Entering in this information logs you onto the server, making you ready to upload files.

Uploading files from your computer to your web host server is easy. The FTP program displays two panels: the left panel contains the information stored on your computer, while the right panel contains the information stored on the host computer. To transfer files between computers, all you have to do is select a file, then drag it into the appropriate pane. For example, if you drag a file from the right pane into the left pane, you will have successfully placed one of your files onto the web host server. If you do it in the opposite direction—from right to left—you will have transferred files from your web host onto your computer. Make sure when uploading files that you keep everything within the same folder you were originally working from. If you change folders, this could mess up links you've established between web pages. Additionally, you want to make sure that your home page is named either "index.htm" or "index.html." Depending on the configuration of the server, you have probably seen default.htm/html as well, they all work the same way.

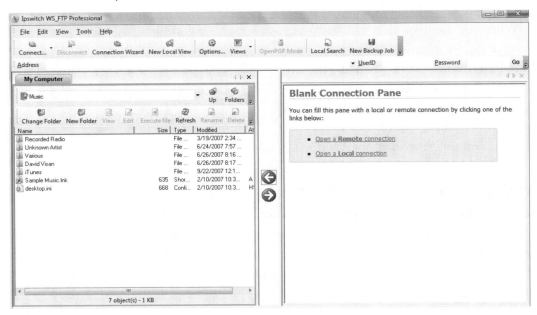

Figure 3-4. Screenshot of WS_FTP—Two Panels

The Web Hosting Companies

I've used a number of companies, including Netfirms, Yahoo!, Bluehost, Verio (previously best.com), Geocities, and GoDaddy as web hosting providers. Netfirms and Geocities offer free hosting accounts, but I would recommend GoDaddy rather than the free accounts. GoDaddy is $9.99, which is attractive for many start-up companies. With multiple options from plain hosting service to shopping carts and blogs, it's a powerful, yet simple, system. (They do try to sell you everything, but ignore it.)

If you're new to internet design, Geocities PRO (http://geocities.yahoo.com/ps/info) may work well for you. You don't have to worry about using FTP programs, setting up your domain name information, or even designing your web site, since they have templates that can take care of all that for you. Everything comes together in a nice package with Geocities, and I recommend it to my newbie friends.

Dealing with Error Pages

Unfortunately, good web page design shouldn't end with only one version of a web site. You'll want to update your site periodically with new information to encourage a steady stream of visitors. In doing so you'll find that you might have to rearrange files, change their names, or remove them completely from your web site. This is not without consequence, because if you don't update the URLs associated with these files, your visitors will see the dreaded 404 "File Not Found" error page. To address this problem, you could use a 301 redirect or a customized 404 error page. This section talks about both these options.

301 Redirects. A 301 "Moved Permanently" redirect is a process that does what its namesake indicates: it redirects old URLs to a new URL. It isn't the only redirect process out there; there are also 302 "Temporarily Moved" redirects, along with HTML meta tag or JavaScript redirects, but these tend not to do well with search engines. In fact, many sites, including high-profile sites, have encountered problems with being indexed in Google when they used these redirects—problems so major that the sites actually got penalized, meaning their listings were completely removed. Don't believe the search engines ever take action? In 2006, Google delisted BMW Germany as part of its anti-spam efforts, so it is possible to be penalized. Use this as a lesson for your own web site. If you're going to do redirects, only use a 301.

> **TIP:** Use 404 error pages to upsell services and drive people to sign up on your site via AdSense referrer pages.

To initiate a 301 redirect you have several methods to choose from. The easiest way is to do it through your web hosting company, as some provide special 301 redirect software. Another relatively easy method is to manipulate your .htaccess file. This file contains instructions for several things, such as error management, security concerns, and specifications for redirection. To obtain a .htaccess file, download it from the root directory of where your web pages are held on your web host's server. If you don't have this file you can create a new one using Notepad. You must save it with the extension .htaccess. In either case, you should include the following line of code (example only):

Redirect 301/old/oldsite.html http://www.yoursite.com/newurl.html

The "Redirect 301" portion of the code tells the browser or search engine that the upcoming link, "oldsite.html," should be redirected to the new link, http://www.yoursite.com/newurl.html." When listing the original URL, omit the "http://www" or the code won't work. If this doesn't result in a successful 301 redirect, try using Apache's mod_rewrite module.

When you've completed the necessary steps to initiate a 301 redirect, test the new link to be sure everything works as intended. If you are involved in any link exchanges (discussed later in this book), make sure you contact the webmasters to let them know your site has been updated. Granted, most of the 301 redirect methods discussed here should automatically transport a visitor to the updated URL even if the original one is entered in, but cover all your bases anyway.

> **TIP:** As a rule, and especially if you have good ranking on certain pages, don't touch or update those existing pages if using 301 redirect. Let them sit, and the search engines will update indexes over time to point to the new page(s).

In terms of search engines, if you use a 301 redirect, you are sure to retain your original rankings. It may take awhile for the new URL to get indexed, but once it does you'll have the same advantages as you did with your old URL.

Customized 404 Error Pages. Some webmasters prefer to use a customized 404 error page instead of the 301 redirects for their missing URLs. Customized 404 error pages are more creative and engaging than the standard "File Not Found" message. Some can be designed in such a way that a visitor barely knows they're on an error page. This is especially the case for customized 404 pages that use the same layout as the rest of the web site. Other customized 404 error pages have a humorous design to entertain the visitor.

Then there are those who try to use the 404 error page as an opportunity to advertise affiliate web sites they're promoting. Customized 404 error pages are only limited by your imagination and creativity.

> **TIP:** An example of how to monetize a 404 page is found at: http://pesonadigital.com/type_anything.

To create a customized 404 error page, you design it as you would any other web page, using the web site creation software mentioned earlier in this book. Once you've completed this step, there are three ways to get your web site integrated with your customized 404 error pages: (1) use the 404 customization option offered by your browser, (2) use Apache or other server software, or (3) use your .htaccess file. If your browser offers 404 customization, use this method over the others, since it will integrate more easily with your web site. If you're trying to integrate a customized 404 error page with Apache, you'll have to insert the following code into your httpd.conf file (which you will have to obtain from your web host if you're using a hosting company):

ErrorDocument 404/yourcustomized404-404.shtml

You would use a similar, yet different coding structure if integrating a customized error page through your .htaccess file. The code for that is:

ErrorDocument 404/404-yourcustomized404-page.html

For the specific codes of other server software, you would have to look for them through Google or by consulting their help or troubleshooting documentation.

CHECKLIST FOR SUCCESS

With your web site complete and uploaded onto your web host's server, you now need to do some "webmaster editing" to make sure that your site is in working order and that it's structured in such a way that it incorporates the principles of good SEO optimization. In this section, you learn about the elements to be reviewed and/or set up when your web site is done. These elements include web site structure, web site title, and web site description.

Web Site Structure

If a web site structure contains complicated hierarchies, it won't index well with search engines. This is why you should stick with the most basic web site structure, which is known as the flat or linear structure. With a flat structure, you have a home page that introduces your topic, then links to various subtopics, which should be listed on the left side of the screen. These subtopics should always be visible; the only thing that should update is the right side of the screen. This would show the current subtopic selected (or the home page). When designing your subtopic web pages, you need to ensure they aren't too far away from your home page. In fact, according to buildwebsite4u.com, it should only take a maximum of two clicks to get from your subtopic page to your home page. Don't make your web site complicated by including subtopics of subtopics. At most, you can add another subtopic link on the left side of the general subtopic screen, or include more detailed information on the specific page of a subtopic. In essence, make your subtopic link pane a clear, keyword-related link for each of your web pages. To get a visual of what this means, take a look at Figure 3-5.

The subtopic links are on the left side of the screen. When you click on them, the right side of the screen updates with the pertinent information. In the screenshot, the subtopic "Cheap Web Hosting" was selected, so the right pane updates with a list of advertising links related to this subtopic. If you click on one of these links, you don't get a change in the subtopics listed on the left panel; instead, you're taken to the advertiser's web site.

Now, don't think that a flat structure alone is enough to ensure that your web site has been designed with the highest capacity possible. Get some human opinions on how your web site is structured. Let people you know online or offline go through the site and note their experiences with it. Ask them to give their general opinion of your site structure: Are there enough or too many subtopics? Does the site look too busy with extra ads? If your site is laden

> ### ▼ Clue to Colors
>
> Many webmasters choose web colors based on the content. For example, health sites may have lighter, soothing colors while exercise sites are bold and bright.

Figure 3-5. Yourdomain.com

with Flash animations or videos that take longer to load, ask if the wait time is acceptable. And don't forget to get opinions on general things related to the design of your site, such as layout, color scheme, and font usage.

After getting a good human opinion, get a computerized analysis of how well your site structure will perform. You can do this with software known as A1 Website Analyzer.

Website Analyzer does what a human eye can't do. It uses a series of formulas to determine the value of the web pages in your site structure. The program will return a "link power" score to tell you about the effectiveness of the web site setup. The program also tests for broken links, as well as providing response times for 404 error pages. Use A1 Website Analyzer to see if the images used on your web site are too big, and have it perform a special test to see if your site can handle increased bandwidth. The data from this analysis are exported to an XML or CSV format.

TIP: Remember to review the accompanying CD for additional software, including more tools at www.jonrognerud.com/amember.

The cost for A1 Analyzer is only $31. This price includes the software and upgrades for two years. To obtain the software, you can either pay the fee upfront, or download the program and try it out before making a purchase. If you do the latter, you're given a 30-

day evaluation period. During this evaluation period you are allowed to try out a full version of A1 Analyzer.

Web Site Title

The web site title appears on the left side at the top of the browser window. Titles not only let your visitors know what your site is about, they are also one of the elements used by search engines to determine what search terms to place your site under. To give your web site a title, you must use the title tag within the <head> portion of the HTML code of whatever web page you want a title for. For example, take a look at the following coding:

```
<head>
<title>Web Page Title Goes Here</title>
</head>
```

This simple piece of code is all you need to create your web site title. Based on this code, what would appear in the browser window is "Web Page Title Goes Here." Of course, you will replace this with your own web site title.

How do you create a title for your web site? Well, as you did with your domain name, you want to include relevant keywords, which you find from the keyword analyzer. If your company name includes a relevant keyword you can include this toward the end of your title. For example, the title "Buy Cheap Computers from Computers-R-Us" lists the keyword "computer" twice and would be preferred for smarter retrieval by search engines. However, the title "Buy Cheap Computers from Electronics Depot" may not do well. This is because it contains two unrelated keywords: "computers" and "electronics." The search engine robot would get confused, because it wouldn't know whether to index the site according to computers or electronics. In this situation, leave the company name out or find a keyword that would match it. In this instance it could be "electronics." The revised title would be "Buy Cheap Electronics from Electronics Depot."

When creating your title, make it brief: that is, no more than 65 characters. A longer title won't increase your chances of getting ranked higher in search engines, since most search engine bots read only the

> **TIP:** Keeping the title close and relevant to your on-page topic is important. A good guideline is 1–2 keywords in the title. Use synonyms, singular words, and plural words to support your topic.

first 65 characters. The rest of the title would get truncated, something that wouldn't look attractive, depending on how your title is worded. Also, don't get lazy thinking that if you put "Home Page" as your title the search engine will show whatever title appears on your home page as your web site title. Not only will it not do this, but you will suffer two consequences. First, the title won't look good to visitors, as they will see Home Page as a title for web pages that don't relate to the home page. Second, the search engine bot will index your site as "home page" which won't get you anywhere with search engine listings. It only takes a few minutes to think of a suitable title for your web page; go on and use this time to think of appropriate titles. It could make a world of difference when it's time for your site to get indexed. You also want your title to be descriptive so that when users bookmark your site, it's easy to remember and access.

Web Site Description

The description of your web site does not appear in the browser like the web site title. Nor is it shown on your web site, once your visitor gets there. Where it appears is in the listings of the search engine results. Whether a keyword-rich web site description actually helps your ranking is debatable. Either way, you want to have your description keyword-optimized for the benefit of your visitors, who can get a clear view of what your web site is all about. A strong call to action with a phone number in the description is a smart tactic to get users to act. I have people calling me direct from organic listings, without ever visiting my page.

To incorporate a description from your web site, as with the title, you use HTML tags. There's a difference from the type of tag you used for title, though. The difference is there's no specific description tag; instead it's a property for what's known as a meta tag. What is a meta tag? A meta tag is a type of HTML coding that provides descriptive information about your web site. Search engine bots read meta tags to determine where to place web sites. The next chapter delves into meta tags, but for now the meta tag code you need for a web site description is:

```
<head>
<title>Web Page Title Goes Here</title>
<meta name="description" content="Your web site description">
</head>
```

The code that has been bolded is the necessary meta tag. The element that lets the search engine know the description is the name property. As you'll learn later, the name property can be set to a variety of elements, but when it's set to "description" the search engine is able to read the description of the web site. In our example, the description is "Your web site description," which would be posted in search engine listings.

However, sometimes search engines treat this differently. Yahoo! will sometimes skip this description, and read directly from text on the page. If you are listed in the ODP project (DMOZ) or Yahoo!, special tags override descriptions from those directories. Google calls these "snippets" (Figure 3-6).

metaname="robots" content="noodp" (Google)
metaname="robots" content="noydir" (Yahoo!)

Figure 3-6. NOODP NOYODIR tag examples

In terms of how to write a description, make it more original than your title. Also, while you do want to incorporate keywords, don't make your description simply a glorified list of keywords. Remember, real people are going to see your description through the search engine listings. If it's not written appropriately, visitors may think the site is not relevant or, even worse, think it's a spam ad. Make sure your description is well written, with appropriate sentence structure and grammar, and keep it short. While there is no consensus on what is considered too long for search engines, most webmasters tend to make their descriptions 15 words long, using one or two sentences.

CHAPTER 4

Competitive Research

ANALYZING THE MARKET

Marian called my office to ask for SEO help for her web site. Marian had an information products web site. She was a speaker, and had hoped to take her knowledge and turn it into passive income so that she could cut down on her travel schedule.

She had spent thousands of dollars on her site and several internet marketing campaigns but had failed to sell more than a few books. "Jon, help! This internet venture is bleeding me dry. What am I doing wrong?" I grabbed a notepad and pen and started to ask some questions. "Tell me more about your target market, Marian."

"Well, internet users."

I asked the question in a different way. "Can you describe your ideal customer? What problems are they trying to solve? How do they decide to buy from you? Are they male or female? What do they do for a living?"

Marian was stumped. We talked for 30 minutes and she could not provide a single detail about her target market. Marian is a highly intelligent woman who had enjoyed years of success in the corporate world. Yet, even she made the mistake that so many make online: She lacked a marketing plan.

Web site marketing is really no different than marketing for other media, such as television, radio, or magazine. While you don't need a marketing degree to successfully promote your web site, understanding the basics of market analysis will get you a lot farther than competitors who don't have this knowledge. What should you know about the basics of market analysis? A market analysis should include: market size, market growth rate, market profitability, industry cost structure, distribution channels, market trends, and key success factors. This section discusses each of these elements in detail.

Market Size

Market size refers to the size of your potential customer base. In the case of internet marketing, a basic keyword analyzer can give you some idea of what people are looking for, at least on the internet. However, it isn't a cure-all, because you have to deal with the element of competition (which is covered in upcoming sections). This is not to say that web site marketing isn't worthwhile, but you may have to use other keywords for marketing purposes. Therefore, you need to know if what you're promoting has a large enough market even when lesser keywords are used. This is why you should also consider offline means of determining your market size. You can find data through the government (Census Bureau, Small Business Administration), industry trade associations, and professional organizations. Even customer surveys. You can also visit your local library's reference section for a wealth of industry data and statistics.

Market Growth Rate

A large market size is nice, but if your market isn't going to grow over time, you won't be able to rely on it for future sales. Conversely, if you find that your market size is initially small, but will grow over time, you may still want to consider using that market outlet.

To determine your market growth rate, first think about any products or services that relate to what you're trying to promote. What keywords are associated with these companies? This is not for the purpose of using those particular keywords, but rather to get a view of how well similar businesses have fared.

Another approach you could take is conduct surveys asking X number of people if they would be interested in your product or service. These surveys don't have to be elaborate. In fact, you could start by asking friends or family. Begin by getting the opinions of at least ten people. You could ask more questions on Yahoo! Answers and epinions.com.

There are other advantages to soliciting feedback from your "potential market." The feedback could uncover potential gaps or flaws. It could also lead you to think of avenues that you would not have pursued.

If the results of your surveys are positive, consider pursuing your business idea as it exists. If only a small group is interested in your project, you have an advantage and a disadvantage. The advantage is that with a smaller number of people interested, you have a niche market you could exploit. The disadvantage, however, is that depending on the size of the niche, you may not get as many sales or leads. If you pursue a niche market, go for one you can dominate. A current trend in business is to "go small" which simply means slicing your market into segments and, rather than trying to dominate a broad slice, dominating a niche. If you do choose a broad, or "popular," market, research the gaps in that market and compete by fulfilling a need that is unmet. For example, in your industry is service a common facet that is lacking? If so, make service one of your core competencies and compete by leveraging that.

> ## Focus Groups
>
> Need an opinion? Create your own focus group to gain information on your market. Invite a group of people from your target demographic to your office or other quiet gathering place and collect your necessary data. People are often willing to participate for something as simple as a paid lunch!

Whether you choose a niche or larger market, all of these principles apply. Use your main site to talk about something that's more popular yet relates to your niche. Look for affiliate programs that promote the more popular market, but leave you a chance to make some money. You can advertise your business as a separate subtopic link or as a separate web site altogether. What happens is that, by promoting a more popular market, you get a number of visitors who will at least get exposed to your business. If you concentrate on the weaker market first, you lessen the chance that you'll get any visitors at all, particularly if it's something that is going to have a higher market growth rate over time.

Market Profitability

Market profitability determines how prosperous a market can make a business. Harvard business professor Michael Porter is famous for his Five Forces of Competitive Position Model. The model provides a simple perspective for assessing

> **TIP:** An affiliate program is like a reseller or revenue-sharing program. I split money with you, depending on what and how much you sell. Often a broker house, such as clickbank.com for digital products, is a great place to begin. They even take care of the monetary transactions for both parties.

and analyzing competitive strength and position. Porter's five forces that drive competition are:

1. Existing competitive rivalry between suppliers
2. Threat of new market entrants
3. Bargaining power of buyers
4. Power of suppliers
5. Threat of substitute products (including technology change)

▼ Porter's Model

Porter's tool was first introduced in *How Competitive Forces Shape Strategy* (*Harvard Business Review* 57, March–April 1979, pp. 86–93). It has since become a widely used and important business strategy tool.

Use Porter's model to analyze each element and assess how each will affect your market profitability. If you're new to business and marketing principles, do a little research and learn how to assess yourself and your competitors. In the internet marketing arena, a quick and easy way to analyze the competitive landscape is to use the keyword analyzer. Highlight one of the terms that pops up. Enter the term into Google or another popular search engine. Take a look at the sponsored listings (these appear at the top of the search engine results) and the pay-per-click ads (these usually appear on the right side of the screen). Note the companies that pop up, and do a detailed search on them. Wikipedia is a good resource because it can tell you all kinds of basic financial information about a company.

For extensive business information, hoovers.com is one of the best sources of comprehensive company data. Some of their information is free, but a paid subscription will give you access to tremendous amounts of key data. Dun and Bradstreet (dnb.com) and Yahoo! Finance are also great sources of company data.

Of most importance is the revenue information: if it has gone up, there will be a little up arrow next to it; if it's gone down, a down arrow. This can give you some idea of whether your own market is going to be successful, but be careful. If a company is making huge amounts of revenue, it could be considered a rival market with barriers to entry, especially if it doesn't have too many competitors. IBM and Apple are perfect examples. If you wanted to try to manufacture a whole new brand of computers, you wouldn't be very successful since these two dominate that scene, with IBM being the leader. Most of the software and peripherals made are created for either of these computers. Obviously, potential customers wouldn't want to buy a computer that they couldn't even use because they wouldn't be able to find software or peripherals designed for the new computer.

However, expanding on the IBM/Apple example, if you were able to come up with a new computer that was significantly cheaper than IBM or Apple machines along with providing your own brand of software customers could buy, many might consider making the switch. So, if a market does have barriers to entry, it doesn't necessarily mean the market is closed to you. You may just need to develop different tactics to get your products or services sold.

Industry Cost Structure

Cost is one of the most important elements when it comes to marketing. Naturally, most consumers want to get the best value for their dollar, but don't get trapped into thinking that lower means better. If you price a product or service significantly below the industry cost structure, consumers might become suspicious. They may think you're charging less because your product or service is not as legitimate or valuable as a more established business.

Consequently, they may buy at the higher price from a different company.

This is why you will definitely want to check out your competitors' pricing before determining the prices for your products or services. The best way to do this is to use online comparison sites. Most, such as froogle.com, show the prices that products or services are going for, but others such as consumersearch.com show this and also provide consumer reviews. The downside to sites like ConsumerSearch is that they tend to be limited in what they show, which is why you want to use more than one of these types of portals.

Once you get abreast of the pricing structure of your competitors, you should set your prices accordingly. As a newcomer to the industry, you don't want to price too high, unless you're offering something spectacularly better than your competitors. On the other hand, you don't want to price too low. You'll want to price mid-range. Many established businesses such as Amazon or Wal-Mart price only a few dollars less than their competitors, yet when they do their promotions, instead of saying such-and-such item is a couple dollars lower, they'll say they're offering a 50 percent discount, or something of that nature. You may want to try that approach for your own business. However, Amazon and Wal-Mart have built-in cost efficiencies that let them price lower; take caution that you run the numbers and understand your costs so you that don't price below your margins.

Keep in mind that what you are really selling to customers is "value." While it's important to understand competitive pricing and to price accordingly, customers pay for the value you offer. Your pricing is not only the result of competitive models but should factor in your cost structure. You may have a lower cost to deliver a product or service and, as such, can price a little lower than your competitors. Be careful, however, when engaging in a price war, for in these wars there are no winners. An old sales adage says that if you win customers on price, you lose them on price. What this means is that when price is the key element in deciding to buy, customers will buy from someone else if they have a lower price. The airline industry is a good example of ongoing price wars. It's far better to create value and sell to deeper needs than price alone.

Distribution Channels

In terms of distribution channels, how are you marketing your product or service? Are you using an online distribution channel or a brick-and-mortar one? Are you using both? If online, how will your service be delivered? For example, a bookseller might use self-publishing portals and affiliates as distribution channels. You may think that how you sell your product or service wouldn't matter in an age when millions of Americans and persons overseas have access to the internet. However, this does not necessarily mean that they'll be comfortable buying over the internet from *you*. A lot of consumers feel uncomfortable buying from new e-commerce sites, especially if their business is exclusively online. They may worry that the site is not legitimate, and they are risking their money. Granted, this may not be as much of a concern if you're selling cheap products, but for merchandise or services that are higher-priced, your company might get bypassed for a more established company with a track record.

While you can control for many of these factors, remember that they call it "building a business" for a reason. Very few businesses skyrocket from $0 to $10 million overnight! You get customers by applying sound business and marketing principles. Customers are taking a risk when buying from you (as they are with every business), but there are ways to minimize that risk for the customer. Money-back guarantees are a classic way to minimize risk. You are assuring customers that they won't lose their money by offering them a guarantee.

> **TIP:** Read the section on conversion/landing pages to see how you can quickly establish trust for high conversion and dollars to you! Hint: logos and testimonials! Also, real-world studies are being made available online at www.jonrognerud.com/amember in the "Conversion" section.

Another way to minimize risk and establish trust is to offer "proof." Testimonials are a wonderful way to accomplish proof of your value. As you obtain customers, ask if they would be willing to provide a testimonial. You could offer an incentive for them to do this, such as a free item or a discount on their next purchase. If they are web marketers, you could offer to promote their web site on yours in exchange for their testimonial. When collecting your testimonials, if your customers will let you, try to include their e-mail addresses, so potential customers will have a way to contact them. Anybody can make up a testimonial, but if you provide an e-mail address, many visitors feel the testimonial is more concrete, because they have someone they can contact.

Another thing you can do is join the Better Business Bureau. This costs a few hundred dollars, but the investment is well worth it. A lot of people trust the Better Business Bureau; in fact, if a business is not established, it's the first resource that I go to for determining whether they're legitimate. Of course, you have to make sure that your business does right by its customers, since the Better Business Bureau will report you, but then again you should be doing that anyway. Besides, businesses that aren't members of the Better Business Bureau also receive bad reports, which is one of the reasons people love the company so much. Once you join the Better Business Bureau, you are able to post their logo on your site. This logo alone will significantly improve consumer confidence in your business. This is particularly the case if you are trying to sell in an industry where the distribution channels have traditionally been through brick-and-mortar enterprises.

Market Trends

Market trends refer to how a market is changing. Market trends include customers, competitors, and the industry as a whole. Being able to determine a future trend and positioning yourself to take advantage of it is a competitive advantage. It's important to understand not only what customers want today, but what will they want tomorrow? Are there unmet needs in the industry? What are your competitors doing? Are they shifting strategies?

Here again is where the survey is a useful tool. However, instead of surveying outsiders, you survey those who have bought from you. Current customers are one of the most valuable and underused resources of any business. Current customers can help you improve your business and develop products and services that have a market (rather than creating something and hoping there's a market for it), and they're an excellent source of revenue (upsells and referrals).

If your business is new and you don't have a customer base, you'll want to conduct surveys on the basis of how customers' needs were met from businesses similar to yours. Again, Yahoo! Answers can be useful for this purpose. If you're carrying out a survey of your own customers, you can do so from their e-mail (assuming they are on your e-mail list) or from a special survey area on your site. (You don't need to have surveys visible from your home page if you don't want to.) You'll want to offer an incentive for the survey,

Lifetime Value

When calculating your marketing ROI, don't forget the lifetime value of each customer. The lifetime value is how much that customer will spend with you over time, rather than a one-time sale. For example, if a customer will buy from you an average of four times spending $2,000 total and you spent $10 to obtain them as a customer, your "profit" per customer is $1,990.

> **TIP:** A free tool (paid services means more features) that you can use to easily create surveys is www.surveymonkey.com.

though many companies seem to have success even when they don't offer survey incentives. If your resources are low, consider trying to get surveys for free, but you'll have to send it to a larger number of people if you don't offer an incentive.

Key Success Factors

What are key success factors? In short, they are all the elements you must have to be successful. For example, commonly accepted key success factors include brand or name recognition, access to unique resources, customer loyalty, financial resources, and access to distribution channels. This section goes through each of these recommended key success factors.

1. Brand/Name Recognition. When you're starting out, you won't have the advantage of a big name, unless you're successful enough to merge with an already established company. So, to build up your reputation, do good business. Make sure you respond to your customers' orders promptly. If you can't, set up an autoresponder and/or hire a person to deal with orders (you'll want to do the latter if your business becomes extremely prosperous). Offer rebates if the customer is dissatisfied with your product or service, Most of all, keep up a friendly persona. Generally, as the adage goes, the customer is always right. This is not always an easy rule to live by, but it's important that a beginning business try as much as it can to observe it.

The more you do good business and the more you promote yourself, the more you will get a name going in internet markets. The speed of information today can help or harm you. If you deliver terrible service, a blogger can write about his or her experience and within hours your name and reputation can be decimated throughout cyberspace. Problems inevitably occur, but be responsive and fix them so that you build a solid foundation of integrity for your company. Of course, with the prevalence of the internet today, a name in internet markets almost guarantees a name in offline markets, although this is not always the case. Specialized services that cater to small niches may only find their fame through search engine placement.

2. Access to Unique Resources. Do you have direct access to a specific market, particularly one that would be interested in the products or services you have to offer? For example, if you sell children's products and you're active at your child's school, the teachers and the parents of the other children could be a perfect base to whom you could market. Your personal connection with this market gives you an advantage as someone serving that market. You have access that another marketer would have to obtain through e-mail marketing, direct mail, or even search engine marketing. Additionally, if your customers like your products, they could use word-of-mouth to market your products further to their family and friends. Don't underestimate the personal element when it comes to marketing.

3. Customer Loyalty. If you do well by your customers, more often than not, they'll do well by you. Recurring customers not only ensure a steady stream of income, they can also do your marketing for you through word-of-mouth and/or testimonials. Existing customers give you unique reach to your target market—other people like them. Too often businesses fail to develop long-term relationships with their customers. Even if you're in a business where repeat sales are years apart, e.g., real estate or automotive, your current customers can be a good source of referrals. Treat them well and not only will they buy from you again, they'll tell others to buy from you, too.

> **TIP:** Don't get caught in having somebody build traffic to your site if you don't have unique and compelling content with a simple "1-2-3" click purchase opportunity. You're wasting your money. Think of traffic in terms of conversion. Checkpoint: if you were a potential customer, would you buy from your own site?

4. Financial Resources. To start your business, you're going to need money. However, depending on what you do, you may not need much money. For example, a virtual service such as word processing wouldn't require much in startup costs. All you really need is a computer and a printer. Even printing costs could be reduced if you e-mail documents to your clients. As long as you can get your web site indexed high in search engines, you could make money without having to invest much.

On the other hand, if you're running a business that requires inventory, you may need to invest thousands up front. If you can't sell the inventory, you would incur a financial loss, which could force you to shut down your business. This is why you need to carefully examine your market before you open your internet doors. If it looks like you're going to make a profit, you can consider getting a business loan so you don't have to risk all your own money. If you're trying to sell a smaller amount of inventory (say, less than $5,000), consider getting a credit card. Credit cards are easier to get than business loans, and the monthly payment even at $5,000 would probably still be affordable.

5. Access to Distribution Channels. Don't limit your advertising to search engines, even if you get a first-place ranking. Other advertising mediums include direct mail, radio, magazines, and, when you really get money, television. Google AdWords, for example, is available for print, radio, video, and mobile. If you're low on funds, you can use the cheap, old-fashioned method of flyer distribution. Make sure to get permission before you distribute your flyers, so you don't get in legal trouble. (I placed a promo business card in an office elevator once, and somebody took the time to leave me a message to stop—in a

> **TIP:** One of the top product lines to get into is information products. They have the lowest overhead and the biggest ROI. There are internet marketers making millions every year selling their own and affiliate market products—no inventory!

not-so-friendly way. I did.) The best marketing strategy employs more than one medium. Again, this is why it is vitally important to develop a comprehensive marketing plan for your business that maximizes your opportunities.

What Happens When You Don't Use Market Analysis. Remember our story of the pizzeria in Chapter 1? While failure to market ultimately led to the demise of the business, the owners made a crucial mistake before opening—they didn't conduct a market analysis. The business was family-run. The family was Italian and loved cooking, and had become legendary for their unique homemade pizza creations. The father and sons had worked in restaurants so were familiar with the industry. It had been a long-held family dream to own a pizzeria. When the space became available they decided that the timing was right.

The location was heavily trafficked and they believed that the other businesses were a perfect complement—no competitors. On the surface it seemed like an ideal location, but deeper digging would have turned up a contrary opinion. The location was conducive to the other businesses.

The surf shop was close to the beach and had convenient free parking. The dry cleaners was a long-established business that offered delivery and pickup service.

However, people on their way to or coming back from the beach weren't stopping for pizza. Those in the mood for a slice of pizza would grab one while at the beach. People leaving the beach weren't stopping, as they were likely eager to get home and get cleaned up from a day at the beach. Just a few blocks down, another busy strip mall offered space for lease. This location was close to nearby businesses and had other food businesses that would have complemented the pizzeria.

What can you learn from this story? Basically, do your homework before you start your business so you can save yourself a lot of time and money. While many business owners have failed, only to find success later, you'll reach your goal much faster with a little advance research. A market analysis is not a guarantee of success. Many factors contribute to success. However, you owe it yourself to be armed with as much information as possible to ensure that your business model is viable. Of course, even the best market analysis can't offer a 100 percent guarantee—you'll never get that in the world of marketing. But if you do it right, you can get perhaps an 80 percent guarantee that your business will be successful. This is a lot better than doing nothing, which would give you a guarantee of 0 percent.

SITE ANALYSIS

Periodically, you should perform a detailed analysis of your site to see if it's still optimized for search engines. To do this you need a software program. You can use a paid traffic and site analysis program, such as Traffic Blazer (which costs $29.99/year and more), or you could use a free site analysis program. A good free site analysis program can be found at linkvendor.com. In fact, this program offers so much of what you need, you almost don't need a paid site analysis program, although a paid program in some instances might be faster than Linkvendor.

> **TIP:** See other tools in the bookmark section of www.jonrognerud.com/amember. An advanced tool like Optilink is used by top SEO firms and marketers to analyze link profiles, a key SEO component.

What do most site analysis programs check for? Use linkvendor.com as a model; a good site analysis program should check for link value, link popularity, domain popularity, IP domains, page rank, SEO comparisons against other sites, your site's SERP (Search Engine Results Page), outbound links, keyword density, cloaked links, how your site is being spidered by search engine bots, and how fast your site is operating. The following paragraphs describe each of these factors, to give you a better understanding of how effective your site really is.

1. Link Value. Internet marketing should not end with search optimization. In fact, one way you can improve your search engine ranking is by linking to established high-trafficked sites. Do this through a link exchange, in which you advertise a webmaster's link on your site in exchange for their advertising your link on their site. Otherwise, you should consider purchasing advertising space from another web site. The best resource you can use for finding link space for sale is through portals such as adbrite.com.

> **Trade Rules**
>
> Keep in mind that while buying and selling links is not recommended by the search engines (Google in specific), you may buy and sell advertising space. Google recommends using a special tag (rel=nofollow) on the hyperlink to not unfairly inflate or pass PageRank.

Before you buy advertising space, however, make sure what you're buying will earn you enough profit. This is where determining link value comes into play. If you're using linkvendor.com as your site analysis program, all you have to do is enter the URL of the web site you want to advertise on, along with the currency in which you would like to see the value. If the resulting link value is high, yet the price advertised is low, go ahead and purchase advertising space from that web site. If the link value is low, and the price is high, leave it alone. If the link value and price match, you can make the call.

The link value tool also comes in handy for determining what you should charge for advertising space once your site is popular enough for you to offer this option.

2. Link Popularity. Link popularity refers to how many web pages link to your site. If you're using the link popularity tool on linkvendor.com, the tool will show how many links are linked to your site on the basis of the most popular search engines: Google, MSN, Yahoo!, Ask Jeeves, and Alexa. It will also list what is being used in your meta tags, your keywords as listed by Alexa, and your Alexa traffic rank. Alexa is a popular site that helps you determine the traffic of a particular web site.

> **TIP:** See the bookmarks section on www.jon-rognerud.com/amember for other tools like www.marketleap.com, a popular free service.

3. Domain Popularity. There's a lot of controversy concerning link popularity, due to link farms and link spam. In response to this problem, Google checks domain popularity, which is how many sites link to your direct top-level domain name, rather than a specific page within your site. The thought behind domain popularity is that if your top-level URL is linked to (rather than a specific page), the webmaster's interests in advertising your site are more genuine.

Linkvendor.com's domain popularity tool returns detailed information regarding your domain popularity. This information includes the number of sites yours serves as a backlink on, your page rank (discussed later in this book), and a number determining the effectiveness of your link, otherwise known as link strength. Next, the web site returns a detailed list of all the sites that link to your domain name. The site tells you the exact URLs of the web sites, the web sites' IP addresses, and the page rank of each site. And even better, you can choose to view your results by listing the URL first, the page rank first, or the IP address first.

The downside to this tool is that it can take a long time to list your results, especially if your site is established. The site even tells you that it can take up to 15 minutes to return results. Unfortunately, there is no way around this. What makes it worthwhile is that it does return a lot of helpful information at no extra cost to you.

4. IP Domains. The IP domains tool (called "Domains from IP" on linkvendor.com) shows the domains that link to your IP address. Knowing which sites also share your IP address can help you investigate if there are questionable web sites that could potentially harm the reputation of your IP address. If one webmaster spams, then everyone on the same IP address is negatively affected, even if they didn't participate. This is why it's best to get web hosts that use separate IP addresses for each of their clients. Yet, if you can't find one and/or you need the affordability of virtual hosting, the "Domains from IP" tool on linkvendor.com can be of great assistance.

5. PageRank. Your page rank is extremely important when it comes to search optimization. Page rank is calculated by a complex formula that takes into account incoming links and their value. At the heart of Google's search engine software is PageRank™. As the name implies, it's a system for ranking web pages. In Google's own words (www.google.com/technology), "PageRank relies on the uniquely democratic nature of the web by using its vast link structure as an indicator of an individual page's value." In essence, Google interprets a link from page A to page B as a vote by page A for page B. But Google looks at considerably more than the volume of votes, or links, a page receives; for example, it also analyzes the page that casts the vote. Votes cast by pages that are themselves "important" weigh more heavily and help to make other pages "important." Using these and other factors, Google provides its views on the page's relative importance.

Of course, important pages mean nothing to you if they don't match your query. So Google combines PageRank with sophisticated text-matching techniques to find pages that are both important and relevant to your search. Google goes far beyond the number of times a term appears on a page and examines dozens of aspects of the page's content (and the content of the pages linking to it) to determine if it's a good match for your query.

The resulting number ranges from 0–10, with 0 being the least relevant to 10 being the most relevant. You can determine your page rank by typing it in Google's toolbar (if you have this installed in your browser), or you can use linkvendor.com. Unlike Google's toolbar, linkvendor.com will tell you if the page rank value returned is accurate.

6. SEO Comparisons against Other Sites. Linkvendor.com puts a little fun in site analysis through its "SEO Challenge" tool. This makes SEO comparisons against other sites. You enter the sites you want to compare, and linkvendor identifies the "winner" and the "loser." The "winner" shows the winning domain name along with a graphic of a crown and a number showing how effectively optimized it is. The "losing" domain name will show the domain name, a trash can graphic, and the same number. Aside from the comedic relief this tool offers, it can actually be a great way to see how your competitors fare when it comes to search engine marketing. If the competing site ranks high, you might want to look at it to see why it's doing better than yours and implement those strategies. You may even want to e-mail the webmaster and see if he or she would be willing to sell advertising space or do a link exchange.

7. SERP (Search Engine Results Page). SERP shows you results from your queries, and you can find out how high your site is in search engine results according to a particular keyword. Wikipedia defines SERP as "the listing of web pages returned by a search engine in response to a keyword query. The results normally include a list of web pages with titles, a link to the page, and a short description showing where the keywords have matched content within the page. A SERP may refer to a single page of links returned, or to the set of all links returned for a search query" (http://en.wikipedia.org/wiki/SERP). With linkvendor.com's SERP tool, you enter the URL you want analyzed, the keywords that pertain to it, and the search engines you want to see results for (which are Google, MSN, and Yahoo!). By selecting the appropriate extension, you can also see SERP data for foreign versions of these search engines. For example, if you wanted to see how your site fares in the French version of Google.com, you would select .fr as your extension.

8. Outbound Links. Outbound links are links on your site that would send your visitors to a completely different site. Having a large number of outbound links is very attractive to search engine bots, so you want to have as many as you can, within reason. Remember, too many outbound links take visitors away from your site, something that you don't want. So make sure that the outbound links are worthwhile, such as affiliate programs or relevant resources. Don't create links for the sake of link-building, as this not only diminishes the value to your potential customers but can also get you into trouble with search engines.

9. Keyword Density. You learned about keyword density earlier in this book, but as a refresher, keyword density is the percentage of times a keyword appears in your web site content. Some of the keyword tools that you learned about earlier, while very useful, lack an element that linkvendor.com has—namely, the ability to show you your exact SERP. Linkvendor.com's keyword density tool shows you the keyword density of each keyword found on your site. It also provides a graphic of the top search engines including Google, MSN, Yahoo!, and Ask Jeeves. If you click on this graphic, you are directed to your exact SERP.

10. Cloaked Links. *Cloaked links* are links that are "hidden" from the view of the site visitor. This could be because they are linked through a banner or button, or through text. Cloaked links are a popular approach used by many affiliate marketers to hide unattractive and intimidating affiliate links that, for the visitor, are hard to remember or even undesirable to click on (since some people may be less likely to click on an affiliate link when they see it as an ad).

When designing your web site, you might have so many cloaked links that you lose track of them. This is where linkvendor.com's cloaked link tool comes in handy. Once you enter the URL, you are shown which links are cloaked. The site shows you graphical versions of these links rather than giving you the specific link itself.

11. Search Engine Spidering Tool. Search engine spiders, also known as bots, scour the web looking for web sites to include in search engine listings. While keywords are important, spiders determine listings by the number of incoming links related to a site (*incoming links* refers to how many web sites link to you). Outbound links can help your ranking, too, though not as much.

Linkvendor.com shows you everything you need to know about how search engine spiders index your site. With your URL entered, linkvendor.com returns meta tag information that's been spidered, text from your web site that's been spidered, outbound links, and incoming links.

12. Site Speed. Site speed is an very important element when it comes to internet marketing. Generally, visitors will only wait up to five seconds for a web page to load, though modem users might be more patient, waiting up to 30–60 seconds. web site visitors might be more understanding if they know the site is complex, which is particularly the case for gaming sites or sites with video. But there is a limit to their patience. If you're unable to get your site delivered within that window of a few seconds, you can pretty much guarantee that you'll lose a great deal of traffic.

Fortunately, there is linkvendor.com's "Speedtester" tool. Speedtester lets you know how fast your site runs for all types of connections including dial-up, ISDN, UMTS, DSL, T1, and T2. The Speedtester tool also returns the percentage of HTML coding you have in relation to the percentage of actual content.

13. Miscellaneous Tools. Site analysis programs may include additional tools that could be of assistance, yet don't relate directly to site analysis. In the case of linkvendor.com, this tool would be its handy "URL Rewrite." If you remember earlier in this book when error pages were discussed, you read about 301 redirects and ways to initiate them. One of these methods is using the Apache rewrite module. If you need the exact coding to determine how to initiate a 301 redirect for your webpage, you can use linkvendor.com's URL Rewrite. You enter your URL and in return you receive a customized Apache rewrite code you can use in your .htaccess file.

Keywords of Competitors

It's important when analyzing keywords that you know which keywords your competitors use, and if you're in the proper league to either continue to use them or try for keywords that are still popular yet not used as often. Some paid keyword analyzers can tell you which competitors use which keywords, but this is often limited to what is used for AdSsense campaigns. AdSense ads are different than regular search engine listings. A good way to determine what keywords your competitors are using is to use a keyword analyzer to extract keywords from their pages, and then copy and paste your selected keyword into a search engine such as Yahoo! or Google to see where they show up.

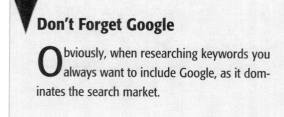

Don't Forget Google

Obviously, when researching keywords you always want to include Google, as it dominates the search market.

Once you've entered your keyword in a search engine, take a look at the results that come up. Don't worry as much about the sponsored listings, as these spots are out of your league if you have limited funds. Focus on the first 10 direct listings of the search engine results. Ask yourself, Do these listings relate to the keyword at hand? For example, when I typed in "cat pictures," I found "Cat Photos," "Funny Cat Pictures," and "Amazing Cat Collection" on the first page of the Google results. You'll note that not every result listed on the first page had "cat pictures." As you learned earlier in this book, having the exact keyword phrase in your title makes you rank better with search engines. Additionally, you can check on the number of inbound links of these sites. Use linkvendor.com to do this. Or, another method is to first put "link:" in front of the URL and put the whole thing into the search engine. (For example, you would use link:http://www.the-page-you-want-to-investigate.com.) The search engine will return how many inbound links the web site has.

Now, what do you do with all this information, particularly if the number is high? Even if the number of inbound links is in the thousands, you don't necessarily have to discount a keyword. In order for inbound links to be useful for search engines, they must relate to the keywords used throughout your web site. For example, if you're looking to rank well for refinancing loans, yet your inbound links are for subprime mortgage loans, you'll get a good search engine ranking for subprime mortgage loans rather than what you originally wanted, which was refinancing loans.

You'll get some legitimate traffic, since some subprime loans are also refinancing loans, but the traffic wouldn't be as good as if you had inbound links that related directly to refinancing loans. If this is what is happening with your competitor's keywords, you can take advantage of it by creating a site with the appropriate inbound links.

How can you determine if a competitor's inbound links relate to the keywords used on their site? Use the "Advanced Search" option of your desired search engine. In the "All of These Words" text box, enter: "link:http://www.the-page-you-want-to-investigate.com."

> **TIP:** I use SEO-Elite, a power SEO tool for checking backlinks. I also use We Build Page (webuildpages/neat-o.com), another excellent resource. Go to the lifetime member portal at www.jonrognerud.com/amember and check the Backlinks Competitive Review video series.

Set the "Display per Page" box to 100 listings. You may initially get a result that says a web site has thousands of inbound links, but what matters are the numbers of results that show up when you scroll down the page. When I did this test for the top-ranking page for cat pictures, I found that although Google said the site had over 400 inbound links, in the first three pages, only one was relevant. You can effectively compete even if a site has a number of legitimate inbound links. The key is to ensure that your links directly relate to the keywords used on your site. If your competitors do not, you may be rewarded with top placement.

CHAPTER 5

Step-by-Step Guide to Keyword Search

Bob was familiar with the basics of keywords. To learn more he decided to use a real estate client as a test case. Bob talked to the client about their web site traffic and told them that he wanted to use them as a case study for improving results. The client happily agreed.

Bob typed "real estate" in the search engine and—no surprise—he got millions of results. He searched for his client's name and was surprised when it wasn't in the top results. He played around with different combinations and took notes on what he found.

Real estate was extremely competitive based on number of web sites returned from initial top-level keyword research and Bob wasn't sure how to get the best results for his client. He had a list of keywords from the client but wasn't sure how to choose the best keywords on which to compete.

Unsure of how to proceed, Bob turned to online webmaster forums for help. A few people pointed Bob in the direction of software programs that would help make keyword selection easier. Bob signed up with Wordtracker and Keyword Discovery, but there was still more work to do.

Earlier in this book you were introduced to the concept of keywords. You were taught how to use keyword analyzers to decide how to write your content. We discussed keyword competition and learned how to determine highly competitive keywords. Now, it's time to delve deeper into every aspect of keyword research.

Begin your keyword research by creating a seed list. You can use Wordtracker or other keyword tools (see Tools for Analyzing Keywords in this chapter) to find the most popular terms in your seed list and reject those that have low volumes. There are many options available if you need help creating your seed list. A few suggestions are listed below.

- Mail, print ads, direct mail, catalogs, and anything that has ad copy related to your site
- Online trend tools such as Yahoo! Buzz Index (buzz.yahoo.com), zeitgeist (Google), hotsearches.aol.com, and google.com/trends
- News articles
- Competition
- news.google.com
- Review hottest bookmarks using sites such as digg and del.icio.us
- topix.net—aggregates
- techmeme
- technorati.com/pop
- Amazon—best sellers
- eBay marketplace research services
- reviews.ebay.com
- Yahoo! Answers
- Google groups
- boardtracker.com
- Review directories such as dir.yahoo.com, dmoz.org, and business.com

Another good tip for analyzing competitors' sites (as well as your own site) is to use Google's "allintitle" or "allinurl" commands. Your title and URL tags help the search engines determine the nature of your page's content. To use the "allin" command for your analysis, for example, in the search box type "allintitle: cat & feline." This tells the search engine to find all sites with both "cat" and "feline" in the title. When I typed this into Google, it returned 512 results. However a search for "cat & litter box" only returned 181 results. The "allinurl: cat & feline" command returned 192 results. Most searchers don't know these commands, but they are good techniques for you to use when researching.

When researching keywords you want to dig deeper into the "long tail." The *long tail* represents the multitude of search terms beyond the top ten or 20 that visitors use to find your site. For example, your keyword may be "chocolate," which drives traffic, but many

Figure 5-1. Allintitle

more visitors combined find you by using "chocolate gifts," "corporate chocolate gifts," and "dark chocolate gifts." While "chocolate gifts," "corporate chocolate gifts," and "dark chocolate gifts" do not individually pull as much traffic as "chocolate," collectively, they pull far more traffic. Think of the long tail as starting with what's popular but continuing to follow that trail to the end. Search marketers are discovering that the long tail is responsible for the bulk of traffic—completely opposite of what was previously believed. However, it's still important to have a balanced focus on both traffic and conversion. Consider what's most important to your business.

Broaden your search to related terms and dig deep again. Organize and prioritize what you find. Many people give scant attention to developing a really great seed list. If you only do the obvious, you'll end up with obvious results—just like everyone else. To get outstanding results from your keyword research, you've got to apply creativity and hard work to the first step, generating your keyword seed list. If you fail here, you fail in search engine optimization.

GENERAL FACTS ABOUT KEYWORDS

Keywords typically range from two to five words, though there are popular one-word keywords. Keywords may also be referred to as search phrases, keyword phrases, or query

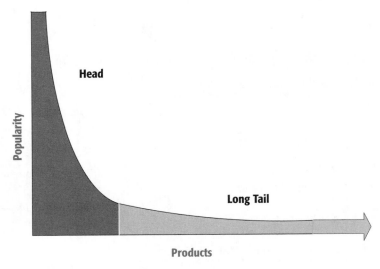

Figure 5-2. The "Long Tail"

phrases. Regardless of what you call them, it's important that the keywords you choose are relevant to your site's goal, theme, and subject matter. Don't optimize for generic keywords (even if they relate to your site) just because those keywords might have more traffic. For example, "real estate" is a generic keyword that gets a lot of traffic. However, if you're a real

estate agent in Sterling Heights, Michigan, a better keyword might be "real estate agent sterling heights michigan." With generic keywords, you might get some hits initially, but they won't convert to sales or leads because the traffic you get is not really interested in your web site. Someone typing "real estate" may have been looking for real estate loans, real estate schools or even information on foreclosures.

When you choose the right keyword combination for your web site, you attract visitors who actually want to see your site—in fact, they were looking specifically for it. In essence, you're prequalifying the lead rather than casting a wide net and throwing back most of the fish! Sometimes there are even cases where you might want to optimize for a less competitive keyword because the few numbers of visitors you get would be highly interested in what you have to offer (especially if there aren't many web sites offering that particular product or service). This niche marketing tactic might generate only a few hundred hits, but if they convert, it's 1,000 times better than the thousands of irrelevant hits you could get from a popular, yet unrelated, keyword. Traffic is meaningless if no one is buying what you have to offer.

Additionally, there are certain types of keywords that are a potential gold mine because they're often ignored by many webmasters and internet marketers. These include misspelled keywords, keyword phrases that use Boolean operators, and advanced search options. If you're new to the internet, you may not be familiar with the term *Boolean operators*, but they really aren't a big deal. Basically, they're special commands you use in a search engine to bring up more specific results. The most popular Boolean operators for search engines include AND, OR, NOT, and " " (double quotes).

Learning how these operators work is not hard. *And* they tell the search engine to look for two sets of keywords (Google, however, uses an automatic Boolean AND, a default). For example, the keyword phrase "necklaces AND earrings," would return results that would include these two words somewhere in a web site. They can be shown individually or simultaneously. If you used "necklaces OR earrings," the search engine would return web sites that contained listings of earrings or necklaces. They would be shown separately. NOT excludes certain keywords from search engine listings. Still using "necklaces and earrings" as the example keyword, if you said "necklaces NOT earrings," the search engine would return only web sites containing the term "necklaces" in their content. Finally the quotation marks "" specify that everything within them must be found on pages, and is returned bold-faced in search engine results. For example, typing "necklaces and earrings" would return search listing results that show these terms exactly as listed. It is important to note that "" allows for more specific results than AND, since AND may or may not return results that show necklaces and earrings together.

So, how would you optimize for misspelled words and keywords with Boolean phrases? Wouldn't this look a little odd in legitimate content? You would be 100 percent correct in this assumption, which is why you would try not to use these throughout your content. The exception could be if a misspelled word is very common and wouldn't look wrong to web site visitors. Otherwise, you would want to put these in the keyword property of your meta tags.

Wait a second … Keyword property of meta tags? More than likely you didn't know meta tags had a keyword property. It's relevant here, where we're doing a detailed analysis of keywords. Basically, the keyword meta tag property tells search engines what keywords you want your site to be indexed by. The syntax of the meta tag keyword property is listed below:

> **TIP:** Since most search engines index documents, you can place misspellings inside PDF, DOC and XLS documents, and they will be picked up. I rank #1 for "whatis seo" in a PDF document. Not highly searched, but it happens. Don't exclude this strategy, especially considering the poor spelling tactics from visitors abroad!

<meta name="keywords" content="enter, your, keywords, here">

In the case of Boolean keywords and misspelled words, you place them where you see the "enter, your, keywords, here." These should be included with your regular keywords. This doesn't guarantee that Booleans or misspelled words will always return your site, but if you don't do it, you won't be able to take advantage of these lesser-used keywords. For search engines today, don't put too much emphasis on the keyword meta tag, as it's largely ignored, but I include it here as reference.

Sour Grapes. Don't think misspelled words are limited to search engine placement. eBay users use the eBay search function to find items of interest. eBay insiders have noted that if you search for misspelled auctions, you can often find deals on merchandise that have few to no bids due to the misspelled word. I read a story about a man who sold a rare type of wine. He misspelled the name of the wine, allowing the winning bidder to buy it for only a few hundred dollars. The winning bidder turned around and sold the wine for over $300,000! Undoubtedly, if he sold it on eBay, he checked the spelling first!

TOOLS FOR ANALYZING KEYWORDS

Earlier you were introduced to keyword analyzers and instructed to either jump to this section for more detail on paid keyword analyzers or use Overture's (now Yahoo!'s) free keyword analyzer tool found at http://inventory.overture.com/d/searchinventory/suggestion.

One note on the Overture tool: you will not receive current results, but searches done six months ago. However, it's still a good tool to help you get started. Good Keywords is another freeware tool that's great for beginners and experts alike, and helps you automate using Overture's database. It can be downloaded from goodkeywords.com. (See Figure 5-3.) Once you start getting some sales, consider investing in a paid keyword analyzer.

Google has a free keyword tool (https://adwords.google.com/select/KeywordTool External) that also shows you advertiser competition, the current month's search volume, and the average search volume (Figure 5-4).

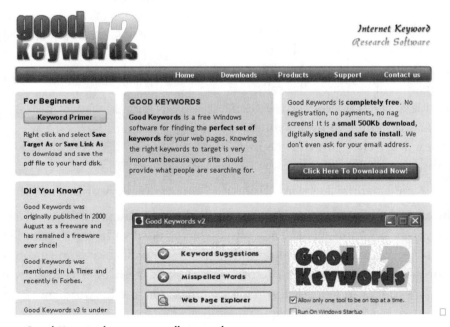

Figure 5-3. Good Keywords—www.goodkeywords.com

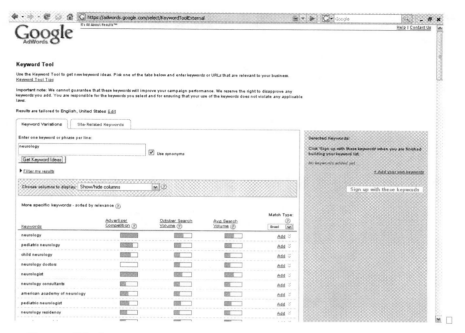

Figure 5-4. Keyword Tool

The tool is helpful not only for PPC campaigns, but for creating your keyword seed list.

The most popular paid keyword analyzers are Keyword Discovery and Wordtracker. The nice thing about these tools is that you don't have to download anything, as it's all available online. The keyword tools identify all the variations of your search phrase, including synonyms and misspellings commonly searched for by those seeking similar sites. They also tell you how many hits a keyword has received (Figures 5-5 and 5-6).

The biggest difference between these tools and free ones such as Overture's keyword analyzer tool is that they contain more detail. With Keyword Discovery and Wordtracker, you get a thorough analysis of your keywords. With Overture's keyword analyzer tool you only get a list of each instance of a keyword and how many people have searched it. In the long run, you'll find that the paid keyword analyzers offer a lot more assistance in your internet marketing campaign than the free ones.

Expect to pay about $50 a month each for Keyword Discovery and Wordtracker.

> **TIP:** If you're researching your existing site or a competitor's, you can also use this simple (and free) trick. Take all the words from your server logs, add to Excel, add <BR> per line, and upload to your server. Then, go to a keyword density tool like linkvendor.com and run the tool against the file. Pick broad match keywords that may have been missed, two or more words. Simple, easy, and free!

Figure 5-5. Keyword Discovery

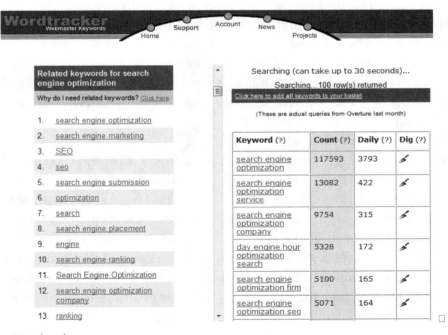

Figure 5-6. Wordtracker

Both, at the time of this writing, have free trials. Use the free trial to evaluate both and pick the tool that best meets your needs. If your budget can afford it, subscribe to both.

What's the best way to use Keyword Discovery, Wordtracker, or a free keyword analyzer? The first step is to think like your customer. Enter phrases that your potential customers may use. For example, if you're a web designer, your customers may enter "web sites," "good web design," "fast web design," or "professional web site." Don't worry about proper grammar or spelling because, as you already know, misspellings are common among search engine users. Improper grammar is also common. Additionally, avoid searching industry jargon, unless your target audience would use the jargon in their web searches. For example, the average person new to internet marketing wouldn't know anything about SEO optimization. So, if they're searching for a book related to SEO optimization, they may instead enter "search engine marketing." More advanced marketers would be acquainted with the term and enter it properly. If you're really stuck on what you should promote in terms of jargon, be on the safe side and try for both, though in terms of search engines the more you can optimize for just one keyword the better.

In the next section we cover a few pointers that will help you manage your keyword research.

1. You say Tomato, They Say Tomatoes. It's important to note both the singular and plural forms of keyword phrases. Even though they are essentially the same, sometimes one form might bring more hits than another. Keep in mind, this goes for the correct form of a keyword along with misspellings. It also applies for keywords using Boolean operators. For example, job seekers may search for "resumes" more often than "resume."

2. KEI – ah! The *Keyword Effectiveness Index* (KEI), found in tools like Wordtracker and Keyword Discovery, determines a keyword's value by calculating its popularity along with the number of competing web sites. A higher KEI means that a keyword may have less competition and would be a strategic pick for you. Wordtracker defines the KEI in this way: "The KEI compares the count result (number of times a keyword has appeared in our data) with the number of competing web pages to pinpoint exactly which keywords are most effective for your campaign."

Wordtracker computes the formula for you, but it breaks down to P, which denotes the popularity of the keyword, and C, the competitiveness. There are other formulas created by search marketers, such as KEI = $(P\char`^2/C)$, i.e., KEI is the square of the popularity of the keyword and divided by its competitiveness.

There is no need to be overly concerned with the formula. KEI helps you find easy-to-optimize secondary and tertiary phrases. If you find keywords with high KEI, by all means use them. Keywords with a low KEI may also be useful if they have a high search value.

3. Export and Sort. Another important productivity feature with Keyword Discovery and Wordtracker is their ability to export files into Excel format. With Excel you can sort your data in a variety of ways. You can also create charts and graphs for it, so you can get a clear visual picture of keyword performance. Then there is an option offered by Keyword Discovery and WordTracker to store your keyword data online, but for many people this feature isn't as useful as storing the data offline.

4. Select Overture in Results. "Select Overture in Results" is a Wordtracker feature only. By looking at Overture searches per month, you can get an idea of the popularity and the perceived monetary value of a search engine phrase. In fact, some keywords are so competitive that the only way you can take advantage of them is through a pay-per-click campaign. The other side to this is that pay-per-clicks are expensive. Some can be as low as a cent or so per click to as high as $63.42 (the keyword "mesothelioma" at the time of this writing is $63.42).

> **TIP:** To get a view into cost per keyword, see Google's own free tool at https://adwords. google.com/select/TrafficEstimatorSandbox. (See Figure 5-7.)

While $63.42 per click is out of most people's budgets, even a keyword that's one cent per click can get expensive if a person gets thousands of hits across multiple keywords and has not monitored the campaign. If you decide to do a pay-per-click campaign, stick with the least expensive keywords and pay close attention to your sales rate. A starting number could be a sale per 500 hits. (This would cost you $5 if the price was one cent per click). If you aren't getting conversions, add more keywords and analyze why your site isn't bringing in sales. To look

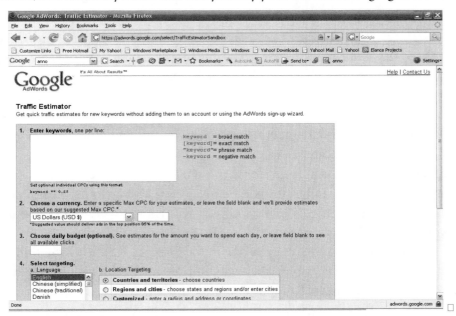

Figure 5-7. Google Traffic Estimator

at this in another way, if you had 100 clicks and 1 percent of the people took the desired action (conversion), your lead result would be one. Move the clicks and the conversion rate up, and you're heading in the right direction. We talk more about pay-per-click campaigns in Chapter 10.

Bob was ready to begin optimizing his first site. Before testing his skills on clients, he offered to optimize his neighbor's site free of charge. He would track the results

> **TIP:** A desktop version keyword tool is found on the CD—GoodKeywords.exe. It uses the overture/yahoo search database, and makes it much easier to manage results.
>
> You can go to www.jonrognerud.com/amember to see videos on how to use both Wordtracker and Keyword Discovery.

and use the site as a test case. Bob knew that he needed a keyword analyzer tool but was unsure which one to use. Using Google, he found Wordtracker, Keyword Discovery, and Ad Word Analyzer. He checked all three sites and decided to use AdWord Analyzer. The program appeared to be as effective as Keyword Discovery or Wordtracker, but with a price tag that was only $97, with no recurring monthly fees. After using the software, Bob immediately encountered a multitude of annoying pop-ups and hyperlinks on things that should not have been hyperlinked (a common characteristic of spyware). Worse, every time he tried to use Google, he was told that he had a virus or spyware program that was trying to break into Google's code. Bob figured out that AdWord was using spyware and other deceptive programming tactics to deliver its keyword analyses. He deleted the software, ran his antivirus and antispyware programs, and went with Wordtracker.

Be careful of third-party keyword analyzers. They might be cheaper, and they might even offer the information you need, but you don't know how they obtain the data. If you can't afford a top-of-the-line keyword analyzer, then it's better to stick with the free programs we've mentioned. As your business grows, you'll be able to invest in other tools.

OPTIMIZATION STRATEGY FOR PRIMARY AND SECONDARY KEYWORD PHRASES

Primary Keyword Phrases

Your primary keyword phrase is a little like your elevator pitch for the internet. It's a single keyword phrase that aptly represents what your web site and business offer. The primary keyword phrase is the main phrase that appears throughout your web site. Because primary keyword phrases tend to be more generic than secondary keyword phrases (discussed in the next section), they are more competitive and harder to optimize.

When determining your primary keyword phrases, be sure to include variations of them. For example, if you wanted to use "home loan" as a primary keyword phrase, you could use "countrywide home loan" as a more specific variation. By using variations of your primary keyword phrase, you prevent the likelihood of using a keyword that's overly broad and not specific enough.

Secondary Keyword Phrases

Secondary keyword phrases are like primary keyword phrases. The difference is that a secondary keyword phrase is not searched on as frequently as your primary. Still using "home loan" as an example, a secondary keyword phrase could be "mortgage loan."

More Suggestions for Choosing Keywords

Generally, the more specific your primary and secondary keyword phrases with related content, the better chance you'll have of ranking high. Think about using keyword combinations that most webmasters ignore, such as three-, four-, or even five-word phrases. You could also include a geographical reference for your keywords to make them even more specific. For example, instead of trying to optimize for "real estate," try for "maryland real estate" and "maryland real estate agents."

▼ **Trend Finder**

You can review search trends using the Google Trends tool found at www.google.com/trends.

Visuwords is an online graphical dictionary and thesaurus. This is helpful in digging deep and coming up with more keywords to research. It's also a fun tool. Quintura is a visual search engine. Quintura calls it a "see and find" search. You type in a keyword, and you get search results on one side of the page and keyword clouds on the other. You hover over a word and it brings up all other related words.

Aaron Walls' SEO book (http://tools.seobook.com/general/keyword/) is a great keyword tool as it pulls in search volumes from Google, Yahoo!, and MSN. From one screen you can link to Wordtracker, Keyword Discovery, Google Trends, Yahoo Suggest, Google Suggest, Google Synonym, SeoDigger, Quintura, and AdWords. Think of it as a one-stop shopping tool for keyword research.

Spyfu (www.spyfu.com) lets you download competitive keywords, rankings, and PPC data. You type in the domain name and receive a list of results. The tool is free but offers advanced analytics for a subscription fee.

Another competitive keyword tool is keycompete.com. You receive the top five results for free. You have the option to buy the full results for your search term for a flat fee, or subscribe (one-day trial, monthly, or annual) for full access.

Additional keyword tools to help you are Yahoo! (http://searchmarketing.yahoo.com/), for which you need an account, and MSN (https://adcenter.microsoft.com/Default.aspx).

KEYWORD OPTIMIZATION STRATEGY

It's a good idea to optimize each of your web pages for no more than two keyword phrases per page, which would include your primary keyword phrase, your secondary keyword phrase, and variations on them. Targeted keyword pages must have your primary keyword phrase and your best secondary keyword phrase. Of particular concern is your home page, which needs to put extra emphasis on your primary keyword phrase. This is because search engines are more likely to give your home page a higher ranking than the other pages on your site (and external links tend to be drawn to the home page most of the time). Your home page will then link to other pages on your site that contain (and are optimized for) your other, more specific keyword phrases.

CHAPTER 6

Psychology of Your Audience

KNOW YOUR AUDIENCE

Janet didn't do much research on her market. She had been coaching for two years and assumed that her online business would be the same as her offline business. In her coaching business she had successfully worked with both men and women of various ages. She had started in her local area and, through referrals and speaking engagements, had obtained clients across the state.

Online coaching was a way for her to cut down on traveling and to develop a secondary income from selling informational products. Janet often met with clients face to face for the first one or two sessions and then continued coaching by phone.

Her practice had been successful and Janet wanted to build up her telephone coaching business, which would allow her to get more done in fewer hours. She also believed that she could eventually make use of virtual web coaching sessions and even group webinars.

The problem was that Janet's success offline wasn't immediately transferable to the web. Janet had failed to assess her online competition and her target market. In fact, she had not clearly identified her target market, so her site and its message were ineffective and captured very little business.

In Chapter 1 we discussed how important it is to have a marketing plan. A key part of this plan is to know your market. While this book doesn't go into depth on how to write a marketing plan, it is important to at least identify basic information about your market. Too many people ignore this key step in internet marketing campaigns, but you need this information. Knowing your market will help you determine what keywords to choose, as well as the direction to take to update your web site.

How do you obtain general information about your audience? What should this information consist of? This section answers those questions by explaining the process of analyzing the psychographics and demographics of your audience, along with the best ways to acquire this data.

Psychographic Analysis

A *psychographic analysis* is an investigation of consumer behavior. It is also called a *lifestyle analysis* or AIO (Activities, Interests, Opinions) because it relies on a number of statements about a person's activities, interests and opinions. In essence, you are determining consumer interest, what they like, and how they live.

A psychographic analysis provides you with information beyond who will buy, or buys, your product or service. It gives you the drivers that make them *want* to buy it. There are a number of approaches to segment your market. The Values and Lifestyles (VALS) approach developed at Stanford Research Institute International is widely used. Some examples of psychographic information you can research include consumer spending patterns, level of brand conscience (for your service/product, are consumers brand conscious?), what influences their buying behavior, and what promotional efforts they respond to most often.

When we discuss landing pages and conversions, we talk more about intent, wants and needs, and how they can be used to leverage content and positioning.

Demographic Analysis

Demographics refers to the physical characteristics of your audience. These characteristics include location, age, marital status, occupation, educational level, disabilities, race, income level, and even an individual's mode of transportation. Demographic trends identify and describe the changes in a population over time. Don't neglect demographic trends when you do your research. In fact, they could be a critical factor determining the success of your business. For example, let's say hypothetically that demographic trends show there's a large percentage of teenagers in the population. You successfully market a product that targets them. However, teenagers only stay teens for seven years. What happens after seven years? If the demographic trends showed that the younger generation, the teens' brothers and sisters, are growing in large numbers, then naturally the former teens will be replaced with the new generation of teens. However, if the demographic trends show that there's a standstill in birth rates, your business that originally marketed to teens might suffer. At that point you could continue marketing your business to the smaller teen population, or you could change the market to the teens you formerly marketed to, who at this point would be young adults.

When doing demographic marketing, it's important to keep mind this is only one component of your analysis. You cannot assume that *all* people in that demographic will behave in exactly the same way. This is known as demographic profiling. Don't completely avoid certain markets just because the data show they might not be interested or eligible. If the data look negative on the surface, see if there is a potential for market growth among that demographic. Video games are a perfect example. When they started out, they were marketed to children and teens. Little emphasis was given to creating games for adults. Things changed as technology improved, especially when the Playstation came out. Now, if the marketing executives responsible for marketing the Playstation console and games had gone with the previous demographic trends, they wouldn't have made much of an attempt to market to an older audience, that is, individuals ages 18 to 90. They didn't, and slowly but surely more and more games for adults were created. Now, it's easy to find video games that are geared to an adult market.

The same principle could be applied to games targeted at women. While that market is still underdeveloped, it's come a long way since video games first came out. There are now more games like The Sims and Dreamfall that try to create an entertaining experience for both genders. Previously, women were so ignored in the video game industry that it was a source of controversy when a gaming company braved the market and produced a game with a prominent female character.

How to Find Out the Psychographics and Demographics of Your Market

To determine the psychographics and demographics of your market there are a variety of sources and methods you can use, including surveys and specialized marketing software. The American Marketing Association (www.marketingpower.com) offers a number of free and low-cost marketing tools. To access the tools, you will need to sign up for a free subscription, but you'll be able to read case studies, research, look up terms and definitions and more.

Hitwise (www.hitwise.com) offers competitive intelligence products and services for online marketing, online advertising, and search marketing. You can obtain in-depth demographic and industry insight. Hitwise is a paid service.

Nielsen//NetRatings (www.nielsen-netratings.com) offers some free data and rankings and also has a number of paid products and solutions for internet marketing and online advertising.

We've already learned about creating surveys for your audience. We won't go into much more detail in this section except to add that there are survey networks you can join if you have the cash. Be careful though, since many of these networks claim to offer money to respondents in exchange for their participation in a survey, but many of them tend to avoid payment. So, if you do decide to use a survey network, research them before you start doing business. Survey networks that don't pay tend to be talked about a lot in message board forums, so an easy way to determine if a survey network is a scam is to enter its name in a search engine along with the term "scam."

The other method to discuss is using software to size up your market. You can obtain demographics info from www.quantcast.com. The software is free; it lets you track your site in their vast database and will create more detail for you by applying a simple script to your page. You can also buy information products or customized lists based on your data sets from infousa.com.

You can obtain keyword competitiveness data from www.keycompete.com or www.spyfu.com.

THINK LIKE YOUR AUDIENCE

What separates the average internet marketer from the highly successful one? It's not necessarily marketing skill in itself. You could have the highest search engine rankings in the world, yet if your copy doesn't touch your visitors' emotional impulses in some way, you won't get sales. Compare that with internet marketers who may not have as high a search engine ranking, but get more conversions because they relate to the consumer better. This section explains how you can relate to your customer better by analyzing the basics in marketing psychology, which would include Maslow's Hierarchy of Needs along with the general thought processes of various marketing groups.

Maslow's Hierarchy of Needs

Maslow's hierarchy of needs is a basic psychological theory that businesses often use to evaluate their marketing tactics. Usually displayed in pyramid format, the theory explains that humans are driven by five levels of needs: physiological, safety, love/belonging, esteem, and self-actualization.

Physiological. Physiological needs, which are at the base of the pyramid, include all the physical needs that must be met for healthy functioning. These include eating, drinking, sex/reproduction, sleep, and eliminating wastes. Grocery stores and fertility clinics are examples of businesses that fulfill physiological needs.

In developed countries creating a business based on physiological needs alone won't guarantee success, simply because there are so many of them already. Businesspeople must give their businesses a unique spin to compete with other enterprises selling products that meet physiological needs. For example, online grocery stores are a limited market. I live in Southern California, where Vons and Albertsons are among the grocery stores that deliver. However, in other areas, even where online delivery exists, the online stores either have limited inventory or don't deliver to certain areas. The need for fast and quick groceries without having to travel to a grocery store is attractive both in the product being provided and the marketing "hook," which would be the online aspect. Of course, a newcomer in that business would have to provide a larger inventory along with making their service available nationwide.

Safety. People cannot be happy if they don't feel safe. So products that ensure the safety of individuals and their families tend to get noticed. Self-protection products such as pepper spray (where legal) and personal alarms are two examples. Products or services that protect the home or the possessions in it, such as a product that prevents a door from opening, are another example. Competition isn't eliminated, as you still need to do your research, but remember that a lot of people are willing to make the necessary investment if they feel they're going to protect their lives, families, or possessions.

Love/Belonging. Everyone wants to feel loved and accepted, so products or services that promote this level of the hierarchy are definitely important. Dating sites are a good example of services that meet the love/belonging need. Social networking sites such as MySpace and Facebook also meet this need. A variant of the love/belonging need is promotion of products that are expected to indirectly meet that need. For example, some weight loss products show a woman as being more dateable or even marriageable after she has lost weight. The products in and of themselves do not meet the love/belonging need, but by promoting how much more beautiful and attractive a woman is to men after she loses weight, companies promoting diet products give the impression that their products are the "solution" to finding romance.

Esteem. Services or products that meet a person's esteem needs give them a sense of accomplishment and respect, both from others and for themselves. An example of an enterprise that meets esteem needs is colleges.

Self-Actualization. *Self-actualization* can be defined as the process of people meeting their goals. Because this is at the highest level of Maslow's hierarchy of needs, it can be hard to define exactly what types of products or services meet self-actualization goals because they differ from person to person. Some markets, such as home businesses, are successful because they meet generalized self-actualization goals—in this case, the dream of being rich and financially sufficient. Others work on the basis of niche markets. The plus side with self-actualization is that it's a market that could be met through products that are low-cost and easy to make, such as books.

THE BASIC MARKETING GROUPS

This section goes into detail about the basic marketing categories your audience will fall into. These categories are age, gender, race/nationality, socioeconomic status, familial status, B2B (also known as business-to-business), health/disability, religion, and occupational status.

Age

The average person lives 80 years, with each period of his or her life offering a different set of interests than before. This section will talk more about these periods and the products and services people are interested in during each period.

Baby/Toddler (ages 0–2). At this stage of life, people are incapable of verbally expressing what they are interested in, yet marketers still take advantage of this demographic. Why? Because while babies and toddlers can't say what they want or need, their parents can. So if you're promoting a product or service geared to babies and toddlers, you should consider yourself to be marketing to the parents. Sure, babies can give cues if they like a certain toy, food, or television show, and parents respond to that. But you need to market your product or service to the parent first before thinking about how the baby will respond to it, though some may consider these things as interrelated.

To get ideas of the types of products geared toward those in babyhood, take a trip through Babies "R" Us or look at the commercials on BabyfirstTV or the PBS Kids Sprout channel.

You can use the internet to search baby products. Use the keyword analysis techniques you learned about earlier to determine which baby products sell the best. You can go right to the source. No, not the babies, but the parents who buy for them. There are a number of blogs and forums for parents. Find out what parents are discussing. You'll discover products they're recommending (or not recommending), as well as unmet needs. Don't be afraid to ask questions, as this could be a potential marketplace for you.

Child (ages 3–12). If you look at most of the commercials that come on during kids' shows, you'll discover what, to a marketer's mind, interests kids. This would basically be toys, sweet foods, and, to a lesser extent, clothes. One neglected market is education, though with games like V-Smile (a special video game system that only plays educational video games) this is changing. Other aspects that are neglected—at least on TV commercials—are products relating to sports and other outdoor activities, and books.

One major disadvantage with this market is the inability of children to buy their own merchandise. They aren't in as bad a position as babies or toddlers, as they can at least verbalize to their parents what they want. However, ultimately the parent is the one who has the final say on whether or not the product gets bought. So, if you're selling a product or service related to the children's market, make an effort to impress the parents. For food, you could emphasize health benefits. For toys, you could emphasize educational benefits. But remember, there are some toys that only a child would see value in; a parent would buy it because their kid wanted it. Marketing a child's love for a product could be the "hook" that gets a parent to buy, even if the product offers no other benefit.

Teenager (ages 13–19). The teenage market is interesting because some teenagers have access to funds through part-time jobs or allowances and they have autonomy to spend it as they choose. Other teenagers may have money but not autonomy; that is, their parents have veto power over books, games, music, etc. Still others may have neither. However, you don't have to worry as much about marketing to their parents, because teens are developing adult interests.

Some things teens are thinking about include dating, education (especially in terms of going to college), friendships/popularity, making money, video games, and buying a car. There are also overlooked niche markets, such as teenage mothers. Generally, they would have the above-mentioned interests, along with the interests an adult would have when it comes to getting things for their young children. Additionally, teenage mothers may be thinking about how to get a decent job without a high school diploma.

Young Adult (ages 18–25). Young adults can be difficult to market to because they usually don't have much money. They're at a point in their lives where they're trying to be independent and maybe they can't rely on their parents for money (although some reports indicate more than 50 percent live at home). For this reason marketers don't hesitate to promote credit cards to this demographic, and their campaigns tend to be successful.

Yet, young adults are complex. Most are trying to find ways to get established. This age group is particularly influenced by their peers. Music, clothing, technology, gaming, cell phones, and ringtones are all products of interest to this market. This demographic, along with teens and tweens, tend to be brand conscious. Influential peer groups include young Hollywood, so products or services approved by rappers, professional athletes, and celebutantes have an almost built-in guarantee of success.

Young Money magazine is a good place to find out what interests the upwardly mobile in this demographic. Its readers tend to be college grads on a fast track to the executive suite.

Adult (ages 25–40). Around age 25, many adults have established a good foundation. Most are no longer students and are a few years into their careers. They have their own cars and addresses (although many return to live with parents). Some are married or thinking of marriage. So, what would they be thinking about as they progress through their adult years? Buying houses is a very big thing to them, along with settling down. If they have already done these things, then their concerns would focus on products or services that could be of value to their families. They are also concerned with improving their financial security, whether it's by getting better jobs, starting their own businesses, and/or improving their credit scores. Some adults are interested in continuing their education to get a master's or even a Ph.D.

Middle Age (age 40–60). Middle-aged individuals have basically accomplished all of the things that adults and young adults are still striving to attain. They have their education, career, house, and family. In fact, when it comes to family, the middle-aged are at the point where their kids are about to move out of the house and start their own lives. For houses, they might be on their second or third house by now. So, what else is there to think about in one's life?

One of the biggest things middle-aged people think about can be summed up in one word: retirement. Even if they have good jobs, without a suitable retirement package they might be forced to continue working even if they don't want to. So, making money and securing good retirement plans are of interest to many middle-aged people.

Some additional concerns could be for their children, especially when it comes to their teens' college education. They think a lot about their health, so supplements might sell well with them. They are thinking about their weight and sexual health (women would be focus on how their bodies are changing through menopause, while men may focused on impotence). Both genders will be thinking about how to address hair loss and graying hair.

The Elderly (ages 60+). If elderly people are mobile and have money, they are thinking about how they can pass their time. This age group loves going on cruises and visiting resorts. They also like spending money on their grandchildren. They probably don't think much about buying additional homes, yet they may want to make investments to remodel their current homes. Or, they may decide to sell their houses and move into assisted living communities.

This is the best scenario with an older person. Scenarios that are not as good are those where the elderly person has to go into a nursing home because of medical problems. Depending on their mental faculties, they might take an interest in which nursing home they go to; otherwise their children may have to make this decision.

Elderly people also think about death. Granted, it's a grim thought, but it's a market that tends to purchase grave sites and insurance policies. They are also thinking about how to set up their wills.

Gender

Things have changed when it comes to men and women, at least in the United States. You can't be sexist and assume that a woman is going to buy a vacuum cleaner just because she's at home. Yet, even with the progress that has occurred when it comes to equality between the sexes, there remain some significant psychological differences between men and women—differences that impact their spending habits.

Women. Most online marketing campaigns market things such as clothes, perfume, jewelry, romance novels, weight loss products, and household supplies to women. While these do seem to do well, some may interpret the perpetual marketing of these types of things to have sexist overtones. However, as with every demographic, don't limit yourself to broad-based assumptions. Women's interests expand beyond these categories. A lot of women work, so products or services that relate to career advancement would be of interest. There are also niche markets among women that a marketer would have traditionally promoted among men. These include sports equipment and video games. Finally, women are often key or primary decision makers for products and services for the whole family. This means that women may make the buying decisions even about products designed for men.

Men. Many of the products marketed to men include sports equipment, grilling, clothes, knives, razors, guns, video games, and, to a lesser extent, cologne. Dieting, a market traditionally geared more toward women, has always been a niche market for men. There is a niche that is virtually untouched—men who are at home during the day. This could be due to working at night or being work-at-home husbands. Either way, it is assumed that some of the types of things that would interest women in terms of cleaning and cooking products wouldn't interest men, though with the growing niche of men at home, that is changing.

Race/Nationality

Marketing by race or nationality is controversial if you're not of the same race as the group of people to which you are marketing. So generally, try to avoid doing this unless you are promoting an enterprise that, due to being clearly geared for a particular race or nationality, wouldn't cause offense if promoted by an outsider. For example, let's say you created a web site talking about colleges, with historically black colleges being one of the subtopics. If you advertise this web page on a "black" web site (such as a message board), you would still be marketing in an ethical manner.

More questionable marketing tactics would be pushing certain products or services based on a stereotype of a race or nationality. An example could be a discounted assumption that the majority of Asians are into education; hence, promoting SAT prep books or software to a mostly Asian audience might not be appropriate. A better marketing approach would be to say that people aged 15–18 are interested in SAT prep books or software, since the SAT is the key for getting into college.

It's important to note, however, that if you are the same race or nationality as the people you are marketing to, you might be able to think of a lot of niche markets, since you are directly involved in the culture. You can think about needs that are being met for other communities, but not your own. You can also market on a more personal/human level. Your visitors will be more attentive to what you have to say if they feel that you are sympathetic to their interests.

Socioeconomic Status

Socioeconomic status refers to what financial class a person belongs to. The main classes include poor, lower middle class, middle class, upper middle class, and rich.

Poor and Lower Middle Class. Poorer people are concerned with finding ways to survive. Since they have limited funds, they don't have money for vacations, investments, or home ownership. However, most do want to find a way out of their situation. if possible. Promoting free government services, especially those that provide employment and/or educational assistance, works well with this demographic. Also, think about promoting resources where they can obtain free health care.

Keep in mind that poorer individuals may not have enough money to afford to surf the internet at home. This means that they have to access it through libraries or college campuses. They may not feel safe making purchases in these environments, since the computers are public. Thus, you may want to consider promoting informational sites. Or, you will want to make sure that they feel comfortable buying on a public computer. Always use SSL (secure sockets layer) for transactions dealing with personal or financial information. Let your visitors know this when they visit your site.

Middle Class and Upper Middle Class. This group is in an interesting position when it comes to their access to financial resources. Although they are far from poor (although many have said the economy is erasing the middle class), they do not have the disposable income that the rich do. Yet, through credit cards and bank loans, they tend to be able to take advantage of the same types of things that rich people do. Middle- and upper-middle-class people go on vacations, buy boats, send their kids to private schools, and buy nice homes and cars. However, many are doing so while getting into a mountain of debt. For this reason, think about promoting refinancing, mortgages, and credit repair with this demographic. Business opportunities are also of interest to the middle and upper middle class, since they still want to make enough money to get to the "next level." And unlike poor people, they have enough money to try out a business opportunity.

Middle- and upper-middle-class people are interested in discounted services and merchandise. Most do not have to pinch pennies as much as a poorer person, but they still want to get the most for their money.

This market also prizes education, both for themselves and their children. Some middle- and upper-middle-class people may be able to pay for their education themselves, though knowledge of loans, scholarships, and free government programs is of interest.

The Rich. Rich people have enough income that they can generally buy whatever they want. In terms of what they buy, they are more interested in the names and labels associated with their merchandise. Extremely rich people will also buy things that people with less money would never dream of, such as islands. The rich are also concerned about education, but for them it would be Ivy League and private schools.

Rich people are also interested in how to make money. While they won't be interested in the so-called "business opportunities" that are advertised on the internet, they are interested in investments.

Familial Status

Familial status can be broken down into singles, married with no kids, married with kids, and empty-nesters.

Singles. Singles are categorized as those who are unmarried or not in a committed relationship. They can live by themselves or have kids. If they have kids, then some of their buying interests would be similar to those of married people with kids.

What are singles interested in when it comes to buying? Matchmaking services are popular with this market, but remember in this day and time many singles don't feel the need to rush into marriage. Other things that interest them could be in the self-actualization area. They may also be interested in social events that would bring them new acquaintances.

In terms of housing, the singles market may not be as interested in purchasing a home, but, on the other hand, many are. Singles with kids will probably feel differently, so don't hesitate to promote mortgage loans with this market.

Married with No Kids. Couples with no kids can either be in the process of having kids or have decided that they don't want kids at all. If a couple is trying to have kids, they will be interested in buying a home for their upcoming family, along with purchasing baby products. If they don't want to have kids, then they could have some of the same interests as single people. In terms of home ownership, it could be either/or for couples who decide not to have kids. They see a benefit to home ownership, and since they're already married, they don't have to deal with the legal issues of ownership that a single person faces when becoming part of a couple. However, a childless couple may not feel as pressed to buy a home as a couple that plans to have children.

Married with Kids. Couples with kids are not in the position to be as interested in social events, going out, or partying as couples without kids or singles. They are interested in daycare/babysitting, products related to their kids' education, and other things related to kids or family. They are interested in acquiring mortgages, and, if they already have one, they might want to refinance.

Empty-Nesters. Empty-nesters are couples or singles whose kids have grown up and moved out of the house. Age-wise they can be as young as 35 (if they had their kids in their teens), but most are middle-aged or elderly. Figuring out how to handle their children's college expenses is a prominent issue with this age group. Older empty-nesters are interested in their retirement plans. Younger, single empty-nesters might be interested in dating at this stage, since their kids are no longer a concern. Both groups may also take more of an interest in social events and vacationing.

B2B

Business owners are interested in products or services that will either help sustain their business or increase marketability or productivity. Examples of products required for the general functioning of a business include office supplies, desks, computer equipment, and industry-specific products (such as a steam cleaner for a carpet cleaning business). web site design is an example of a service that could increase marketability for a business, while an electronic envelope stuffer could increase productivity.

Health/Disability

A lot of marketing potential is available when advertising to this market, but you have to make sure you hit a niche market rather than something general. For example, if you ran an AdSense site for progeria (a condition that causes children to age prematurely), you might get more clicks than if you ran an AdSense site for high blood pressure. While high blood pressure would offer more in terms of general searches, the competition would be so fierce that you wouldn't be able to rank high anyway. Progeria offers much less competition, so visitors would be more likely to go on and click through to your site.

Religion

Religion opens up many doors for niche markets. Examples could be Christian movies, books, video games, or clothing. There are many more niches, including those with no direct tie-in to the religion itself, but to their interests—for example, family-oriented movies or games.

Occupational Status

For certain types of jobs, people may need to purchase supplies that are not available where they work. For example, teachers often purchase art supplies, paper, and other materials for their classrooms with their own money. There are also industries where a person may have to take a test to get licensed for their occupation. In this case they would be interested in buying training materials, which can be in the form of books or computer software.

MARKETING

The marketing terms and categories may be a lot to take in at one time. However, it's a key ingredient in your success. The discipline of marketing is important because it uncovers whom we should target, why, and how we should reach them. For example, many marketers believed that making things pink was a good tactic for marketing to women. Make it pink and pretty and women will come. Wrong! Some women hate pink and most want clear-cut solutions to their problems. Many are making buying decisions for the whole house, so presenting them with enough information to make those decisions is a good strategy. Your market should drive your messaging and not the other way around. This is no less important in search marketing. Take the time to understand, identify, and properly target the right audience and you'll get a tremendous return on the time invested in doing so.

CHAPTER 7

SEO Ethics

Janet began writing articles about coaching topics to boost her visibility online. She loved writing and felt that she was providing good information that would boost her other marketing efforts. She started posting to three or four sites initially but then found software that would post to hundreds of sites at once. She tested carefully and tried to provide useful content.

Janet had also learned the value of keyword descriptions and tags. She found popular keywords and used them in all her articles. She did the same thing for her web site. A woman named Nina, who was an SEO expert, found Janet's site when searching for keywords Janet used. The problem was that Janet's content had nothing to do with the keywords used.

Normally, Nina would have been irritated and continued her search, but she had a feeling that Janet's intentions had been good. Nina read through her actual content and thought Janet had a lot to offer. She e-mailed Janet and they connected by phone the next day. Janet was shocked when after they exchanged greetings, Nina said, "Did you know that you were practicing forms of black hat SEO?"

Throughout this book you have learned how to design your web site, how to look for the right keywords, and how to consider the psychology of your audience when writing your content and/or choosing your keywords. We've also touched on several search engine optimization principles. Now, it's time to roll up our sleeves and discover the ins and outs of search engine optimization.

In this chapter you learn basic search optimization guidelines, along with the more specific guidelines of Google search engine optimization. Why Google? Well, because Google consistently leads all others in search engine traffic. It makes sense to optimize for the greatest amount of traffic and your efforts will be rewarded across the board.

SEO ETHICS AND GUIDELINES

A discussion of search engine optimization would not be complete without addressing what happens when good SEO goes bad. As with other things, many of the practices that are frowned on were once legitimate. However, when good practices are overused or used for bad purposes, it penalizes everyone.

SEO, like every other discipline, has those who follow legitimate, industry-accepted practices and those who strive to "trick" the system with dirty tricks. Industry insiders refer to unethical or unfair practices as black hat SEO.

The terms "white hat" and "black hat" were actually taken from old cowboy movies (commonly called Westerns). In these movies the good guy always wore a white hat and the bad guy always wore a black hat. So the sheriff of the town would ride in with a white hat to fight off the robbers who wore black hats. For ages in Western history, black has often been associated with darkness, shadows, and evil, and white has stood as a symbol of goodness and purity.

In the cyberworld, the term "black hat" was first used in reference to hacking, but the basic principles are the same when it comes to search engine optimization.

However, there's debate about what is "unfair or unethical." A common thread to what is black hat is "unfair manipulation." Some would argue that SEO in and of itself is a manipulative tactic. After all, the purpose of SEO is to manipulate the search engines into ranking your site higher, right? Wrong! SEO and SEM (search engine marketing) are equivalent to creating advertising messages for television, magazines, or other format. You strive to gain the attention of your target audience—the audience that needs and desires what you sell. You aren't trying to twist their arms and falsely manipulate them into buying your product or service.

This false assumption about sales and marketing is why so many fail at the practices. If you believe that selling is mind manipulation, you may trick a few people into buying your goods and services, but you won't create long-term, sustainable relationships. My goal with this book is to share with you good, sound practices and the underlying principles that will not only help you earn money today but well into the future. I believe good business is based on relationships, and a foundation built on deceit and trickery does not support that goal.

What is considered black hat SEO varies. Sometimes black hat is designated by search engine guidelines. The practice itself may not be unethical but simply scowled on by the search engine. There are black hat practices that intentionally set out to harm the competition. These tactics are widely embraced as wrong. Black hat sometimes involves property rights (stealing content from others). The biggest debates about black hat are practices so designated because they result in "unnatural rankings." It's important to understand the many facets of SEO so that you'll know what not to do. Some practices that may appear harmless can get you in trouble with search engines. I believe that if you aren't hurting anyone, you're following the best rule. For example, if a mother searches for a baby stroller and is taken to an adult site instead, that could be considered "hurting" another person. Don't do that.

Webmasters who use white hat SEO techniques are as concerned about their visitors' experience on their web sites as they are with ranking high on search engines. Thus, they concentrate on creating content that both their visitors and search engines are hungry for, forming legitimate relationships with other web sites for link building, and proper use of meta tags. You have already learned how to create appropriate SEO-optimized content along with how to use meta tags. You were introduced to link-building concepts, but only the basics. Before we can delve more deeply into what you need to do to embark on a successful link-building campaign, we have to lay a foundation of the rules.

WHAT YOU SHOULD NOT DO: BLACK HAT SEO

So let's talk about black hat SEO. Black hat SEO optimization has no consideration for web site visitors. Its only goal is to get ranked high in search engines. Black hat SEO optimization techniques are considered "spamdexing."

Spamdexing (content spam, link spam, and cloaking are examples) is a practice that tries to manipulate the search engines' indexing to produce higher ranking results. An example of spamdexing is keyword stuffing. In *keyword stuffing* you stuff your web pages with competitive keywords simply to manipulate search engines rather than deliver useful content to the user. The content may not even make sense. It's simply a trick to manipulate the engines to rank you higher. You can also "overstuff" the page's meta tags.

Duplicate Content. As Google defines it, *duplicate content* means you have the exact text on a different page in the same site. This also applies to sister sites or sites to which you are heavily linked. Avoiding duplicate content doesn't mean that every single word on all of your pages must be unique. Black hat duplication is copying and pasting the same paragraphs from one page to another. This practice can, and most likely will, drop your site's rankings and possibly exclude content from the main index. Syndicated content is not treated as duplicate content, so if you carry a news feed on your home page that may also be found on 1,000 other web sites, the search engines won't drop your ranking for it.

Note that syndicated content (distribution of pages/content via syndicated networks) is highly contested in terms of how much it can affect your site in the rankings, and it is a much-discussed topic in search forums and at search conferences. Suggestions about "freshness" of data and origins are still being offered.

Link farming is the process of exchanging reciprocal links with web sites to increase search engine optimization. The idea behind link farming is to increase the number of sites that link to yours, because search engines such as Google rank sites according to, among other things, the quality and quantity of sites that link to yours. In theory, the more sites that link to yours, the higher your ranking in the search engine results will be, because more links indicate a higher level of popularity among internet users. However, search engines such as Google consider link farming to be a form of spam and have implemented procedures to banish sites that participate in link farming, so link farming has garnered negative connotations across the internet.

> ### ▼ Make It Yours!
>
> One tip to try to make syndicated content yours is to interlink to other articles and posts on your own site, and brand it in resources boxes and elsewhere. But realize that many syndicated networks remove links in the middle of the content/article, and allow "resource box" (bottom) links only.

The difference between good link building and bad link building is how it's done. Link spamming is another type of link farming in which you use software to generate lots of links over a short time. Google in particular looks unfavorably at lots of links over a short time, and not built naturally, with varying anchor text changes. In fact, Google refrains from the use of the term "reciprocal link exchanges" in its documentation.

There are many service providers who promise to help you boost your link popularity by automatically entering you into link exchange programs they operate. The programs often link your page to web sites that have nothing to do with your content. Users should be aware of the repercussions of this action, as the major search engines penalize sites that participate in link farming, thereby negating the intended effect. A link farm is a web page that's nothing more than a page of links to other sites.

As I said earlier, some practices are black hat because the search engine frowns on the practice. For this reason, it's important to read the webmaster guidelines provided by the search engines. Google, in particular, may punish you by banishing your site to the still-existing supplemental index (fondly known as Google Hell) and you may not even understand why or how you got there!

That's why you must understand the good and bad so you'll know what not to do.

Google's supplemental index is like the digital basement. You're still listed on Google, but not in the more visible core index. Relegation to the supplemental index can significantly impact your revenues. A few things that can relegate you to the basement are duplicate content, a lack of links to other quality sites (yes, confusing, you can't have too few or too many), and pages with only a few words and pictures and little content.

> **TIP:** Good, unique titles and internal link structure, deep linking, and unique content for every page will help you get back out of the supplemental index or prevent banishment in the first place. If you must include text on your page because of a requirement from an organization (often found in the real estate field, for example)—add the text as an image (gif/jpg) to the page, so search engines don't penalize you for duplicate content.

Office politics have made their way to cyberspace, as well. Black hat sabotage is unfortunately alive and well in search engine marketing. Using black hat SEO, a competitor can harm your site rankings. In a practice sometimes called *Google bowling*, someone else frames your site for link spamming. They generate automated links to bad neighborhoods and make it appear that you're guilty of link spamming. Google then drops your search rankings.

One of the most famous examples of link spamming was a "miserable failure." Thousands of links using "miserable failure" in the anchor text pointed to www.whitehouse.gov, President George Bush.

When asked about negative SEO, Matt Cutts, a senior software engineer for Google, offered this comment: "Piling links onto a competitor's site to reduce its search rank isn't impossible, but it's extremely difficult. We try to be mindful of when a technique can be abused and make our algorithm robust against it. I won't go out on a limb and say it's impossible. But Google bowling is much more inviting as an idea than it is in practice." (*The Saboteurs of Search*, Andy Greenberg, Forbes.com, October 2007)

Content Spamming

Content spamming involves tricking a search engine into thinking a web site has relevant, keyword-rich content when it really doesn't. Some of these methods create web site copy that not only is irrelevant but cumbersome for the web site visitor to read. Others show nothing to the visitor, but are still considered black hat. The specific types of content spamming are outlined below.

Keyword Stuffing. Keyword stuffing comes in four categories: content keyword stuffing, image keyword stuffing, meta tag keyword stuffing, and invisible text keyword stuffing.

Content Keyword Stuffing. Remember when you learned earlier that your content should have a keyword density of no more than 2–5 percent? When it has a keyword density that's higher, not only does its ridiculousness negatively affect your credibility in the eyes of your visitors, it's also flagged for spam.

Don't confuse legitimate SEO writing with keyword stuffing. More than likely, even if you're an average SEO writer, you won't do keyword stuffing. Writers who do keyword stuffing do it on purpose and know that their content looks crazy. They don't care about their visitors; they just want to rank high in the search engines and hope that the visitor will concentrate more on the banner or link ads than the content. An example of keyword-stuffed content could be as follows:

> Cheap Laptops.com offers the best in cheap laptops. The cheap laptops available from Cheap Laptops.com are as low as $300! Not only that, but the cheap laptops from Cheap Laptops.com make the cost even cheaper with its free shipping, available for a limited time. Also, the cheap laptops are not cheap when it comes to the brands available. With Cheap Laptops.com, you can buy Sony, Gateway, Dell, Toshiba, Acer, HP and more. Just because Cheap Laptops.com offers cheap laptops doesn't mean that you'll have to settle for generic brands. Indeed, you won't be able to find cheap laptops anywhere else but from Cheap Laptops.com. So come on down and get your cheap laptop today from Cheap Laptops.com. You'll be happy once your brand new cheap laptop from Cheap Laptop.com comes in the mail. On top of that with Cheap Laptops.com you don't have to pay shipping for your cheap laptop. Try getting that from Amazon, eBay or other sites selling cheap laptops. I guarantee you won't be able to find free shipping on cheap laptops at any place other than Cheap Laptops.com.

See how insane that is? And can you guess the keyword density for that awful content? With as many times as "cheap laptops" appears, you would think the keyword density would be crazy, like 20 percent. But it was only 8 percent, not much higher than what you can legitimately do, which is 5 percent. Don't worry. More than likely, you won't produce such trash because you're not trying to. For comparison purposes, below is an example of appropriate SEO writing that adheres to the guidelines you learned earlier in this book.

> If you're looking for a good deal on laptops, look no further than Cheap Laptops.com. With Cheap Laptops.com, you can buy laptops for as low as $300. Some of the brands that are available include: Sony, Gateway, Dell, Toshiba, Acer, HP and more. Additionally, as an added bonus, the site is offering free shipping for a limited period of time. So, if you're looking to save money on your next laptop purchase, consider visiting Cheap Laptops.com.

The keyword "cheap laptops" is used only three times, yet since there are only 75 words it still has a keyword density of a healthy 4 percent. This copy is significantly easier to read, and more important, won't get flagged as spam. In the long run, you'll want to stick with this type of copy. The first one may get you a high ranking for a short time, but once search engines catch up to the spam technique, your site will get banned.

It should be noted that there's an even more blatant variant of content keyword stuffing. This form may have legitimate content in the areas of the web site that are most likely to be visited (such as at the top or, more commonly, toward the middle of the page), but at the bottom is garbage. It's usually not even in the form of content, but rather a bunch of keywords.

Image Keyword Stuffing. While Google and other search engines can't read images or text that might be on them, they do read what is in the 'alt' attribute (often incorrectly referred to as an image tag), which offers a description of what an image is. It's not used much anymore. The proper way to use the alt attribute is shown below:

<IMG src="yourimage.gif" alt= "short description of your image"/>

The IMG is the tag that tells the browser an image is about to be shown. The "src" attribute is where you enter in the name of your image along with its extension. Then there's the "alt" that spammers love to exploit. The normal use of the alt tag is to place a one-word description of your image. It can be a keyword *if the keyword relates to the image.* If it doesn't relate, then you should say what it is. For example, if "yourimage.gif" was a picture of a purse, the alt tag should say "purse." But the following is what a keyword stuffer would do:

<IMG src="purse.gif" alt= "coach purse, designer purse, chanel purse, wholesale purse, louis vuitton purse, gucci purse, prada purse, dooney bourke purse, replica purse, vera bradley purse, purse party, handbag purse, coin purse, discount coach purse, baby phat purse, juicy couture purse, coin purse, knockoff purse, dog purse, purse forum, photo purse"/>

They fill the "alt" tag with keywords unrelated to the image. The hope is that by doing this the image gets indexed in the image results of Google or other search engines offering an image-based search. When images are displayed in these listings, the web site that contains them is also displayed. Of course, the keyword stuffer won't get this result, and if they do it's temporary. This tactic, being not as "bad" as other ones, may not get the site totally banned, but it certainly will get the web site to receive a lower ranking.

TIP: The alt attribute was developed for 508 accessibility reasons, and may possibly help lift relevancy for keywords slightly on a page in some search engines, but not for Google.

Meta Tag Keyword Stuffing. From your newly acquired knowledge of meta tags, can you guess where keyword stuffers would do their dirty work? Yes, in the title tag. Keyword stuffing the title tag can cause lots of keywords to show up in the title browser and make the site look unprofessional. Another black hat technique is to spam the keyword and description attribute. It's not uncommon to stuff so many keywords into these attributes that the HTML code is pages long.

Invisible Text Keyword Stuffing. *Invisible text* is the practice of putting lists of keywords in white text on a white background. This practice is to get more spiders to crawl the site. The webmaster makes the text the same color as the background, so it's invisible to the visitor. Regular content would appear in a table or image, so that it's still visible. The hope is that the search engine will index a site that, to the naked eye, looks legitimate.

Gateway or Doorway Pages

Gateway or *doorway pages* are small web pages that contain a small amount of content and link to a legitimate web page. They used to be considered a white hat SEO tactic, until people started using them strictly for the purpose of tricking spiders to index the site higher.

Scraper Sites. *Scraper sites*, also called Made for AdSense sites, are created from programs called article generators. Article generators scrape the internet looking for highly ranked content. They take bits and pieces of this content from one web site to another to create a new article. The problem with this is if the content is not rewritten, the webmaster is breaking copyright law by using it. Of course, the black hat SEO optimizers using this technique don't care about the law, or their visitors' experience. For this reason you'll find that most scraper sites are laden with ads or serve as doorway pages to other sites.

> **TIP:** You'll find article/content generators listed on the accompanying CD.

Don't think that article generators are all bad. In fact, they can be a helpful tool in creating content. The key to remember is that what they show is a source of research only. You don't own the copyrights to the content they create, which is why they need to be rewritten. If you use an article generator, use it to find ideas, rather than something that can write content for you. In fact, I view them as elaborate keyword analyzers.

Hidden Links. To create hidden links, webmasters do the same thing as they would for hidden text; they make the background the same color as the text. This gives the appearance of a lot of outbound links and even reciprocal links. You might be wondering how they could have reciprocal links if they're hiding the links. Doesn't the process of getting reciprocal links require that the other webmaster's links be visible on the page? Well, what a webmaster could do is *initially* show the webmaster they're doing a link exchange with the links shown visible and that their web site/links have been posted. But after a few weeks, they'll assume the webmaster won't be interested in seeing the site anymore, so that's when they change the color of the text to render it invisible.

Sybil Attack. According to Wikipedia, a *Sybil attack* is a black hat SEO optimization technique in which webmasters take over the reputation systems of various types of networks, whether they are message boards, blogs, or social networking sites. They create dozens of IDs, using each one to help improve the reputation of one main ID. With this high reputation, they then start posting their ads, hoping that they don't get noticed because of their reputation.

A variant of the Sybil attack is when webmasters create a lot of sites that link to one another. Many of these sites offer nothing relevant and some may even be spam blogs.

Spam Blogs. *Spam blogs*, also called *splogs*, are the blog equivalent of link farms. They post links to hundreds, maybe thousands of sites, in hopes that they get rated high in search engines. In terms of content, if they offer any, it tends to be plagiarized content from article generators. Whether they have content or not, they extensively promote any affiliate programs of which they are a part. The splog may also use other techniques discussed here with the false hope that they can get listed even higher in search engine results.

Spam *in* Blogs. Keep in mind the keyword for spam in blogs is the word "in." They aren't the same as spam blogs. In fact, the blogs themselves usually are legitimate. The problem comes in the comment section. What webmasters do is make spam comments to help promote their web sites or affiliate programs. They hope they get the advantage of traffic and a one-way link. What's more likely to happen is that they'll anger the blog owner, who will ban them and remove the spam comment. If a search engine finds out about this, they could end up as many black hat sites do: banned.

Wiki Spam

Introduced in the late 90s, wikis are a special kind of site that lets users post and edit web sites as they see fit. They're most commonly used for informational purposes, with wikipedia.com being the most popular example. In terms of *wiki spam*, Wikipedia puts it in five categories: article spam, link spamming, source soliciting, spam bots, and canvassing.

Article Spam. While writing articles about your web site can be an excellent white hat SEO tactic, it can become black hat when they're placed on inappropriate web sites. Wikis not geared for advertising are an example. If a spam article is found on Wikipedia, it can be deleted with the {{db-spam}} command. A person could also use Wikipedia's proposed deletion option or list it on Wikipedia's "Articles for Deletion" section. However, sometimes Wikipedia leaves the article up to be rewritten in the more encyclopedia-like tone that Wikipedia uses. Note that Wikipedia doesn't discourage articles about companies; they just have to be written properly. You'll learn some tricks you can use to meet Wikipedia's guidelines so you can promote your site. You won't be able to promote affiliate links, but you can talk about a general, top-level domain web site.

Wiki Link Spamming. In the case of Wikipedia, there are two places where links are allowed: at the end of the article in the list of sources and in the section to the right of the article in a grey box that shows contact information. If a link is listed anywhere else, it's considered spam. If a web site is listed in the right place but doesn't relate to what is being talked about, it's still spam.

Another type of link spamming that has become popular is *video spamming*. Webmasters create a video promoting their site and on the video blatantly advertise their URL. While this isn't wrong to do, placing it on an informational wiki is wrong. Informational wikis are not for self-promotion but for information and resources.

As wikis are user-generated and may depend on volunteers, it may take a while for all of their spam links to get lifted from the web site. So this leaves the potential that webmasters might see the links before they get removed.

Source Soliciting. *Source soliciting* is when webmasters go on "article talk pages" to solicit editors to use their web sites. They make the claim that their web site could offer more content to an article. Following are a few guidelines that wikis use to distinguish a legitimate post from solicitation:

- If the solicitation is made anonymously
- Whether the solicitation was made through a template or a category
- Previous discussion on why the suggested source should be used
- Whether the source is controversial
- Whether the source appears commercial

Spam Bots. *Spam bots* are used to collect e-mails from various web sites on the internet or to post spam on various sites. In the case of wiki spam, the spam bots place advertising links on articles they find. The purpose is not advertising, but the hope that search engines see that they have several one-way links from popular web pages. Wikipedia is fighting back against the spam bots through *sysops*, which is another name for Wikipedia administrators. They block any spam bots that they find. Of course, webmasters may face even more consequences, as the use of spam bots is against the law. If spam bots make any edits, legally it can be considered a defacement of another person's property. It makes no difference that the property is virtual rather than hard content. If spam bots are consistently used, sysops may complain to ISPs, which could lead to prosecution.

Canvassing. *Canvassing* is the process of sending messages to Wikipedians in hopes of starting discussions. It is not considered solicitation because the initial message may not have the tone of an ad. The canvassing techniques used by spammers include friendly notices, cross-posting, campaigning, vote-stacking, and forum shopping.

Friendly Notices

Friendly notices are messages that on the surface seem to be focused on genuine interest in improving a discussion. However, the webmaster's true intent is to advertise his or her web site.

Cross-Posting. Cross-posting is the act of posting the same message to multiple forums, mailing lists, or newsgroups. Editors solicit discussions outside of the wiki by e-mailing other users. This can be considered a form of e-mail spam. Wikipedia suggests that contacts should only be made on related WikiProjects and only a limited number of legitimate friendly notices should be used.

Campaigning. *Campaigning* is e-mailing editors who have "predetermined" points of view on an article. The correspondence may seem legitimate, but it's only a front to draw the editors into a spam advertisement through their e-mail box.

Vote Stacking. *Vote stacking* is similar to campaigning and is the process of sending several "talk messages" to editors who have a definite opinion on a certain subject. Rather than spam in their e-mail inboxes, it comes through the wiki's internal chat or talk message system.

Forum Shopping. *Forum shopping*, also known as "asking the other parent," is when a user asks for several opinions of fellow visitors until they get one they like. For example, if the user's spam article was blocked, and an internal review indicates that the block was proper, it is overall not OK to ask for yet another review. Forum shopping can be considered internal spam, and you can be permanently blocked. With forum shopping they get an additional opportunity to promote URLs or affiliate links. This technique is viewed as spam since there are more appropriate steps a webmaster can take if they think a legitimate article got unfairly blocked.

Page Hijacking

Page hijacking is a black hat technique that can be scary, especially if it's done on sites where people freely give their private information. In this case the webmaster copies a legitimate web site that later redirects visitors to malicious web sites. In fact, even the hijacked page itself could be malicious. For example, it could ask for important information such as passwords, Social Security numbers, and credit card information. People give them out because they think they're visiting a legitimate site. Usually people are linked to the phony site by a spam e-mail saying that their account is in jeopardy if they don't verify it. They are further fooled because the webmaster uses cloaked links to make them think they're clicking through to the real site. Thankfully, spamming technology has not progressed enough that black hat webmasters can get to the top-level domain of a web site they're hijacking. They may have similar domains, but not the top-level one. Additionally, people should be aware that companies that store their personal information won't use e-mail as a medium to ask them to update their accounts.

Referrer Log Spamming

When you click on URLs of other sites on your own, the server that hosts the other site keeps track of the specific web page that was used to click to the other site's URL. Black hat webmasters use robots to hijack these logs and update them with inappropriate information. This information would be the web pages associated with the spammer's site, not the original one. The problem in all of this is that search engines use referrer logs to help determine the link popularity of web sites. If the log contains inaccurate information, the wrong person gets credit for the linking arrangement, since search engines use link-counting for improved search rankings.

Miscellaneous Black Hat Techniques

1. Mirrored Web Site. This process involves hosting web sites with content that's the same but uses different URLs to fool the search engine into thinking it's different. This is not URL redirecting, which is pointing various URLs to the same web site. With URL redirecting there is only one web site. With *mirrored web sites* there are several web sites, each with different URLs.

2. Cloaking. The *cloaking* involved with black hat SEO is not the legitimate cloaking that you learned about earlier in this book. With legitimate cloaking you "hide" affiliate links or cumbersome URLs in place of hyperlinked text. With black hat cloaking methods, you're not involved at the link level, but rather at the site level. Black hat webmasters create a web site that's designed to rank high with search engines but it is cloaked in favor of a more normal-looking web site. Cloaking is sometimes called *IP-delivery*.

THE CONSEQUENCES OF BLACK HAT SEO
Supplemental Index Hell: How You Got There and How to Get Out

As mentioned earlier, when Google excludes certain pages from appearing in the results pages, those pages that are left out and shown in what Google calls the "supplemental index." Pages in the supplemental index may show up in search results, but pages in the main index are always given priority. With Google being the most powerful search engine, getting into their main index and out of the supplemental index should be one of your top priorities.

There are many reasons why your web page might end up on Google's supplemental index. You may not have enough content on your page to justify putting the page in the main results. Too much duplicate content can also hurt your chances and land you in the supplemental index. Too many query strings in the URL of your site can make finding your page difficult for Google's crawlers.

Also, *orphaned pages*, pages that aren't linked to any other inside your site, can hurt you. Avoid having the same titles and descriptions on every page, as this can land you in the supplemental index, as well. All this can cause problems with the crawlers, as they see just another form of duplicate content.

The linking structure of your web site can also get you into the supplemental index. If all you have are reciprocal links with potentially bad neighbors, this increases your chances of getting dumped into the supplemental index. Check to see if a page that no longer exists has an old, cached version of itself in the supplemental listings. That can drag the rest of your site down as well.

Should your web site be afflicted by any or all of these problems, fear not. There are ways to get out of the supplemental index and back into the main results. If you're in the supplemental index, you are being crawled. Google does know you're there. But you'll have to take action to get into the main index.

Eliminate all duplicate content issues on your web pages. This is most likely your largest concern and should be dealt with as soon as possible. Google wants every result to be unique, as users get frustrated dealing with the same information page after page. Keep every page on your site as unique as possible. Also, improve the content you already have.

Shorten filenames for static web sites, or decrease the number of folders used, as this decreases the complexity of your URL. Give each page a unique and descriptive title, as well. This keeps the crawlers from finding more duplicate content in your pages' titles and descriptions. Simply using the company name or web site name on every page won't help the search engines specify the content subjects and topics on each page.

Improve your site architecture. Every site you want to have indexed by search engines should have links to it. Use a sitemap to make sure there's a link to every page. This might not be enough, so make sure you use links all throughout the site, whenever relevant. If you have no links to a particular page because you'd like that page not to be found, put that page in your web site's "robots.txt" file. This tells the search engine to ignore that site.

Google considers how far a page is from the home page. Although this is impossible with larger web sites, a good rule of thumb is that all pages should be accessible from the home page in two clicks or less. Look for relevant pages that can link together. Use links in the text of articles, and at the end of articles, to related pages. The sitemap also works well here.

Get listed in directories Google trusts. Yahoo!, Open Directory Project, Business.com, Microsoft SBD, and LinkCentre are all good examples. You could start a blog and link to a different inner page every day, or write and submit articles with links to different inner pages. If you trade links with other web sites, do so only with relevant, non-spam sites, and encourage them to link to your inner pages. Also, make sure that your content hasn't been stolen, as Google might be ranking the plagiarized content instead of yours.

If all else fails, there are more drastic measures you can take. You can rename all the pages in the supplemental index and save them as new, with new URLs. Link to these "new" pages prominently on your site, and use a 301 redirect from the old URLs to the new ones. This takes a lot of work if you have a lot of pages in the supplemental index.

Finally, tell Google what's going on. If you feel you've exhausted every option, use the sitemaps to send your URL directly to Google. Also, be patient. Google isn't known for quick responses when webmasters push to have their pages put back into the main results index.

You now are aware of most of the major black hat SEO techniques used by webmasters. What would happen if you decide to use these techniques for your web site? Well, initially, you may get positive results. The search engine would temporarily be fooled into thinking that you've initiated a legitimate link-building campaign and/or your site contains highly relevant content. Of course the keyword here is *temporarily*. You might get a high ranking for a couple weeks, but when the search engine finds out what you're doing, you could (1) lose your page rank, (2) get removed from the search engine results, or (3) get your site permanently barred from the search engine.

So, you might be thinking, if you can get indexed high initially, why not take advantage of that and risk the consequences later? After all, can't you create another web site if you get banned? There's a problem with that strategy. First of all, if you create a web site with irrelevant content, it's not going to do well with your web visitors. They'll see it once and never visit your site again. This is not what you want. You want your site to be designed so well that visitors decide to bookmark you and visit your site again. They won't do this if your site is only an elaborate advertisement. Things are even worse if you use more blatant black hat SEO tactics, such as content keyword stuffing, that make your site look like it's not legitimate.

What would happen if you used black hat SEO tactics on a legitimate site? You may get a few leads or sales, but you would do so at a great risk: getting banned from search engines and potentially getting reported to your ISP for spam. If you're reported to your ISP, you could in extreme cases be barred from the internet, period, at least through that ISP. You might even suffer legal consequences, since customers who spam can ruin an

ISP's reputation. Another consequence might be getting banned by your affiliate network or pay-per-click program *forever.* The ends do not justify the means.

Do not be fooled by the growing subculture of black hat webmasters who use black hat SEO techniques and are proud of it. There are several message boards and even books promoting black hat SEO techniques. There was even one web site that talked about the "myths" of white hat versus black hat SEO. Be aware that there are no myths with white hat SEO. White hat SEO is what you're supposed to do. It may take a while to get the results you want, but you have nothing to feel guilty about when you use white hat SEO tactics. You also have nothing to hide because you followed all of the appropriate guidelines when embarking on a search engine optimization campaign.

GOOGLE GUIDELINES

Each search engine has guidelines for web-masters. It's worth the effort to read them so you don't inadvertently break a rule. Google has an entire webmaster console with tools to help you drive traffic, manage analytics, and more. There's also a blog with frequent updates on Google developments. For your convenience I've copied the guidelines from Google below (http://www.google.com/support/webmasters). Note that they are frequently updated, so it's always a good idea to check online for the latest information.

> **TIP:** Use the site: command in Google to list all currently indexed pages. Compare the results to your source pages to make sure they match.

Google's Webmaster Guidelines

Following these guidelines will help Google find, index and rank your site. Even if you choose not to implement these suggestions, we strongly encourage you to pay close attention to the "Quality Guidelines," which outline some of the illicit practices that can lead to a site being removed from the Google index or otherwise penalized. If a site has been penalized, it may no longer show up in results on Google.com or on any of Google's partner sites.

You can review design, content and technical guidelines, as well as quality guidelines at google.com/support/webmasters.

When your site is ready:

- Have other relevant sites link to yours.
- Submit it to Google at http://www.google.com/addurl.html.
- Submit a sitemap as part of your Google webmaster tools. Google uses your sitemap to learn about the structure of your site and to increase coverage of your web pages.

- Make sure all the sites that should know about your pages are aware your site is online.
- Submit your site to relevant directories such as the Open Directory Project and Yahoo!, as well as to other industry-specific expert sites.

Design and Content Guidelines

- Make a site with a clear hierarchy and text links. Every page should be reachable from at least one static text link.
- Offer a site map to your users with links that point to the important parts of your site. If the site map is larger than 100 links, you may want to break the site map into separate pages.
- Create a useful, information-rich site, and write pages that clearly and accurately describe your content.
- Think about the words users would type to find your pages, and make sure your site actually includes those words.
- Use text instead of images to display important names, content, or links. The Google crawler doesn't recognize text contained in images.
- Make sure that your TITLE tags and ALT attributes are descriptive and accurate.
- Check for broken links and correct HTML.
- If you use dynamic pages (i.e., the URL contains a "?" character), be aware that not every search engine spider crawls dynamic pages as well as static pages. It helps to keep the parameters short and the number of them few.
- Keep the links on a given page to a reasonable number (fewer than 100).

Technical Guidelines

- Use a text browser such as Lynx to examine your site, because most search engine spiders see your site much as Lynx would. If fancy features such as JavaScript, cookies, session IDs, frames, DHTML, or Flash keep you from seeing all of your site in a text browser, then search engine spiders may have trouble crawling your site.
- Allow search bots to crawl your sites without session IDs or arguments that track their path through the site. These techniques are useful for tracking individual user behavior, but the access pattern of bots is entirely different. Using these techniques may result in incomplete indexing of your site, as bots may not be able to eliminate URLs that look different but actually point to the same page.
- Make sure your web server supports the If-Modified-Since HTTP header. This feature allows your web server to tell Google whether your content has changed since it last crawled your site. Supporting this feature saves you bandwidth and overhead.

- Use the robots.txt file on your web server. This file tells crawlers which directories can or cannot be crawled. Make sure it's current for your site so that you don't accidentally block the Googlebot crawler. Visit http://www.robotstxt.org /wc/faq.html to learn how to instruct robots when they visit your site. You can test your robots.txt file to make sure you're using it correctly with the robots.txt analysis tool available in Google webmaster tools.
- If your company buys a content management system, make sure the system can export your content so that search engine spiders can crawl your site.
- Use robots.txt to prevent crawling of search results pages or other auto-generated pages that don't add value for users coming from search engines.

QUALITY GUIDELINES

These quality guidelines cover the most common forms of deceptive or manipulative behavior, but Google may respond negatively to other misleading practices not listed here (e.g., tricking users by registering misspellings of well-known web sites). It's not safe to assume that just because a specific deceptive technique isn't included on this page, Google approves of it. Webmasters who spend their energies upholding the spirit of the basic principles provide a better user experience and therefore enjoy better ranking than those who spend their time looking for loopholes they can exploit.

If you believe that another site is abusing Google's quality guidelines, report that site at https://www.google.com/webmasters/tools/spamreport. Google prefers developing scalable and automated solutions to problems, so we attempt to minimize hand-to-hand spam fighting. The spam reports we receive are used to create scalable algorithms that recognize and block future spam attempts.

Quality Guidelines—Basic Principles

Make pages for users, not for search engines. Don't deceive your users or present different content to search engines than you display to users, which is commonly referred to as "cloaking."

Avoid tricks intended to improve search engine rankings. A good rule of thumb is whether you'd feel comfortable explaining what you've done to a web site that competes with you. Another useful test is to ask, "Does this help my users? Would I do this if search engines didn't exist?"

Don't participate in link schemes designed to increase your site's ranking or PageRank. In particular, avoid links to web spammers or "bad neighborhoods" on the web, as your own ranking may be affected adversely by those links.

Don't use unauthorized computer programs to submit pages, check rankings, etc. Such programs consume computing resources and violate our Terms of Service. Google does not recommend the use of products such as WebPosition Gold™ that send automatic or programmatic queries to Google.

Quality Guidelines–Specific Guidelines

- Avoid hidden text or hidden links.
- Don't use cloaking or sneaky redirects.
- Don't send automated queries to Google.
- Don't load pages with irrelevant keywords.
- Don't create multiple pages, subdomains, or domains with substantially duplicate content.
- Don't create pages that install viruses, trojans, or other badware.
- Avoid "doorway" pages created just for search engines, or other "cookie cutter" approaches such as affiliate programs with little or no original content.
- If your site participates in an affiliate program, make sure that your site adds value. Provide unique and relevant content that gives users a reason to visit your site first.

CHAPTER 8

Link Love

Bob continued working on his real estate client's site. He had some success with keywords but the site rankings were still very low. Bob began reviewing successful sites in the real estate industry, as well as top-ranked sites in other industries.

Bob noticed that most of the top-rated sites had inbound links. He had always written them off as "internet marketing garbage," but it was clear he had been wrong about their importance. He contacted a few site owners to ask about linking but didn't receive any responses.

With a little more research, Bob found that there were a few guidelines to follow when asking for reciprocal links, which he wanted to start with. He also discovered that he needed to carefully check the sites he wanted to link with to make sure their practices were in line with the search engines' guidelines.

To get an understanding of why links are important, a background and position is necessary. Success in search engine optimization comes from continuously focusing on and achieving three things.

We refer to these three essentials as "the SEO tripod":

1. Content (optimized!)
2. Link counts (how many links point to your web site)
3. Link reputation (what those links say about you)

If you're selling shoes and somebody links to you with "buy red shoes" in the anchor text (the blue underlined text) on an outside, high-quality, related web page, you're being smart about your linking and search optimization.

If your destination page is created with up-sell messages and easy navigation, you're moving in the right direction.

When these three legs are balanced and working together with high relevancy and structure—both internally and externally—you're creating a solid foundation for high search rankings and traffic.

Internal structure and link profiles are important, and getting links from authority web sites and avoiding technical problems (like a JavaScript redirect) are top goals.

Figure 8-1. Tripod

While most of the text in this book speaks about Google, this tripod model works for all search engines. However, MSN and Yahoo! seem to favor content more. A recent site I tested ranked very well for Google by using a link program I initiated, but until I added more content, Yahoo!, Live (MSN), and Ask were trailing behind. However, Google provides 64 percent of search engine traffic (comScore, September 2007), so it's important to get rankings there.

For more competitive keywords, it's easier and faster to get listed in MSN and Yahoo! (in that order) by creating solid content and using complementary long tail keywords. These lower searches can help build your traffic and click stream data while building out toward Google.

WHY LINKING?

Google in specific is big on links. The linking algorithms sit as a core element of their search engine. According to Matt Cutts, "Google is getting better at understanding the properties of link quality. The search engines optimize results by counting quality editorial votes as links and they help to influence their relevancy algorithms." (http://www.mattcutts.com/blog/indexing-timeline/)

As you've seen, we talked about the importance of the web in the "rise of search engines." In that section, we also learned about the new search engine by Google and how they were able to beat out AltaVista (the best search engine at the time) and Microsoft.

▼ King of the Search World

Did you know that Microsoft (Bill Gates) said they were going to take the search world by announcing a catalog of over 4 billion web sites? Well, the day (in 2001) of that announcement, Google informed the world that they had indexed 8 billion web sites. Google's scale is amazing, and via intelligent, home-grown computer systems and software, they not only have provided huge infrastructure cost savings to their company, but have built a proprietary system that some say is the true "search engine secret." Google was providing 100,000 million searches a day in 2001, and now (Sept. 2007) is providing 37 billion searches worldwide. What was their biggest problem? Not their search engine algorithm—but power (electric). More specifically, figuring out how to run over 400,000+ servers (est.) worldwide and not consume all the power from the entire city of New York!

When Larry and Sergey (referred to as the Google Guys) wanted to "download the entire web to their desktop," it was no small feat and required a grand vision that could not stray. This drive and vision to create the most relevant search engine was found by (almost) accident, and developed into a white paper, "The Anatomy of a Search Engine" (http://infolab.stanford.edu/~backrub/google.html). The paper offers insight into how Google manages links. It says: "We assume page A has pages T1...Tn which point to it (i.e., are citations). The parameter d is a damping factor which can be set between 0 and 1. We usually set d to 0.85. There are more details about d in the next section. Also C(A) is defined as the number of links going out of page A. The PageRank of a page A is given as follows:

$$PR(A) = (1\text{-}d) + d\ (PR(T1)/C(T1) + \ldots + PR(Tn)/C(Tn))$$

Here's a Google fun fact (and potential *Jeopardy!* answer): PageRank was the brainchild of Google founder, Larry Page, hence the name PageRank.

PageRank is now "marketing spin" and creates "controversial discussions in thousands of search forums." Most search marketers mention that it's outdated and doesn't get updated often (every three months as of last count) and that other pages will rank high on the search engine, even with a lower PageRank.

The paper is a quality background read, and you should note that the PageRank and TrustRank (voting and authority) remain as important today as they were then.

We have not yet discussed TrustRank. The TrustRank algorithm was created by Zoltán Gyöngyi and Hector Garcia-Molina, both from Stanford University, and Jan Pedersen from Yahoo! In their abstract, "Combating Web Spam with TrustRank," they conclude: "Search engines are today combating web spam with a variety of ad hoc, often proprietary techniques. We believe that our work is a first attempt at formalizing the problem and at introducing a comprehensive solution to assist in the detection of web spam. Our experimental results show that we can effectively identify a significant number of strongly reputable (non-spam) pages. In a search engine, TrustRank can be used either separately to filter the index, or in combination with PageRank and other metrics to rank search results."

> **TIP:** Example: If you get links from 100–200 sites with low confidence or relevancy to your site, you should instead try to go for 10–20 highly trusted links. If you were able to get one link from CNN, it would outweigh many other poor-quality links!

Rather than focusing on "on-page content" (content on a page) and meta tags and internal structure (very important) the Google Guys decided to pursue the "citation" model from their academic world. In this model, white papers, theses, and special reports would be referenced in "footnotes" as citations by professors and engineers, authors and speakers. Brin and Page decided that testing for "links/refs" would also be a good way to build "votes of confidence" for any subject matter—and it would be related and have a high vote of confidence.

As this work grew from the now-infamous garage in Silicon Valley into a full-blown project close to Stanford University, it became apparent that the "link citation" theory was more than valuable—it worked so well.

I mention this background and the tripod model because it's the way you need to look at your optimization—a complete model of not only links and backlinks, but content and site architecture.

So, now that you know why links are important and have more background on search engines and the 100+ factors that make up the Google search engine, let's talk about how to structure sites and get links.

General Link Advice

To get high search engine rankings you should provide quality inbound links to related, quality page contents. Make sure to always build links—we talk about the various types below—and the more you can get (without spamming), the better. Use the competition in your niche to figure out which links are high-quality and where they link to/from. Studying the competition will help you get a higher ranking faster, and you won't be doing it blindly.

Make sure to follow the list of top directories. This is list to start with:

- dmoz.org
- yahoo.com
- business.com
- joeant.com
- gimpsy.com
- botw.org

Other directories include:

- wowdirectory.com
- Thisisouryear.com
- skaffe.com
- searchsite: free
- addyoursitefree.com
- Splendes.com
- excellentguide.com
- uncoverthenet.com
- spheri.com
- sezza.com
- elib.org
- fatinfo.com

As with all things on the web, this list can change by the time this book is printed. Many free sites are switching to paid submission only or have closed free submissions. The list is simply a guideline to get you started.

> **TIP:** Research the competition and get placement in vertical directories for your business. The Bookmarks section on the member site contains massive lists, and is updated there.

Some paid directories are created not only to make money for their creators, but to provide a firewall to protect themselves from spam. Google and others also value these directories as providing better-quality links, and if you can afford it, it's wise to belongto them.

Vertical Directories and Lists

- ISEDB.com
- Searchengineguide.com

Directory links can be good for your ranking and strongly elevate your brand. The assumption is that if somebody has the money and is willing to pay then it's likely they don't have a spammy site. Some of these insist on company names, not keywords, but don't try to trick the system. You can establish unique domains with keywords to it with a redirect, but it's considered tricking the system. Better to do it right.

> **TIP:** The Strongest Links (www.strongestlinks.\com/directories.php) web site has a listing of directories along with their Alexa and PageRank rankings, saturations and fees. As you consider which directories to list in, this site is a good resource to help you prioritize.

In Chapter 1 we talked about social search and user-driven content. We also introduced you to tagging and bookmarking. In your marketing efforts, it's important to take advantage of the social web to build links and your brand. The list below is by no means comprehensive, but a sample of social media to consider in your marketing efforts.

- Digg
- Del.icio.us
- Technorati
- Netscape
- Newsvine
- Ma.gnolia
- Shoutwire
- 43 Things
- WikiHow
- StyleHive
- Wetpaint
- Yahoo! 360
- Ning
- The Best Stuff In The World
- Yahoo! Answers
- Flickr
- Reddit
- Squidoo
- LinkedIn
- Wikipedia
- StumbleUpon
- Facebook
- YourElevatorPitch
- BlueDot
- JotSpot
- Shadows
- Furl
- Frappr
- MySpace
- Ridiculous

Yahoo!

Yahoo! is one of the most complicated. Go to yahoo.com and select the "More Services" link and then click on "D:"—Directory link. You are now in the directory (dir.yahoo.com).

> **TIP:** Use tools like onlywire.com and social-poster.com to get your content updated to several Web 2.0 locations quickly.

To locate the best place for you to list in the directory:

1. Locate a competitor; type in the name.
2. Click on it and you'll see the breadcrumbs link to where it's located.

Yahoo! search has nothing to do with the directory. You have to enter the directory to see your listing. Think in terms of alphabetical listings. If you're deeply nested in the tree, it may not be the best place for you. Once you've typed in the competitor's name and found your place, click "Suggest a Link" to sign up for Yahoo!.

Directory submission is $299 annually and does not guarantee inclusion. Adult sites are charged $600. Your next step is to accept the terms of service—print, read, and understand them. Once you're in, there are four steps to update your listing:

1. Understand the cost.
2. Submit the site—don't need to get the keywords in each link, don't sell in the description, be factual—no sales pitch. Look at some existing listings.
3. Credit card info—Visa/MasterCard and billing address.
4. Submit the actual content via a review and confirm.

Wait at least seven business days for a response. It's not immediate.

Don't forget that many people do a local search for businesses and services in their area. You should also build local and regional links from sites such as Yahoo!

> **TIP:** Use roboform.com to save your info securely—great time saver!

Local, Google Local and through local organizations such as your chamber of commerce.

Link In, Link Out

You should link out as well as getting links in. In my business dealings with clients, I often come across a "not me" attitude. Web site owners feel that linking out to somebody else they don't know is a mistake. Imagine if this were the case in the social network—the blogosphere!

> **TIP:** Create an Excel worksheet to track names, titles, keywords/phrases, dates, pricing, comments, etc., for all links and directory tracking.

Exchanging links with other, related web sites is good practice, and get links where the competition is getting them, too. However, I would not pursue an automated link program for reciprocal links. It's not highly valued, and if not done right (lots of research needed)—you could end up in an FFA (free for all).

If you're a local merchant or provide services locally, you should submit to your niche, local directories. Adding yourself to Google Local and Yahoo! Local is a start. You can also try paid services like truelocal.com or local.com.

I recently visited a local chamber of commerce, which is a great way to create online and offline visibility (especially if you go to all the events and promote yourself and your services). Your local chamber and other trade organizations are intelligent options to include in your marketing strategy.

> **TIP:** Tool to find hubs: www.linkhounds.com/hub-finder/hubfinder.php

I have also talked about research that can help you get links from hub sites.

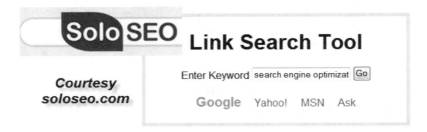

Figure 8-2. Great Way to Find the "Add Link" in Google

When links are coming back to you, instruct (kindly) the webmasters to use keywords for which you are you are trying to optimize. Make it natural and mix it up—link to the home page, inner pages, and deep/lowest pages in the web site structure. Make sure the relevant links point to the correct pages; don't just link to the home page—a common mistake.

TYPES OF LINKS

1. PageRank, natural link equity (people enjoy your site)
2. Links by "aggression" (somebody might not like you)
3. Contextual and navigation
4. Bartered links (as a favor in exchange for something)
5. Link exchanges
6. Paid links (pay for directory, links from partner and commerce sites)
7. Manufactured links
8. Automated links (i.e., link exchange programs, gotlinks, linkmetro)—use with caution
9. Ripped-off links (spam comments on blogs, automated form posts, etc.)—black hat strategy.

The goal of linking is to build relevant links. Links are like "votes" for your site, as each link functions as a "recommendation" from another site to check yours out! So, now for the important question: what can search engines do with links?

1. Easily identify the links as two-way links, three-way links
2. Adjust or weight those links
3. Determine the type, the source, the target, the age of the link, combination of things
4. Although it isn't an exact science, search engines can spot paid links
5. Filter by source (reputation passing and PageRank via outbound links, Google-specific)

The search engines also know a great deal about your site, and the technology continues to advance. The search engines know:

1. Age of site, domain name, history
2. IP and address history
3. Easy to find one-, two-, three-way links
4. Trust and authority
5. Topic and type (commercial/informational)
6. Default "link weight" (low quality may drag them down, or treat them equally)

All links are not good links. The weakest link types are:

1. Link farms
2. Link spam (comment spam)
3. Web spam

4. Paid links (we'll discuss this later)
5. Run of site (more links on many different sites/pages than on one site)

Remember that you're aiming for long-term success and not a one-time or short-term benefit. Choose quality over quantity. You're not simply building links for search engine position, but always keeping your customer in mind. Good links will bring you long-term success, so opt for authority and trust.

One-Way Links

One-way links are those in which another web site advertises your URL without requiring that you link back. Google places more value on one-way links because they show that other web sites truly see worth in the information you're offering. This is all in theory, of course, since there are web sites on which you can post your URL for payment. However, you'll want to take advantage of both free and paid one-way linking situations.

1. Free One-Way Linking Opportunities

Online Writing Portals. *Online writing portals* are communities to which you can submit articles to be read by other members of the portal or by the general public. There are also sites that allow you to pay to have your content submitted to a network of directories (such as isnare.com). Many online writing portals offer payment along with exposure. Some that offer payment do so in what is known as AdSense revenue sharing. For those portals you must first have an AdSense ID number, which you obtain by signing up at https://www.google.com/adsense. You then provide your AdSense ID to the writing portal. You write an article, which you submit into their network. AdSense ads are shown alongside your article. Depending on how the revenue sharing system is set up, you'll receive revenue a certain percentage of the time when the AdSense ads alongside your site are clicked on. For example, if you write for an online writing portal where they offer revenue sharing 50 percent of the time, your ads will be shown half of the time, while the ads of the portal will be shown the other half of the time. If the ads showing during your half of the time are clicked on, you receive revenue, which shows up in your AdSense account. However, the portal receives the revenue for any clicks that occur during their half of the time.

Other examples of writing portal payments include payments based on the number of views your article receives and upfront payments. Some, such as publishing portal Associated Content, allow for both. Generally, these types of portals offer a higher potential to profit from your content. With revenue sharing you have to get clicks in order to make a profit. In fact, you could have 100,000 views, but if no one clicks the AdSense ads during your allotted time, you won't make any profit. Compare this with sites that pay per view: 100,000 views for maybe $.01 per impression (the exact cost depends on the portal, keywords, and content you're using) would yield $1,000. Upfront payments are even better because you get compensated for your writing, as well as getting exposure to your web site. Yet you need to be careful that you're not writing an advertisement when you write articles for writing portals offering upfront payments. You also aren't allowed to promote affiliate links (at least in the case of Associated Content). So make sure that when you're writing your articles, you direct the visitor to a top-level URL instead of an affiliate link or a subdomain.

There are also online writing portals where the only compensation you receive is a traffic boost to your web site and the potential for even more one-way links. These sites are known as free article directories. How they work is simple. You start by writing an article for them. Since they aren't offering payment, you advertise any link you want, whether it's a top-level domain name, a subdomain, or an affiliate link. However, many have a limit to the number of links you can include in the article body. Some may only allow a link in the resource box (information at the bottom of the article that contains your name, brief bio and contact info, such as e-mail or web site). You write your content and submit it to the directory. Some sites such as EzineArticles (one of the largest), ArticleAvenue, and iSnare require you to sign up (membership is free). Others like GoArticles or ArticleCity simply require you to post and submit your article.

Each site has guidelines regarding content, hyperlinks, and word count. Read the site's guidelines before submission to prevent your article from being rejected (you can fix the error and resubmit). Once your article is posted, your content is offered to other webmasters as public domain. (Some

> **TIP:** I started bringing traffic to my site via article writing, and it was and is my preferred choice for quality traffic. I always recommend this as a good SEO and traffic strategy.

sites give you the option to opt out of your work being used without permission; read the guidelines). This means they can post it for free on their web site. Yet don't think that you are giving away your writing work, because there is a catch to this. The catch is that in order for webmasters to legally post your work, they must keep the article intact. They cannot alter it in any way. Do you see the advantage? Basically, they're required to advertise your URL (which is in the resource box most often). So when they get traffic, their visitors will be exposed to your URL, which they are free to click on if you're advertising an offer that interests them. In terms of one-way links, you get the one-way link to the free article directory along with any one-way links that could occur when webmasters decide to post your article on their web site.

The other benefit to writing articles is that it gives you more ways to appear in search engines. Don't forget to post your content to your own site—and spend a little time making changes to avoid duplication issues.

> ### ▼ More on Links
>
> **M**any of these sites only allow one or two links back to your site, and only from the resource box. A relevant link that cites your web site in the middle of the page content, within text that supports the anchor text/URL, is a highly qualified link! Google uses latent semantic analysis (LSA & LSI), defined in wikipedia as a technique in natural language processing, in particular in vectorial semantics, to analyze relationships between a set of documents and the terms they contain by producing a set of concepts related to the documents and terms. See http://en.wikipedia.org/wiki/Latent_semantic_analysis for more.

What's the best way to write articles for online writing portals? Should you write differently for free network sites versus the paid networks? The answer to the latter question is no. The reason behind this answers the first question: online writing portals are interested in the same thing you are—search engine optimization. They need to rank high so they can get AdSense revenue or get exposure to their own services, products or affiliate advertisements. A good tip to follow is to offer your best. Do not write artificial keyword–stuffed articles for the sake of driving traffic. Writing articles does more than boost your search traffic; it can also boost your credibility with potential buyers. Every eyeball on your article is a potential customer. Give them useful information and demonstrate your value in your field.

Write for the customer first, but of course you still need to do your keyword research. In the case of paid online writing portals, if you can write an article on a more popular keyword, you might be able to make more money, since a popular keyword equals more clicks. For free article directories, writing for a popular keyword means you'll get more webmasters interested in promoting your content.

The only restrictions you need to keep in mind are that you can't plagiarize and you can't use private label content. You might be wondering why you can't use private label content if you legally own the rights to the writing. This is because with most private label content, you're not the only one who owns the rights. There are exceptions. If you buy content with full rights from networks such as Constant Content or of course from ghostwriters, you can be assured that only you are getting the article. In cases like these, you could submit the article to online writing networks without penalty (unless another webmaster has plagiarized the work, which you can find out through services like Copyscape). However, most private label situations are not like this, especially in the case of memberships (which is the most popular way private label content is sold). What happens is the content gets posted elsewhere by other people who also own the rights. Some may even try to post it on online writing networks themselves. Since the content is viewed as not being original, doing these things could ban a webmaster from any type of online writing portal.

What you can do with private label content is use it to get ideas on how to write your own articles. If the private label content is in Microsoft Word format, you can use Word's AutoSummarize feature to highlight key points in the article. These highlights can appear in the article or in a separate document. Regardless, you can use these key points to form the basis for a new article. This method is preferable to rewriting the content, because you're less likely to borrow exact phrases from the original content. Of course, if the private label content has an identifiable author, you could put the phrases in quotes and cite them at the end of your article. This method is acceptable to most online writing portals, since they realize you may still need to do research to write your content. However, if the content does not have an identifiable author, you need to avoid borrowing phrases. Maybe one or two here or there won't get noticed, but doing it too often could make the portal you submit your works to classify it as duplicate content. This means that your content is found on other sites, making it invalid for submission.

There are thousands of article directories and publishing portals in addition to the few mentioned in this section. To get you started, here are a few:

- Helium
- EzineArticles
- iSnare
- Searchwarp
- Getmyarticles
- Goarticles
- Alumbo
- ArticleAvenue
- ArticleCity
- Articlesbase
- Marketing-Seek
- Upublish
- PromotionWorld
- American Chronicle (must be approved)

Classified Ads

Online classified ads work just like print classified ads. They allow people the opportunity to post advertisements for things they are selling, business opportunities, or jobs. Most online classified ads offer free

> **TIP:** Craigslist.org still has good visibility with search engines, but has also been victimized by spam.

submission, but if you upgrade to their paid packages, they make your ad more prominent. For example, they might bold your ad, allow you to include pictures, and, depending on the site, allow your URL to be clickable. These things don't matter much for link building, though they increase the chance that your URL will get viewed by visitors.

Message Boards and Online Groups. Message boards, which are sometimes classified as a type of group, are forums in which a group of members exchange text messages. These messages are put in different categories called threads. While most message boards leave communication on the board, some allow members to receive new posts through their e-mail (this is an option popular with Yahoo! Groups). Members are free to talk about anything they want, and usually they can post links to their URLs. However, it's important that if they advertise, they follow the guidelines set forth by the webmaster of the message board or group. Some webmasters don't care if you're advertising, just as long as it relates to the thread at hand. Others allow you to advertise only in a special section of the message board. The downside to these types of sites is that your ads are clearly shown as ads, which tend to draw people away from wanting to see them. This is a big disadvantage if you want to get your site seen, but in terms of link building it doesn't matter. You get the advantage of a one-way link just by posting your URL.

> **TIP:** Check out Yahoo! Groups and Google Groups, and depending on your topic, set up your account to e-mail you when topics change. Good for research and feedback.

However, if you want the advantage of one-way linking and traffic, consider joining message boards exclusively designed for advertising. You could use a search engine to find these boards, or you could search the three main sites offering groups. These are AOL, MSN, and (my personal favorite) Yahoo!. Many folks on these message boards are internet marketers, so keep that in mind when you post your message. They tend to be more responsive to ads promoting business opportunities, cheap advertising, or free advertising. They may also be interested in link exchanges (which are discussed more when we cover ways to get paid one-way links).

Finally, some networking sites offer opportunities for free exposure. A relatively new feature on LinkedIn is an "Ask" section where you can post answers to questions posted by other LinkedIn members. You can demonstrate your expertise in your specialty by answering a question. All your contact info is visible so those interested in knowing more can send you an e-mail or visit your site.

Free Online Press Releases. A press release is a public relations announcement distributed to the news media and other targeted publications. Online press releases unfortunately are overused and abused. Many barely pass as readable and are hyperbole disguised as a press release. However, a well-written, targeted release is still an effective marketing tool.

To get an idea of how press releases are written, visit the press or media room of any large company. All are written in the same journalistic style—they start with a compelling, descriptive headline, then a nugget that introduces the story and tells the "Who, What, Where, Why, When, How" in summary. That's followed by the body, which provides detail, and the release ends with a close and information about your company. With online press releases, you also want to optimize using keywords. Optimize the headline and the body of the copy. When posting your press release on a free online press release site, you get the advantage of one-way linking and traffic. In this case, it's both traffic to the free press release site and any traffic that might be generated if your press release is chosen to be promoted elsewhere. You can also pay for online press release distribution. One of the largest sites is prweb.com, which offers additional services, such as RSS feeds, SEO, choice of geographic distribution, and more. Many online marketers don't realize that you can submit your press release directly to targeted publications and media. You can hire a PR specialist to put together a targeted media list for you, use online software (such as that offered by Mass Media Distribution), or put together your own list.

> **TIP:** I recommend building press release management into your SEO strategy. Distribute new, fresh releases as often as you see fit, but only if you have something worthwhile to say. Remember: Users first, search engines second! It can bring massive and targeted traffic, just as articles do.

Controversial Free One-Way Building Methods. Controversial one-way link-building methods include banner and link exchange networks, autosurfs, and safelists. Banner and link exchange networks are those in which members submit their sites in exchange for viewing other people's sites within the networks. Autosurfs are similar to banner and link exchanges, except that they pay their members to view the material. Safelists are web sites where members post their links with no obligation to view other people's ads. All of these networks may offer a credit system in which the more ads you view, the longer you can show your ad in their network.

Why are these methods controversial? And if they're controversial, why are they still being listed as white hat SEO tactics? First off, they're controversial because of those who abuse an otherwise ingenious marketing approach; for example, sites that don't pay. Additionally, many internet marketers don't like them because they feel the traffic isn't genuinely interested in what is being advertised. However, does this mean there's anything ethically wrong with them? Most people joining these networks know what they are getting into. It's not like they're being thrown advertisements against their will, as they would be if their e-mail inboxes were being spammed or if they received pop-ups. So ethically, I don't see a problem with them, which is why I still list them in this section.

genuinely interested in what is being advertised. However, does this mean there's anything ethically wrong with them? Most people joining these networks know what they are getting into. It's not like they're being thrown advertisements against their will, as they would be if their e-mail inboxes were being spammed or if they received pop-ups. So ethically, I don't see a problem with them, which is why I still list them in this section.

Directories

Webmasters who own directories allow one-way linking because not only do they get a moment when their ads are seen by those submitting their links, they also get the advantage of outbound links (discussed earlier in this book). To find directories, search "free directories" on your favorite search engine, or you can visit rankready.com. Rankready is not a directory in itself; instead it's a free service that advertises web sites offering free ads in their directories.

As we talked about earlier, directories are an important tool in your SEO efforts. The top directories are Yahoo! ($299 per year) and DMOZ (Open Directory Project), now owned by Google. DMOZ is free, but it typically takes a long time to get approved and listed. In addition to the ones already listed, there are other paid directories that may require payment or reciprocal linking (discussed in the next section). If you do reciprocal linking, you don't get the advantage of having a one-way link, which is what search engines prefer to see. And if you pay for a link, you are using a paid method of one-way link building. Check out the next section to learn how you can determine whether it's worth your while to pay for a listing in a directory; in my opinion, adding random directories is not worthwhile and certainly not for link/spam techniques, but if the directory follows the guidelines set forth in the next section, it might be.

Paid One-Way Link Building

Paid one-way link building involves buying advertising space from a web site.

Unlike free one-way link building, the paid version allows you to get one-way links that better match the keywords found throughout your web site. Because you are paying for the link, the provider ensures that the keywords are a perfect match to your requirements. This section explains in detail the process to go through to determine what sites you should use for paid one-way link building. You also learn about how to find paid one-way link-building opportunities.

TIP: To see a diagram of an optimally structured paid link page, visit the member site.

We talked about link spamming and the fine line that must be walked when building your links (build quality links and build gradually). Your strategy should include both paid and free links. Paid links are fine, as is regular advertising, but Google recommends using them only with "rel=nofollow". This values the link from an advertising perspective, but not a "PageRank citation perspective," which they consider deceptive. Keep this in mind as we go through the next section. Search engines aren't perfect, but they typically can detect paid links in the right or left columns of your site. They can also detect the number of paid links. It's far better to have links in the body of your site content rather than on a sidebar list or the bottom of the page. Of course you'll want to integrate the links with relevant content with good anchor text.

What You Should Look For in Sites Offering Paid One-Way Link Building

1. Linking Format

Make sure that the site where you plan to advertise offers its linking format in HREF code. HREF is a special HTML tag that creates hyperlinks. The syntax for HREF is:

<a href="yoururl">Your Desired Keywords</a>

As you can see, HREF can help you create keyword-centric links. Place your URL where you see "yoururl" and the text to describe your link in the section where it says "Your Desired Keywords." To find out if the site you want to advertise on uses HREF format, use "View Source" from your browser. Right-click on the page your link will be advertised on and select "View Source." Note: This command might be worded differently, depending on the browser you use.

From there look for HREF coding. A quick, easy way to locate this would be to go to "Edit" and select "Find" within the program. That opens after you select "View Source." Type "HREF" in the text box at the bottom of the program. The program then highlights any instance it finds of HREF.

But, don't think that because you see HREF, you're home free. There are other elements that you need to look for when looking at the HTML coding of the web site you intend to advertise on. These elements are explained in more detail below:

- Make sure there is no coding that indicates redirection, as this puts a negative effect on your site's page rank.
- Make sure that JavaScript isn't used. The difference between linking with straight HREF and linking with JavaScript is that the word JavaScript is listed as one of the HREF properties.
- Make sure that the HREF property "rel=nofollow" isn't used. "rel=nofollow" lets a search engine know the link being advertised has not yet been approved by the webmaster or is a paid link. When a search engine sees this property, it ignores the URL, and spiders don't follow any URLs that are listed this way. It's up to you if you decide to pay for it when it has less of an effect. You'll get traffic, but not link juice (Google frowns on this).

- Make sure the "robots" property associated with meta tags on the page doesn't have the attribute "noindex." The "robots" property communicates to search engine spiders or robots what you want to get indexed in search engine listings. "noindex" indicates that you don't want the following URL to be indexed in the search engine results. Don't be alarmed if you see the "robots" property, since it's not "robots" that's the problem, it's the "noindex" property. If you see "index, follow," your URL will be included for search engine indexing. Keep in mind that capitalization of the tags or properties doesn't matter. I see many web sites with "index, follow." This isn't really needed, and since it's especially powerful and easy to change, I don't include it.
- Professional webmasters may use the robots.txt file: a special search engine instruction file found under the root of the site. You can check to see what has been included/excluded by going to http://www.domainname.com/robots.txt. (Substitute your domain name for "domainname.com." If you get a 404 error, that means robots.txt is not in place). These techniques should assist in link discovery and help you find out where they may be deceiving you.

2. Number of Backlinks Associated with the Site

Simply defined, *backlinks* are the links that advertise a particular web site. They could be one-way links or reciprocal links. There are a number of easy-to-use, tools to check the number of backlinks a site has, including iwebtool (www.iwebtool.com/backlink_checker), SEO Elite, and the Google Webmaster tools. Alternatively, you could use a free tool like marketleap.com. If the site has a lot of backlinks, you'll want to advertise with them. Don't necessarily discredit sites that don't have as many backlinks, especially if they offer affordable advertising options. You would still get the advantage of a one-way link, which search engines prize. This is even better if the web site you're advertising on directly relates to the keywords used throughout your site. Keep in mind what you read before: the number of backlinks (quantity, popularity) is important, but so is the relevancy (quality, reputation) of the site and pages.

3. Check the Site's PageRank

As discussed, PageRank is a relevant measure. To find PageRank, use linkvendor.com or Google's toolbar (http://toolbar.google.com).

4. The Web Site's Alexa Rating

Alexa.com is a web site that shows the traffic rankings of web sites. However, alexa.com is unable to distinguish between "legitimate" and "non-legitimate" traffic. For example, if a site "buys" traffic, this would be included with its alexa.com results. The problem with buying traffic is that you don't know for sure if you're getting real visitors. Sites that use expired domains tend to get real visitors, so their type of traffic is legitimate. However, there are many more sites that use bots to generate false traffic. Since you don't know if a site's traffic ranking has been affected by this type of traffic, don't get too excited if the web site you want to advertise on has a high Alexa rating. Alexa is most often used by technical people, and so the data is demographically skewed. Although it's better than nothing, use it with caution and follow the other guidelines set out in this section for determining whether you want to spend your money advertising on a particular site.

5. Check to See If the Web Site Is Listed on Google or Other Search Engines

This guideline might be obvious, yet it's very important. Type in keywords that relate to the site and see what pops up on the major search engines. Look through the first 50 listings (although it's optimal that the web site appear in the first ten listings). If the site isn't there, you don't want to advertise with them.

> **TIP:** A quick way to check search engine inclusion is to take a string or sentence from the webpage and put "" (quotes) around the expression and Google search. If listed, it will show up. Be sure to include enough words to make it unique.

6. Make Sure the Cached Version of the Web Page Contains the Links

Cached web pages are backups of the regular page. According to GoogleGuide.com, they are "snapshots" of the original web site. They're just as important as the regular version of the web page because they show when the regular web page is unable to show. Googleguide.com says the situations in which this could occur include congestion on the internet, an overloaded or very slow web site, or a webmaster removing web pages from their site. If advertising links don't show in the cached version of a web page, you're not getting the most advertising value for your dollar. This is a disadvantage to both you and the site owners, since outbound links increase the chances that the site will get a higher ranking in search engine results.

7. The Relevance of the Site in Relation to Your Own

With free one-way linking situations, you don't have the advantage of determining whether the site best reflects the keywords you might be promoting. You only get the advantage of showing search engines that you at least have some one-way links. However, if you're paying for advertising, you want to make sure that the site relates in some way to your keywords, especially your primary ones.

How to Find Paid One-Way Linking Opportunities

The quickest way to find paid one-way linking opportunities is to type in your primary keyword and see what web sites come up in the first ten listings. I know this might seem to be clichéd advice, but hey, don't underestimate it. How can you lose if you advertise on a site that you know ranks high on a search engine? The only downside to this method is that, depending on the keyword you're promoting, the web sites that rank higher may take advantage of their position by charging outlandish advertising fees.

Another thing you can do to find paid one-way linking opportunities is to use adbrite.com or services like it. Adbrite.com is a service that allows people to sell advertising space. You can buy text links, banner space, full-page ads, a special type of pop-up known as an inline ad, and video advertising. When you're more established, you might want to look at the other advertising options. For now, since you're mostly concerned with search engine optimization, go for the text links. Don't forget to go through the previous steps mentioned on how to determine whether or not you should advertise with a particular site. Just because Adbrite lists a site doesn't mean it's the best one for you. Alternatively, you can find web sites to advertise on through eBay.

> **TIP:** On the member site, you'll find more information on web sites to peruse.

Lastly, don't rule out advertising on some of your favorite web sites. If they aren't visibly offering an advertising opportunity on their web site, e-mail them and ask if they would be willing to sell ad space. You can also do this to initiate a link exchange, which is the focus of the next section.

Reciprocal Linking

Reciprocal linking is when a web site links to you in exchange for your linking to them. Reciprocal links aren't as valuable as one-way links in the eyes of search engines because there's always the chance of people abusing the system with them. However, they count enough that you shouldn't overlook them.

You need to have a page rank of at least 3 before most webmasters will consider linking with you. However, take a look at some of the guidelines specified in this section even if you haven't yet achieved this page rank. Why? Because there are a lot of webmasters like you who are interested in reciprocal linking but don't have the advantage of a high page rank. Remember, linking to someone, even if their page rank is low, is better than not having any links.

That being said, you're ready to learn what to do to prepare your site for reciprocal linking. First, you need to have a web page on your site that says "Related Links" or "Resources." Avoid the temptation that many webmasters fall into of saying "Sponsors" or "Affiliates" or "Links." If the webmasters you want to exchange links with are savvy, they'll realize that titling their link sections this way makes them less likely to get their URLs seen. This is because people don't like being advertised to. Most visitors have no reason to visit a "Sponsor" or "Affiliate" page. However, they may be curious about "Related Links" because they think they might receive more content that relates to what they're looking for.

Next, make sure that your "Related Links" page is as optimized as it can be with key-words related to your site. You should even place keywords in the advertising descriptions of the sites you're posting. If possible, include content on the "Related Links" page. The best approach for creating keyword-optimized content on your "Related Links" is to include detailed descriptions of the sites. Since these sites should relate to your keywords anyway, it shouldn't be too hard to come up with keyword-rich content that accurately describes the purposes of these web sites. The people linking with you will appreciate this as well, since by providing a description, you're offering a way to convince visitors that they should look at the sites listed.

You will need a "Link to Us" code. With the "Link to Us" code, webmasters get HTML code they can use to easily link to your site. Plus, the link provided through this code would be cloaked, which offers a better clickthrough rate than those that are uncloaked. To initiate a "Link to Us" code, say something like "Easily link to us by using the follow-ing code," then provide the necessary HTML linking code. This syntax of this code is:

<A HREF="http://www.yoursite.com"> **Your Primary Keyword**></A>

Enter a short description using your primary keyword to tell what your site is about.

Does this look familiar? It should, because it's the HREF tag discussed earlier. This is the general tag you need to link to web sites, at least if you're doing it through HTML coding.

Now what you need to do is start posting web sites with which you want to exchange links. To find them, use the methods discussed in the section "How to Find Paid One-Way Linking Opportunities," as the principles outlined there also apply to reciprocal link-ing. After that, you should see if the webmaster of your selected web site is interested in a link exchange. Some sites let you submit your site instantaneously, so you don't have to e-mail the webmaster asking permission to embark on a linking exchange. Others require an e-mail (even those that may have a "Link to Us" code). To e-mail the webmaster, look for a Contact Us section on the web site. If a Contact Us section isn't provided, you can use a Whois utility, which can be found through domain name services, to deter-mine their e-mail address. All you need to use these utilities is the domain name of the person you want to contact.

> **TIP:** Visit the member site to see videos on how to use tools such as a professional link-building system, Arelis, from International Business Promoter (IBP).

Following are a few suggestions for proper e-mail etiquette when requesting link exchanges.

1. You should *want* to link to their site. I know … you might be thinking, why link to their site if you don't know for sure they'll link to yours? The answer is because by linking to their site first, you're showing intent that you are genuinely interested in a link exchange. Some webmasters won't be interested in a link exchange if they see that

the person e-mailing them hasn't started the link exchange first. If in the end you find that the person doesn't hold up his or her end of the bargain, you can always remove the link from your web site.

2. Let the webmaster know clearly in the e-mail subject line that you intend to link to his or her site. It could be as simple as "Link Exchange from Your Site to the Webmaster's Site." By doing this you are stating your intention, which saves the webmaster valuable reading time. He or she is also more likely to open up your e-mail.

3. Make sure your writing style is friendly and personal. Show that you have genuine interest in the person's web site and describe the benefits of linking to your site. Talking about how much traffic you get is a big plus (if you get a lot of traffic). You might want to include a screenshot of your traffic (most web hosting programs have options in your account manager that let you track your traffic). Alternatively, you could find your site through alexa.com and provide the specific URL that would show your alexa.com rankings. If you don't get too much traffic, try to sell yourself by explaining more about the audience that you *intend* to market to. Webmasters are interested in promoting themselves in niche markets, and if they think your site is going to be popular in a niche market, you may be able to win them over and get them to participate in a link exchange.

4. Don't threaten to delete their links from your site if they don't respond within a certain time. Link exchanging with another site is a privilege, not a right. If webmasters are interested, they'll respond saying they'll exchange links with you. If this is the reply you get, give them some time to put your link on their sites, about a week. If they don't do anything, e-mail them again asking if they're still interested in the link exchange opportunity. Hopefully, they'll reply saying "yes" and put your link on their sites. If they aren't, then delete their links from your site.

5. Keep your e-mail condensed. You should have no more than two short paragraphs of three to four sentences. Make sure that it's grammatically correct, because if it isn't, the webmaster might get the impression that your web site isn't worth linking to. Most e-mail providers have a spell checker. Take advantage of it.

6. Only send one follow-up request. Bombarding a webmaster's e-mail is annoying and could be considered spam. In fact, some people may even report you to their ISPs if they think you're spamming them. This could ban you from doing e-mail marketing with anyone else using that ISP. Remember, most webmasters respond to the first e-mail if they're interested in a link exchange. The few that don't will definitely respond on the second e-mail. If they don't, assume they're not interested and move on.

7. Don't use this as an opportunity to advertise affiliate web sites you might be a part of. Yes, it might be tempting to tell a webmaster about the latest server that's out there and collect a hefty commission, but forego the temptation. Trust me, if their sites are

up, you can be assured that they already made their hosting or server decisions. If you must refer to an affiliate link, add "(aff)" at the end of the link as an indicator.

8. Use commonly accepted e-mail etiquette. Be professional and concise. Avoid using words in the subject line that may tag your e-mail as spam (such as "free").

On the upside, you're getting a chance to get your site advertised to that many more people. If your site just happens to relate to things that webmasters are interested in, then you might get a lead or sale from them when they visit your site to consider doing a link exchange with you. Let the site do the advertising for you, not your e-mail. The average response rate is about 1 percent. So if you send out 1,000 e-mails to webmasters asking for participation in a link exchange, that's a possibility of ten sales. Okay, maybe it sounds desperate, but as far as I'm concerned, all types of traffic count.

> **TIP:** Continue testing different messages, content and structure. I have moved up in the response rates, and 3–5 percent isn't uncommon, moving higher with testing.

Do you have all eight of those suggestions in mind? Good. Now you're ready to learn how to automate this process, if you have the money. The wonderful little program that helps you to do this is called SEO Elite. The program scours the web looking for possible reciprocal web sites based on the keywords you provide for it. You can also use the program to find keywords. The program has a built-in Whois utility to help you figure out the e-mail addresses of webmasters who don't post them on their web sites. Once the program collects the e-mail addresses, use it to send an e-mail to all of them. Optilink is another professional program that is a must-have for the professional search marketer. Optilink is a little harder to learn and not as automated with e-mail exchange tracking. My online membership area has videos that explain how to use it and provide you with some advanced techniques.

As you go through the process of acquiring reciprocal links, there are some other things you need to keep in mind. First, remember that search engines want to index sites that would be of real value to a visitor. When their bots encounter reciprocal links, you want to give the impression that you exchanged links because your web site and its contents are that good for the other webmaster. So, if you are obtaining an abnormally high number of reciprocal links, your site may not get indexed as high or may even be penalized because it's seen as trying to cheat the search engine's algorithm. This is why you want to build your links gradually. In all likelihood, if you receive 100 reciprocal links in a month, it won't raise any red flags. However, if you build 1,000 links a month, watch out, as search engines will consider this link spamming and penalize you.

While the principle is true, please note that it's also relative. If we use news powerhouse CNN as an example, they most certainly receive many more than 1,000 links per month and they're not penalized. That's because history, patterns, and marketplace are also factors, and not simply "the rules." Also make sure that you offer some variations in your linking code. This is because search engines don't want to see that your web site is linked to hundreds of other sites with the same code and description. It doesn't see this as being a natural link-building method. Consequently, you should periodically update your "Link to Us" code. Use different primary keywords, or even secondary keywords, along with different descriptions.

Additionally, you should make sure that not too many links on your site are reciprocal. Remember when I said earlier that one-way links are what search engines prefer to see? Do you also remember I said that reciprocal links have lost some of their emphasis because of the potential for abuse? This is why you want to keep your percentage of reciprocal links relatively low.

In terms of where your reciprocal links point to, avoid the temptation to always have it be the home page. First of all, from a marketing standpoint there are situations where the more specific content is provided on a subtopic web page, the more value it would have for a web site visitor. Secondly, search engines don't like to see it. When it comes to natural link buiding, you're not always going to want to provide links to your home page, as you would want to promote other web pages, as well. Search engines are leery when they see otherwise. Remember the silo approach discussed in Chapter 3? This also applies to how you build your links. Group the links by like content to create relevancy and you'll be rewarded with higher search rankings (and happier users!).

Outbound Links

Outbound links, as you've learned previously, are links that you post on your site that point to other sites. These can be provided through webmasters who decide to pay you for ad space or simply because you think a web site has relevant material. Google doesn't penalize you for getting outbound links from advertising, though you want to make sure the links relate to the keywords featured on your site.

So, what are some ways of finding outbound links? Remember when Adbrite and eBay were discussed? Well, feel free to use them. You may also want to have an "Advertise Here" section on your web site. In this section you can create a form for webmasters to fill out to automatically send you an e-mail request. You can create forms in any web site creation software or use HTML if you're more technically inclined. Alternatively, you could show your e-mail address, though make sure you don't use your main e-mail address. This is because spammers often collect e-mail addresses posted on web site to do their dirty business. In fact, even when you vie for traffic exchanges you should probably use a separate e-mail address, though it's not as essential.

For free outbound links, you can do a keyword search and subsequently link to the sites that you feel relate well to your site. If you need content for your site, you could create outbound links by linking to articles from the free article directories talked about earlier in this book. However, be careful. The downside to free article directories is that there is the possibility that the content may have already been used by another webmaster. If it has been, and you post it on your web site, Google could flag you for duplicate content, making you rank lower, if at all. So, copy and paste a few words of the article into the search engine text box. See how

> **TIP:** The number of outbound links on a page should not exceed 100, as a general recommendation. Google looks at the total counts on a page, and that's true for your own site, as well as others that link to you. The idea is that if it's drastically more than that, it could be considered spammy and not as valuable.

many results come up. If a lot of webmasters are using the content, reconsider using the actual content. However, this doesn't mean the link the content is promoting isn't of any value. In fact, if that many webmasters are putting it on their sites, the links probably are valuable. Create your own article (using the free article as a guide) and place the link on your web site. Of course, if an article submitted to a free article directory is new, then you can go ahead and put the article and the link on your own web site.

How to Legitimately Post on Wikipedia

It's important to keep in mind that Wikipedia and sites like it are informational in nature. Self-promotion is prohibited, but giving general information about a business, product, or service is acceptable.

Make sure your articles have an encyclopedia-like tone. Wikipedia offers some guidelines you should follow when writing for their site:

1. **Know your intentions.** As an internet marketer your natural urge is to advertise, advertise, and advertise even more. Don't do this if you want to take advantage of Wikipedia. In fact, since you know you might be biased when it comes to your own site, consider having a ghostwriter write the article. It won't cost much to get a ghostwriter to write one article, plus you will be able to get a viewpoint that's less subjective.

2. **Use cited text in place of links.** Wikipedia frowns on redirecting visitors to other sites. This is why when referring to another site, it's better to paraphrase what the site says than cite

> **TIP:** Wikipedia is an authority site, but there was too much spam being injected, so Wikipedia implemented the rel=nofollow, which quickly removed spammers. It's still valuable as a source for traffic and reference. (You have probably noticed how often listings show up with Wikipedia at the top in Google results).

the reference at the end of the document. And you definitely shouldn't use affiliate sites as references, as this could be seen as advertising.

3. **Don't put ads in the references section.** References are what a writer has used to help create an article. In other situations you could use an affiliate link as a reference, but article writing for Wikipedia is not one of them.

4. **Don't make your article sound like an endorsement of your web site.**

5. **Avoid spam radar.** A few things that could set off the spam radar are links at the top of an unordered list, putting more emphasis on one product over another when listing links, adding too many links mentioning the same product or service, and adding the same link to other articles.

6. **Use the talk page.** It's OK to ask editors if a potential article meets Wikipedia's requirements. However, only do it once and don't put in anything else that could be construed as an ad.

7. **Don't use external links in your signature.** While doing this is fine for many message boards, don't do it when writing for Wikipedia.

8. **Look at other Wikipedia articles.** Yes, this might be another obvious suggestion, but how else are you going to determine what Wikipedia likes if you don't do this? Do searches on some famous companies as well as smaller ones. Pay particular attention to how the articles for the smaller companies were written, since it can be a lot harder to get an article about a no-name company accepted over one that has already been talked about before.

9. **Use rejection as a learning experience.** If your article is rejected, don't be discouraged. You can use the experience as a learning tool to figure out more of what Wikipedia wants.

> **▼ TIP:** To see the "rel=nofollow" links and who uses them and where, install the SEO for Firefox plugin by Aaron Wall (see my free lifetime membership site for "firefox plugins"). Once installed, refresh the pages, and the links show up highlighted in red.

CHECKLIST FOR SUCCESS

Now that you know the ins and outs of linking, you're well on your way to building a brand and making money online. Below is a list of what SEO pros consider necessary in order to consider linking with a site. It's also a handy comprehensive reminder of how to build links the right way.

1. Build links from related or complementary web sites—in other words, topically related.

2. Don't worry about PageRank, see number 1 above.

3. Links should contain varied, targeted keywords/key phrases as text hyperlinks.

4. Reciprocal links are OK, but make sure you offer readers value and the site isn't a link farm.

5. Links optimally should be followed by a short description of the target web site also containing related keywords. Top links are contained within the *body* of the page using keywords/text to help describe the link.

6. Don't build all the links on the same day (or within a short time period); avoid any penalties and avoid "run of site" links, showing up on all pages.

7. Links should not be from framed pages.

8. Links should not be through a JavaScript or redirect scripts.

9. Get links from top-valued directories, research categories.

10. Build quality links from trusted sites. Avoid bad neighborhoods.

11. Links should not be on Flash sites or pages.

12. Links should not include a "nofollow" tag or any other robot tags (unless it's a paid link).

13. Don't link with penalized or banned sites.

14. Avoid link farms, link exchange sites, and link clubs.

Link Terms

anchor text: The text associated with a hyperlink.

one-way link: A hyperlink that points to a web site without a reciprocal link; thus the link goes "one way" in direction.

link: A citation from one web document to another web document or another position in the same document.

link baiting: Targeting, creating, and formatting your content or information in a way that encourages your target audience to point high-quality links at your site.

link building: The process of building links. Can be inbound or outbound.

link burst: A rapid increase in the quantity of links pointing at a web site.

link churn: The rate at which a site loses links.

link equity: A measure of the strength of your site based on inbound link popularity and the authority and quality of the sites providing the links.

link farm: A web site that links to other sites without regard to content or relevancy. Free For All (FFA) pages are examples of link farms.

link hoarding: Keeping all your link popularity by not doing outbound links or only linking out using JavaScript or redirects.

link popularity: A measure of the quantity and quality of inbound links pointing to a particular web site. This feature is used by search engines for positioning of web pages in their indexes.

paid links: Links purchased for advertising.

reciprocal links: Links exchanged between two sites.

Link-Building Resources

The following sites are great resources to add to your arsenal of tools.

1. **www.ericward.com/articles/index.html.** Site offers great article by Eric Ward, one of the web's very first link builders. He worked on the first link requests for amazon.com. I signed up for his paid newsletters and resources. Excellent.

2. **www.wolf-howl.com/category/link-development.** Michael Gray writes with humor and intelligence on link development. He likes to challenge Google directly at search engine conferences!

3. **www.stuntdubl.com/category/link-development.** Todd Malicoat, known as "Stuntdubl" online, provides heavily researched and highly valuable discussions on link-building practices.

4. **www.seobook.com/archives/cat_seo_tips.shtml.** Aaron Wall's SEOBook is one of the most respected web sites on the subject of SEO.

5. **www.copyblogger.com.** Brian Clark's Copyblogger is an excellent site for learning how to write great content, a critical part of successful link building.

6. **www.jimboykin.com.** Jim Boykin's blog and discussion of his "link ninjas." His site is an invaluable resource for link building. He also has top tools for SEO analysis and link building at http://www.webuildpages.com/tools/.

7. **www.toprankblog.com/category/seo/link-building.** Lee Odden's Online Marketing Blog, read by many. A great resource for how to acquire links.

CHAPTER 9

Ready to Launch

HOW TO SUBMIT YOUR SITE TO SEARCH ENGINES AND DIRECTORIES

Janet had been told that the search engines would "find her" if she optimized her site correctly. However, after four weeks she was beginning to wonder if the search engines had taken a wrong turn.

Frustrated that she was still not receiving as much traffic, she turned to the experts for help. Janet found out that it was actually not inaccurate that the search engines would find her, but there was action she could take to become more visible in cyberspace.

Janet listed the directories and began submitting her site, beginning with Yahoo! Directory. Within less than two weeks Janet started to see results from her efforts. Finally, she felt like she was making progress.

This section talks about how you can submit your site to Yahoo!, Ask Jeeves, MSN, and AOL. You will also learn how to submit to the Open Directory (DMOZ). It's not a search engine, but it's vital in helping you get noticed by search engines. You also learn why you shouldn't use submission services or submission software. The only topic that isn't covered in this section is Google, which is talked about in the next section.

Best Opportunity for Fast Indexing

Search engine indexing is how information is collected, parsed, and stored in search engine databases to facilitate fast and accurate information retrieval. The search engine index design uses interdisciplinary theories from linguistics, cognitive psychology, mathematics, informatics, physics, and computer science.

Search engine optimization is about creating a site that meets search engine criteria.

Automatic versus Manual Submission

Search engines don't like automatic submissions. They get millions of attempted automatic submissions each day, and as a result, go to great lengths to try to stop them, such as requiring passwords and/or fill-in details before the submission is accepted.

Automatic submission software is banned by many search engines and directories because it can't always place links in relevant categories. Whether you hire a directory submitter or use submission software yourself, you are setting your site up for failure. Getting too many incoming links too quickly or submitting the same site to the major engines repeatedly can be seen by search engines as spamming and get your site banned.

There are few benefits to using a paid submission service, although the promotions tout that these services know of places to submit that you are unaware of. The best submission services take the time to educate their clients on submission with the expectation that they'll be able to do the job themselves next time.

Submitting your site manually gives you control over where you'll be listed. Automatic submitters may list your site with an engine you've never heard of outside the United States. Or, worse, they could be associating your site with sites that you find objectionable, such as pornographic sites. When you submit your own site, you decide what category to list in. You don't want your site to end up in the general directory or the miscellaneous category where it may never be seen.

Every site should be marketed differently, and submitted to different engines and directories depending on its intended audience. Automatic submission doesn't do this.

Manual submission is the only way to choose the descriptions and keywords that you think will be most effective in promoting your site, as most engines and directories allow you to choose your own.

Common Myths of Search Engine Submission

Here are some common myths about submitting your site manually.

1. Search engine submission requires enormous research.
2. Almost every search engine and directory has a link labeled "Add a site" or "Submit URL," which takes you directly to their submission form. All you have to do is follow their rules and enter your information carefully.
3. Web sites should be listed in all search engines.
4. If you list your web site with the top-tier search engines, it will find its own way into the second tier and beyond. In fact, you don't even have to submit your site at all for it to be listed—search engine spiders are constantly combing the web and will eventually find your site on their own if your site contains links to other sites.
5. Web sites should be listed on a weekly or monthly basis. Continually submitting your site can be classified as spamming and result in your site's banishment from a search engine's database. As a general rule, don't resubmit a new version of a page unless you have an unfavorable ranking.
6. Good submission is costly. The truth is you don't have to pay a submission service to submit your site to the search engines. Submission to most major search engines is free.

Search Engines and Directories to Submit to:

- http://dmoz.org/
- http://dir.yahoo.com/
- http://www.joeant.com/
- http://www.skaffe.com/
- http://www.bluefind.com/
- http://www.zeal.com/
- http://www.goguides.org/
- http://www.gimpsy.com/
- http://www.wowdirectory.com/
- http://www.sevenseek.com/
- http://www.thisisouryear.com/
- http://search.looksmart.com/Submission Service Claims

How Long Does It Take to Get Listed?

Here are estimated waiting periods for some of the more popular search engines:

MSN	up to two months
Google	up to four weeks
AltaVista	up to one week
Fast	up to two weeks
Excite	up to six weeks
AOL	up to two months

| HotBot | up to two months |
| iWon | up to two months |

How often should you resubmit? Well technically you don't have to resubmit! Once your site is indexed, simply keep adding search-friendly content and there's no need to resubmit. You should, however, be familiar with your site statistics.

Look at your web site statistics for robot visits.

- Google monthly (using links is the strategy I recommend)
- DMOZ (two months and "good luck")

Robots.txt

The robots.txt is a simple text file that is placed in your root directory. It directs search engine robots/bots/spiders/crawlers.

- It saves your bandwidth. The spider won't visit areas where there is no useful information.
- It gives you a very basic level of protection. It keeps people from easily finding stuff you don't want easily accessible via search engines. Some webmasters also use it to exclude "test" or "development" areas of a web site that are not ready for public viewing.
- It cleans up your logs. Every time a search engine visits your site it requests the robots.txt, which can happen several times a day. If you don't have one, it generates a 404 Not Found error each time. It's hard to wade through all of these to find genuine errors at the end of the month.
- It's good programming policy.
- Pros have a robots.txt. Amateurs don't. What group do you want your site to be in?

This is more of an ego/image thing than a "real" reason, but in competitive areas or when applying for a job it can make a difference. Some employers won't consider hiring a webmaster who doesn't know how to use one, on the assumption that they may not know other, more critical things, as well. Search engines work the same way; it's sloppy and unprofessional not to use a robots.txt.

HTML Code versus Text

Your web site is like an iceberg: You only see the top bit in your browser. Search engines look at your whole source code. Search engines are constantly spidering the web and indexing pages for search data.

You need to consider your HTML-code-to-text ratio. How much of your web page is HTML markup and how much is text that the search engines will read? This is important because search engines only read and index the text of a page and they only go so far into a page to read either HTML or text. So if your web page is mostly written in HTML code, the search engines might not read all your text.

So what is the desired ratio? The higher your text content the better. Thirty percent or more is not bad. You can check the ratio of your site at www.holovaty.com/tools/getcontentsize/. How much your ratio affects your overall rankings in search engines may never be known. But it's another important factor to consider when optimizing your web site.

W3C Standards. Adhering to W3C Standards helps your sites maintain code that's clean and more easily spidered and indexed by the search engines. Often when a search engine spider encounters bad code, it leaves the page or doesn't perform a deep spider.

The World Wide Web Consortium (W3C) develops interoperable technologies (specifications, guidelines, software, and tools) to lead the web to its full potential. W3C is a forum for information, commerce, communication, and collective understanding. Information related to this organization can be found at www.w3.org.

Let the Spiders Do the Walking

Like search engines, directories can aid your web visibility. Following is a list of directories and your options for submission.

1. Yahoo! Directory. The first thing to do is submit your site to the Yahoo! Directory. This web site contains a detailed compilation of web sites that can be browsed by visitors through certain categories. Unlike Yahoo!'s search engine, Yahoo! Directory is powered by editors rather than robots—all the more reason to be sure your site has followed all the white hat techniques outlined earlier in this book.

What connection does the Yahoo! Directory have with the Yahoo! search engine? It's generally accepted that you have a greater chance of getting your site listed higher if you submit to the crawler-based Yahoo! search engine. This isn't a guarantee, but either way you have nothing to lose by submitting to the Yahoo! Directory.

To submit to the Yahoo! Directory, use their "standard" submission service or their "Yahoo! Directory Submit," which charges a fee. The standard submission service lets you submit your site in general categories at no extra cost. You're not allowed to submit to commercial categories. If you try to submit your site to a commercial category using the standard submission option, it won't be allowed. Instead, Yahoo! Directory will force you to upgrade to Yahoo! Directory Submit.

How does Yahoo! Directory Submit work? First, you must pay an annual fee of $299, for non-adult sites and $600 for adult sites. What you get according to Yahoo! Directory is an "expedited review" of your web site(s)—that's right, you can submit more than one, though you have to pay $299 or $600 for each submission. You'll get a response within seven days indicating whether or not your site is accepted. If it's accepted you'll have to pay $299 or $600 once a year to keep your listing in the directory, at least if it's a commercial site (non-commercial sites aren't charged the recurring fee). The upside to the paid submission is that your site gets reviewed quickly; with the standard submission service you may not get your site reviewed at all. The downside is that you're paying a lot of money for a service that can't guarantee you placement (although if you're promoting a business you must use the Yahoo! Directory Submit).

In terms of getting your site accepted, what matters is relative content. When it comes to the standard submission option, you want to ensure that your content is not commercial in any way. For example, if you're running an online clothing store, more likely than not this won't be acceptable with standard submission. However, if you submitted a site that talked about how to be fashionable with a certain collection of clothes, this would be accepted, even if the article provided a link to your web site. Yahoo! Directory would choose the latter site because it's seen as being informative and more helpful than the actual store.

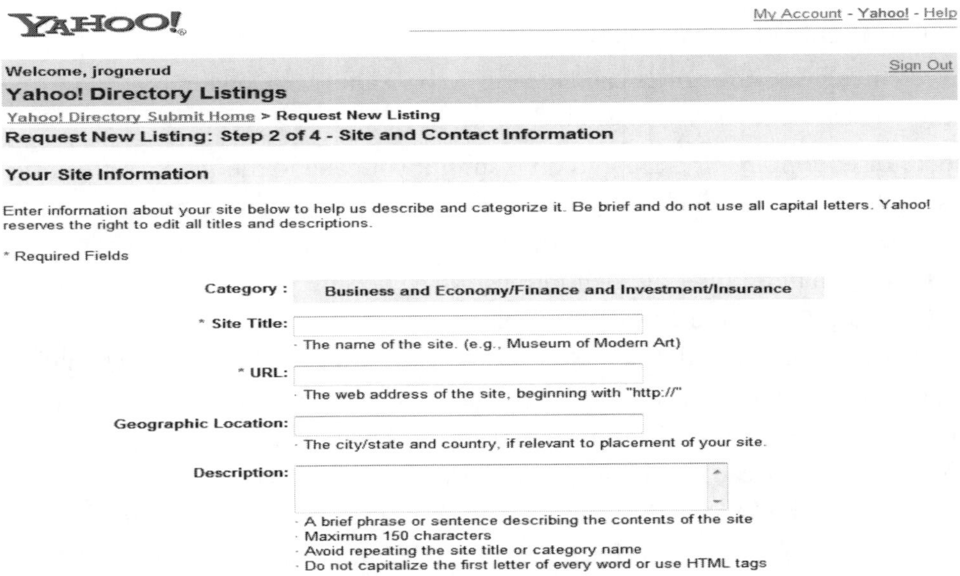

Figure 9-1. Yahoo! Directory Entry

If you do use the Yahoo! Directory Submit and you choose not to pay the renewal fee (if it applies to you), your listing will be dropped by Yahoo! Directory. However, this may not have a negative impact on search engine crawlers. If you get an initial boost from the Yahoo! Directory, there's greater potential that others will want to link to you. This is even more true if you follow the link-building specifications laid out in this book. This may be enough to keep your high ranking with the other search engines, including Yahoo!. If it isn't, you can always submit your site again through Yahoo! Directory Submit.

To submit a site to the Yahoo! Directory, you need to visit dir.yahoo.com. If you want to use standard submission, select the "Suggest a Site" link at the top right corner of the non-commercial category page you want your site to be indexed to. Note: You'll have to look closely, since "Suggest a Site" is in a smaller font. You could use the same method to use Yahoo! Submit, or you could use the home page. The category you choose doesn't matter as much, because the editors working for Yahoo! Directory choose the category for you.

2. Yahoo! Search Engine. With your site submitted to the Yahoo! Directory, you're ready to submit your site to the Yahoo! search engine. If you performed your quality link-building work, Yahoo! should be able to pick you up automatically. Otherwise, you can use their URL submission form, which can be accessed by going to search.yahoo.com. Enter the URL you want to submit. You'll probably want to submit only your home page, though you can submit individual subtopic pages as well. When you submit the web page, be sure to include the whole URL including the "http://www." If you don't include http://www, the page will prompt you to enter the proper URL. Also, make sure that you don't submit your site twice, as you may get penalized.

Yahoo! also offers Search Submit. With Search Submit you must pay an annual subscription fee in addition to payment per click. Don't confuse this program with Yahoo! Sponsor Search, which lists your site in certain commercial categories. The monthly fee for Sponsor Search ranges from $5 to $30. These are pay-per-click programs that show ads on the right side of search listing results. You pay when visitors click on your ads. With Yahoo! Search Submit, your site is shown just like other normal search engine listings. However, you do have to pay for it. If you run out of money, you might lose your listing, though sometimes you won't.

Is it worth using Search Submit? It is in the sense that you can get your site indexed immediately. However, it offers no benefit when it comes to your ranking. The payment structure for this program is not as attractive as other pay-per-click programs, since in addition to PPC you also have a subscription fee. For this reason you may prefer to spend your money on Yahoo! Search or Google AdWords. In fact, these are a great way to test the advertising value of your keyword, at least if you want to see results before your site gets indexed.

3. Ask. Ask Jeeves doesn't offer a free URL submission page nor does it offer paid submission. However, the search engine periodically crawls the web, indexing sites on the basis of how many times they appear on other sites. So, again, there's value in building valid links.

4. MSN. MSN Search, also called Microsoft Live Search, doesn't offer free URL submission or paid submission. It uses its bot, MSNBot, to crawl the web in search of relevant sites.

5. AOL. AOL Search is powered by Google's search engine technology. So once you submit your site to Google (which we talk about in the next section), you also get your results shown in the AOL Search listings.

6. The Open Directory (DMOZ). The Open Directory is a special directory built by volunteers that serves as a guide to the internet. The Open Directory is now owned by Google.

Many of the most popular search engines, including Google, pull results from and point to the Open Directory, so trying to make your web site a part of it definitely doesn't hurt. Plus it's free. The only major problem with the Open Directory is that you won't get a guarantee that your site is accepted, nor can you estimate how long it will take to get a response (if you get one).

To submit to the Open Directory, you need to select the category you want your page to show up on. Use the "Suggest URL" link; it can be found on the category page near the top. You are then directed to a form that requires you to provide your site URL, title of the site, site description, and your e-mail address. It takes about three weeks for your site to show up in the directory, and if it doesn't you can resubmit.

GOOGLE'S GUIDELINES

Meet Google, the "coolest kid" on the cyberblock!

Google is popular, and popularity means it may be tough to get in initially. Even if you do everything right, it could take months to see results, at least if you use their URL submission page. However, there is hope! There's a method that you'll learn in a moment to get indexed in 24 hours, so don't even bother submitting through the URL page. But before we get to that, you should know about the guidelines you must follow to ensure that not only does your site get listed, but that it also doesn't get banned. You also learn about elements of your web site that Google won't look at. Then you'll get to read the juicy stuff on how to get your site indexed in less than 24 hours.

1. How to Get Google to Read Your Keywords First. Google's bots read your web pages from the topmost left corner of your site to the bottom right. However, most sites are designed with all of the links on the left side, and the content on the right. In fact, earlier in this book you learned that this is the recommended web site design you should use. Yet the problem with this design is instead of seeing your content first, Google sees the links first. Your links may not be seen to be as optimized as your content.

One solution is to use three panes rather than two. Keep the normal left and right panes, but add an extra pane at the top left of the layout. Don't put keywords in this extra pane. With this area "blank" when the Google bots read the site, rather than going for the links as they normally would, the bots see that a portion of where the links are is "blank." This then forces it to read the content first, which is more keyword-rich than the links.

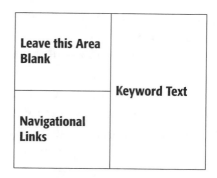

Figure 9-2. Table Structure Optimized for Google

Note that not all search engines read sites this way, which is why this guideline was provided in this special section dedicated to optimizing for Google. You could be on the safe side and use the layout anyway, especially if you do plan to submit to Google, which you should. It doesn't take away from the look of the site, and by using it you ensure that your content gets read first. If you don't use it, you aren't giving yourself the best opportunity to rank highly in Google search engine listings. Making tables isn't very hard to do. Most word processors and even WYSIWYG HTML editors provide them, so take advantage of it.

2. Things That Google Ignores. There are some HTML attributes that Google pays no attention to when it goes through its crawling process. While you won't get penalized if you use these attributes, why waste your time with them if they're not going to count anyway?

Of course, there are exceptions to these rules, as noted in the numbered list below. There are also some elements listed that you will choose not to include.

1. **The keywords and description attributes of the meta tag.** Yes, I know earlier I talked about how wonderful this code is and now I am listing it here as unimportant. Remem-ber that this list is what Google ignores so it does not negate my earlier advice. The keywords and description attributes are still read by other search engines. However, the boost you get from having them isn't as much as if you follow the other techniques, such as proper link building. If you submit to Google only, you may not want to include the keywords attribute, but focus on a smart "upsell" or "positioning," "branding" of your message in the description attribute. Other search engines use them, so you should go on and include them.

2. **The <!--comments--> tag.** The comments tag is an optional tag designed more for the web site designer than for search engines or browsers. You use it to make personal notes related to what the upcoming coding does. It's especially useful if other web-masters are working on web pages that have been started by someone else. Still, it isn't a necessary tag, so you can omit it if you want.

3. **The <style> tag.** This tag has attributes that specify what your site will look like. This deals with styling of your page (CSS). If you're using extensive CSS, include the file as an external reference.

4. **The <script> tag.** This tag lets the browser know that a block of JavaScript code is about to be initiated. While Google ignores the information in this tag, it's still useful if you want to take advantage of JavaScript. You would use JavaScript when you

want to run applets, special programs that run in a separate browser window. Use of this tag may or may not be optional, depending on what your site is for.

5. **Duplicate links.** If you have duplicate links to the same page, Google only counts the first one.

6. **Interlinking to points on the same page.** Interlinking involves picking a point on your web page called an anchor that you want another anchor to link to. This practice is commonly used when web sites present very long copy on the same page. Readers can click on links throughout the document to jump to other parts of the document. It's very effective for increasing readability, but it's another optional device. Worst case, you could break up the copy and make more subtopic links.

7. **Graphics, animation, and video.** Google pays no attention to these types of content, but it may notice the descriptive attributes surrounding them and certainly their URLs.

8. **Boolean words.** We discussed these earlier. They are words like *a*, *an*, *the*, *is*, etc. If you're optimizing for Google only, don't bother including these keywords.

3. How Not to Link to Sites That Are in a Bad Neighborhood. You learned a little bit about this earlier. Basically, sites that are in a bad neighborhood are those that post on link farms, splogs, or other sites using black hat SEO techniques. Stay away from these types of sites. Do you know that if a person you're linking to posts on these types of sites, you could get in trouble with Google as well? It's unfair, but true. And don't think that because a site has a good page rank today that tomorrow they won't use black hat techniques that would mess up your site. This is why you need to keep your eye on the sites to which you link.

One way you can do this is to read the page rank bar on the Google toolbar. This is better than using linkvendor.com, because it tells you if a site has been banned, whereas linkvendor.com may not. If the page rank bar is gray, that indicates a ban. However, don't confuse being banned with having a page rank of 0. Just because a site has a 0 page rank, that doesn't mean it's linking to sites in a bad neighborhood. It could just mean that not enough time has passed for the webmaster to get the site to rank high enough in search engines to receive a higher page rank. Recently, for example, there was a proxy problem (now fixed) that erroneously returned sites with a page rank of 0 which in fact were ranked higher.

You can use SEO Elite to determine a site's page rank. To do this, you first open the program and select radio button 4. Enter the URL of one of your links, then select "Google PR" from the checkboxes. Click "OK." You're shown a report that displays the page rank for each of the web pages within the site you're linking to. Be on alert for those with a rank of 0. As you already know, this doesn't mean they're linking to bad neighborhoods, so you'll need a method to find out for sure. Now select radio button 6. Through this you can see if the site still appears in Google's search engine listings. Next, select the

Google checkbox. If it returns 0, you know the site no longer appears in the search engine listings, and you should stay far away from it.

4. How to Get Your Site Listed in Google in 24 Hours or Less. Wouldn't it be nice to start seeing your site in Google's search engine results in 24 hours or less? Earlier we explained that if a site is crawled but not yet indexed, the results aren't visible to search users.

For example, if you enter the full domain of your site with the "http://www." and your site hasn't been listed yet, it won't show up in Google's results. When your site does get indexed, if you enter the full URL, you'll see your site listed. This listing contains the URL, the title of your web site, and a description.

To get your site indexed quickly, you won't use Google's submission form (google.com/addurl.html). Using this method may take 2–6 weeks to get your site indexed.

So, what do you need to do to get your web site indexed in 24 hours or less? The first step is to visit Google and enter a broad, generic keyword that's relevant to your site. This is the rare time that the broader the keyword, the better. Don't worry about trying to go for niche markets with this step, because you're going to want to have access to sites with the highest level of traffic. Once you enter the keyword, you see the Google listings. Use the "Page Rank" indicator on the Google toolbar to see what the page rank is (or you could use SEO Elite or LinkVendor, but doing it right from the browser is faster). To refresh your memory, the higher your page rank, the more web sites that are linking to you. Keep an eye out for sites that have a page rank of 5 or higher (with the higher ranking being the better one). Visit each of these sites to see if they offer a link exchange. Remember, if they do they'll advertise it in the same way you did yours, through a "Link to Us" web page or something similar. Look for the contact information if it's listed. If it's not listed, use the Whois utility found through domain name services or SEO Elite to find their e-mail address. Use the same methods of e-mail etiquette you learned about before and send them an e-mail asking if they're interested in a link exchange. Remember to post their links on your site first before you send out the e-mail. And don't forget that you can still purchase advertising on the resources given throughout this book. Just make sure the site you choose has a page rank of over 5.

If you advertise your site on a site with a page rank of 5, your site will get indexed in three days or less. If you advertise your site on a site with a page rank of 6, you can get your site indexed in less than 24 hours.

> **TIP:** Domaintools.com is a must have tool to review domain information. The Reverse-IP tool will tell you if there are many sites within one IP.

CHAPTER 10

Food, Gas, Great Web Site—Next Exit!

As a Southern California resident, traffic is a big part of my life. While traffic on the interstate is a headache, traffic on the information highway is a great thing. In this chapter we look at techniques for driving lots of traffic to your web site, including the long-awaited discussion on Pay-per-Click.

We've discussed some traffic sources in previous chapters. Listed below is a beginning checklist that includes the sources we've already discussed. For up-to-date lists, visit the member site.

- SEO
- Pay-per-Click (i.e., Google AdWords, Yahoo!, MSN, Miva, Enhance, 7search)
- E-mail marketing and subscription lists
- Trading traffic links
- Buying traffic links (see comments about Google's standards)
- Earning traffic links (articles, press, blogs, Web 2.0 services, etc.)

- Joint venture (JV) deals
- Affiliate programs
- CPA affiliate programs
- Link bait
- Link love via other blogs
- Viral marketing (videos, word-of-mouth, widgets, etc.)
- Offline marketing
- Banner ads
- Pop-ups
- Co-registration

In addition to selling your product or service, there are a number of other ways to make money from your web site, including:

- AdSense, Yahoo! Publisher Networks
- Sell advertising space on your site(s) (assuming you have more than one domain)
- Push your own affiliate programs
- Sell your own products directly from your web site
- CPA, Cost Per Action Networks (like hydranetwork.com, where you get paid when a lead is closed on your behalf)

Your site can make money even if you don't have a perfect design. Remember Janet's beautifully designed first site, which generated no revenue? Yet there are numerous examples of sites that are not "award-worthy" but generate a great deal of traffic.

We want to look to building traffic, not making a site completely perfect at first. All that will follow.

TRAFFIC DRIVING TECHNIQUES
Blogs

One of the fastest ways for you to build traffic to your site with minimal effort is to create a blog. Last year, I created a blog and within 24 hours of being indexed (I got a link from another PR value 3 web site), I was ranked #1 for a phrase keyword (small searches). You can build content yourself or outsource the writing to a ghostwriter. The content doesn't have to be long. A short post of 100–200 words is acceptable, and sometimes shorter will do. Testing and monitoring is key.

Blogs are a great way to naturally attract search engine traffic. Most of the time, blogs already have optimized site architecture, clear navigation, and the innate potential for good linking. Intelligently linking your site with a well-created blog can increase your traffic. In fact, blogs can get so well indexed that you have the potential to show up for any number of four-word phrases relevant to your industry, if done correctly.

Use a keyword that gets a moderate level of targeted traffic. It might not bring the most traffic, but it often brings the most profit through more subscribers and sales. If possible, narrow the scope of your blog discussion to a two- or three-word phrase that has a high yield of traffic, yet little competition. Set up your blog to repeat keywords that you want to target just enough times to establish a theme. You can take full advantage of this in your post titles, category names, and the pages' URL names. Sparingly include the "moderate" keyword you selected before in your title and description. All those link-backs will contain the keyword term you want the most attention for.

Post in a timely fashion. You can get better results by updating or pinging just once during one of the three best times during the day: early in the morning, at least before noon, or late at night (thinking internationally here as well). Monitoring when the search engine's crawlers visit your site can help as well. You can increase the number of crawler visits by blogging on the time or period they come to your site. The more you post, the more the crawlers have to go through your content. This could cause the crawler to split its job into several visits, whereupon you have even more content.

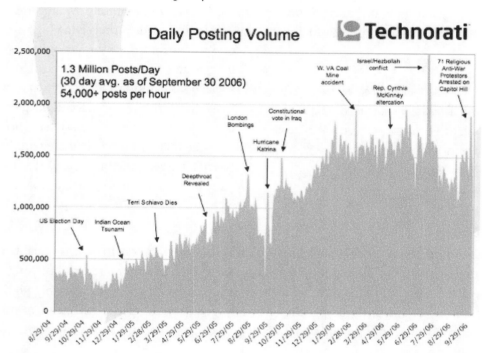

Figure 10-1. Blog Posting Volume

Most blogs have RSS (rich site summary or really simple syndication) as a default, but make sure you set up and test your blog to use RSS feeds. RSS is a way to deliver web con-

> **TIP:** Many bloggers have noted that it may take a couple of days for your post to work its way through the blogosphere to readers. If you post too often (unless you have a well traveled, established site) your posts will get pushed down quicker and potentially not read. Start off by posting two or three times per week for maximum visibility. Many bloggers who are hyperactive post two or three times a day, every day! You can write several posts in the morning, and use the scheduling function in the blog to distribute entries throughout the day, week, or month. This is a great timesaver and it helps if you plan to be on vacation. You can write posts in advance and they'll be released in your absence.

tent that changes frequently (i.e., news sites, blogs). For more on RSS visit www.whatisrss.com. You'll want your blog to display headlines from other RSS feeds, as well. This is because whenever a search engine bot crawls your site, it almost always sees something new, and you provide dynamic links that are relevant.

"Tagging and Pinging" refers to having your blog posts automatically tag and then ping bookmark sites to have the new blog posts automatically added. For receiving high-quality, one-way links from other webmasters, tagging is not the best way to go. However, social bookmarking and tagging can be used to pick up the traffic needed to gain the attention of other webmasters, who can then see that you have great content. If you haven't posted anything new, don't ping your blog, as it'll be regarded as spamming.

> **TIP:** A top blog tracking site, www.technorati.com, will automatically see your post and "auto-ping" by itself. Pingomatic.com and pingoat.com are additional resources to use.

Articles

We discussed article writing in Chapter 3. Articles are a great way to develop quality content on your web site. You could publish articles written by other authors, but you'll find those articles on hundreds of other sites as well. If an article on your site only points to the web site of the author, you can probably guess where traffic will head next. The author's web site could possibly pick up the ranking points, and your copy of the article might be ignored.

On the other hand, should you start creating your own original articles, you might be tempted to keep them for yourself. However, your best bet is to offer your articles to other site owners. If your articles are good, and contain valuable information, you will see an increase in traffic and sales. Boosting your presence on other sites can do the same for your rankings.

Make sure each article you release has a number of unique text strings. This can be used to monitor who is using, or misusing, them. Sites that don't appear in major engines may be harder to track, but they are also less of a threat.

Press Releases

Press releases are another way for you to increase your web site traffic. Users will be able to easily see what's going on with your business, and will more likely be drawn in to the rest of your site. Make sure to include "For Immediate Release" and "For more information, contact:" followed by your contact information in the first lines to make it easy for visitors to find you.

Create a compelling headline to make your release stand out. Keep it short, active, and descriptive. Hook your readers with the first paragraph. Include and summarize "The Five Ws": who, what, where, when, and why (and add "how" for good measure). If your readers can't easily follow your articles, they'll find another site that can explain more clearly.

Put the most important information at the beginning of your press release. Never wait until the end; doing so is a bad writing practice. Don't sell, but answer questions. This is one of the biggest frustrations users experience, and will quickly turn them off to your site. Avoid saying that something is "unique," or "the best." Instead, show how people will benefit.

Getting a non-biased source, such as an expert in the field or product reviewer, is helpful. Provide all possible contact information; the more users you can speak with personally, the better. Proofread everything, and don't let a single spelling or grammar error slip by. You'd be surprised how impressed visitors are by such a simple concept. Also, end your press release with ###. This lets the editors know they've successfully received the whole release.

Finally, think differently about your project, and don't do what everyone else does. Use relevant and original content in your press releases. You'll find them a useful means of increasing your web site traffic.

PAY-PER-CLICK ADVERTISING

Pay-per-click is an advertising technique used mainly on web sites and search engines. Advertisers bid on "keywords" or phrases that they think potential customers would type in the search bar when they're looking for that type of product or service. Usually ads are placed in order from the top in conjunction with the bid amount. The higher the bid, the better the placement. These ads are called "sponsored links" or "sponsored ads," depending on which search engine you're using. They appear next to or above the results of the original search. The advertiser pays only when somebody clicks on their ad.

Figure 10-2. Google PPC Ads

Bidding for ad space on popular search engines such as Google and Yahoo! can be competitive and costly. The top ten pay-per-click search engines and the minimum deposits they require are as follows:

Pay-per-Click Search Engines	Minimum Deposit Required
1. Google AdWords	$5
2. Yahoo!Search Marketing	$5
3. ABC Search	$25
4. SearchFeed	$25
5. 7 Search	$25
6. MIVA (formerly FindWhat)	$50
7. Enhance Interactive	$50
8. Findology	$25
9. MicrosoftAd Center	$5
10. Ask.com	$15

Figure 10-3. PPC Search Engines and Deposits

Types of Pay-per-Click Advertising

There are several types of pay-per-click advertising. The most popular is keyword advertising. The keywords that are bid on can be words, phrases, or even model numbers. The ads will appear in the order of the amount bid, from highest to lowest. Software and other services are available to help advertisers develop keyword strategies.

Product pay-per-click advertising lets advertisers provide "feeds" of their product databases to search engines. When users search for a product, the links to the advertisers who bid for placement appear with the highest bidder appearing most prominently. The user can sort by price and click on a feed to make a purchase. Bizrate.com, shopzilla.com, nextag.com, pricegrabber.com and shopping .com are popular product comparison engines, also known as price comparison engines.

Service pay-per-click advertising is similar to product PPC. "Service engines," such as Nextag, SideStep, and TripAdvisor, offer advertisers the opportunity to provide feeds of their service databases, which appear when users search for that particular service. As usual, advertisers who pay more are given better ad placement. However, users can sort their results by price or other methods.

Pay-per-call advertising is similar to pay-per-click advertising. Ads are listed in search engines, and directories and publishers charge local advertisers for each call they receive as a result of their listing. This form of advertising is not limited to local advertisers, as many of the pay-per-call search engines allow nationwide companies to create ads with local telephone numbers.

When conducting a PPC campaign, bidding on particular words and phrases achieves a particular position in PPC search results. The amounts of bids by

> Agencies such as Adify and Tribal Fusion build vertical networks for publishers and advertisers by aggregating audiences into relevant vertical networks. This is one method of reaching a very targeted audience and controlling who and where your message is seen.

competitors are displayed, and you can choose how much you will pay for a specific position. Your web site needs no manipulation or changes to conduct a PPC campaign. However, every time someone clicks to your web site from the ad it will cost you.

Determining the most effective keyword terms is critical to the ROI. You need to experiment to find the most effective keywords. Refer to the Keyword Guide in Chapter 3. You can use the same tools to find keywords for your PPC campaign.

Negative Keywords

Another consideration of keyword selection in PPC campaigns is the search for words to eliminate. Due to the cost-per-click factor, to avoid paying for web site visitors who have no interest in the product or service offered, certain words and terms must be excluded from the campaign. These words are referred to as *negative keywords*. These negative keywords must be designated in AdWords campaigns to increase conversion rates.

"Negative keywords" refers to the words, terms, and phrases advertisers would not want to cause their ad to be displayed in search results.

Suppose an online store sells chess games. The store's Google AdWords campaign has an ad group with these phrase-matched keywords:

- chess game
- chess games

The keyword research tools reveal many keyword phrases that are searched relating to chess games that aren't related to buying chess games.

For example, using the Overture (Yahoo!) search term suggestion tool showed these results for the keyword phrase "chess game":

- 22,421 chess game
- 14,842 play chess game
- 3,231 online chess game
- 774 chess game image
- 567 chess game software
- 321 chess game clip art
- 263 chess game results
- 185 chess game organizations

There would likely be no benefit for the store that's selling chess games to display an ad in search results for several of these keyword phrases. Adding "-software" to the ad group prevents the ad from appearing for that particular search phrase. Keep in mind that several search term suggestion tools don't differentiate between singular and plural forms of keywords. So in reference to the example, designate the following terms as negative:

- play
- online
- image
- software
- clip art
- results
- organizations

Once designated, if any of these negative keywords are in a search phrase, the ad does not appear in the search results.

When creating SEO or web content, these same negative keywords could be beneficial.

These words and phrases are synonyms or alternatives to prevent keyword overuse that causes search engines to eliminate a page or site.

Landing Pages

When developing PPC campaigns it's a good idea to create specific pages for visitors to land on when they click the ad. This type of page is called a *landing page* or *lead capture page*. If you're running multiple PPC or ad campaigns, you can have multiple landing pages. The landing page displays content aligned with the ad. You can optimize with keywords and phrases related to the ad. Landing pages allow you to test the effectiveness of your campaigns by measuring click-through rates.

The two types of landing pages are transactional and reference. *Transactional* landing pages call for the visitor to take an action. That action could be to sign up for a newsletter, purchase a product, or complete a form. When the visitor takes the desired action on a transactional landing page, it's a *conversion*. *Reference* landing pages present information to the visitor. For example, a domestic violence nonprofit might run an ad to raise awareness. Their landing pages might offer information on how to help domestic violence victims or how to identify domestic violence.

Check below for a list of top things to test in a landing page. It's an important study, so make sure to test every component if you can.

- Headline—a strong, compelling, problem-solving headline, relevant to topic
- Price of offer—test different prices
- Bonuses or other incentives
- PS (p.s.)—at the end of your sales letter, many will scroll down your page and read this
- Guarantees—for example: "90-day guarantee or your money back"
- Audio—test with auto-play or not
- Body copy—short and long copy, maximize use of white space, and make it short; web readers "scan" the page
- Header image and/or banner—test by turning it on and off, different sizes and colors, too
- Site color/fonts—red and blue fonts work well; test it all
- Sub headers, taglines—compelling "problem solvers"
- Images, "hero shots"—personal pictures of people, then things
- Testimonials!
- Videos—upload a video to YouTube and make sure to brand it on your page
- Buttons—different colors, different text in buttons (not just "submit," but "Yes, download the free white paper," etc.)

- Your logo—show it/don't show it; you'd be amazed what turning it off may do
- Credibility, legitimacy—VeriSign logo, BBB, Hackersafe, Visa/MC, etc.
- Test your sign-up forms, short versus long (short forms work better, but test this)

HOW TO CONSTRUCT A PAY-PER-CLICK ADVERTISING CAMPAIGN

1. **Decide what your advertising budget is and what level of risk you are willing to take.**
   - Larger search engines are less risky, as they already have excellent market coverage and typically offer excellent customer service.
   - On the other hand, it's more expensive to achieve a top ranking on the largest search engines.

2. **Decide which search engines you want to use.**
   - Ask for recommendations from friends and business associates.
   - Do your homework. Research each option carefully.
   - 99 percent of the time I recommend starting with Google.

3. **Decide which keywords you want to bid on.**
   - There are plenty of free tools available on the internet to help you research keywords. They give you the current bid prices for certain words and phrases currently running on different search engines.
   - Pick your keywords wisely, as they can range in bid prices from $.10 to over $10.
   - Don't limit yourself to one keyword or phrase. Large corporations often have thousands of keywords.
   - Follow the keyword research steps outlined earlier in the book.

4. **Pay special attention to the design of your landing page.**
   - This page must make it clear what products you sell, the benefits of buying these products, how to make a purchase, and why your product is better than your competitor's.
   - Your business's home page is usually not a good choice for a landing page. If visitors want to learn more about your company, they will do so on their own initiative.
   - The fewer clicks that a visitor has to make to get to the purchase screen, the more visitors will convert into customers.

5. **Begin the bidding process.**
   - Most search engines have automated the bidding process, so you don't have to actively participate in the process. They stop when they reach your maximum bid.
   - Personal involvement is a good idea, at least at first.
   - Be sure to carefully read the search engine's terms of use. Look for minimum bids required, deposits required, and what happens if you have to cancel your campaign.
   - Usually, PPC search engines allow fewer than ten ads to appear on a search results page.

PPC Monitoring and Management Services

Many companies offer PPC monitoring and management services. These companies can be an integral part of any PPC campaign. They automate many of the

> **TIP:** The membership site contains more examples of landing pages and conversion and PPC techniques.

processes you need to perform to protect your investment. They have the added advantage of being independent of the PPC search engines and offering unbiased answers and advice. Here are some of the more popular services available and the companies that provide them.

PPC Management Services:

- Atlas OnePoint
- Dynamic Bid Maximizer Advance/Overture
- Google AdWords Report
- PPC Bid Tracker

PPC Research Tools:

- Wordtracker
- Compare Your Clicks
- PPC Bid Reporter Professional
- Keyword Monster

Click Fraud Monitoring:

- Who's Clicking Who
- Click Lab
- Ad Watcher
- ClickDetective
- ClickForensics

Ad Tracking:

- Adtrackz
- Hypertracker

Click Fraud Facts

According to *In the News*, up to 20 percent of all pay-per-click traffic delivered to advertisers originates from false sources, not from potential customers. The majority of click fraud originates from two sources: competitors and web site owners. Competitors want to drain your advertising budget by producing false clicks that you have to pay for, even though they aren't viable leads. web site owners sometimes work in tandem with search engines by agreeing to feature their ads and provide their customers with more exposure. In return the web site owners receive part of the revenue generated by each click. Thus, some of these web site owners try to generate as many clicks as possible to increase the profitability of their agreement.

Click fraud has become enough of an issue to attract the attention of major publications, such as *The Washington Post* and *Business Week Online*. According to www.end-ofclickfraud.com, if an organization spends $15,000 on PPC advertising distributed among the top-tier search engines, such as Google or Yahoo!, and is paying between $0.50 and $1 per click, on average, they could be losing as much as $2,220 to fraud.

THE PROS AND CONS OF PPC
PPC Advertising Cons

1. It's very easy to get caught up in a keyword bidding war and spend more than you could ever recoup.
2. Your ROI can be hard to measure. Some PPC search engines provide customers with measurement tools, but these aren't always accurate. Most of the smaller PPC companies don't even provide tracking methods.
3. You can spend advertising dollars just to generate junk traffic. PPC services distribute some of their results to other search engines, allowing your listing to show up in the nether regions of the internet.
4. PPC advertising requires you to pay more when more traffic is generated. Natural search engine optimization lets you invest a set amount of time and money to achieve a better rank, and your cost goes down as you attract more traffic.

PPC Advertising Pros

1. Pay-per-click can generate traffic immediately.
2. Pay-per-click ads can be adjusted in hours or days in response to market behavior.
3. Pay-per-click advertising can be a bargain if you choose your keywords wisely.
4. Pay-per-click can guarantee ad placement for a relatively small portion of your marketing budget.
5. Access to rich information about keywords and performance of those to "conversion."
6. Use these results to push over to SEO and content build out.

WHAT ROLE SHOULD PPC ADVERTISING PLAY IN YOUR MARKETING STRATEGY?

Most businesses can't afford to rely on pay-per-click advertising alone. It's too expensive to keep up with the ever-rising bid amounts for advantageous keywords. However, there are certain instances in which PPC advertising can be invaluable.

If you're starting a new campaign to draw attention to a new product or service, PPC is a great way to create a buzz.

1. If you sell a product or offer a service that consumers can purchase immediately upon arriving at your web site, PPC is effective.
2. If you can find keyword(s) that create a market niche for your organization, PPC provides cost-effective advertising. For instance, if you can generate traffic with a highly specific keyword, such as "perfectpoint pencils" instead of "pencils," PPC may be a good option.

Google AdWords Marketing Mistakes...

1. Not designating a spending limit. This can put you out of business fast.
2. Not knowing your conversion rate. Many new marketers choose high-priced words without basing their bids on research. If you don't know the conversion rate of the product you're selling, then start slow and low.
3. Insufficient keyword research. Most people use the Google keyword tool, including your competition.
4. Not writing effective ads or customizing them for each keyword.
5. Ignoring daily stats and failing to track and analyze results. You need to keep daily records.
6. Quitting too soon. AdWords takes time to learn.
7. Not knowing when to quit. If you're not converting enough to make a profit, then make changes.
8. Breaking the rules. Many people think they can beat or cheat the system. Others don't know better and place pop-up ads or link to inappropriate sites, thus getting their accounts revoked. If you're going to play the game, take the time to learn the rules.

TESTING AND MONITORING

In the end, you want more traffic coming to your web site, and you want those users to find what they need on your pages. There are many ways you to monitor, test, and reconfigure your site to bring in the most quality users.

Track your hits from month to month. Then you can see if you're on the right path with your site, as you can see your traffic increasing or decreasing. Also, monitor the entrance and exit pages for traffic. This shows you what page is bringing in the most visitors, and which page could be causing them to leave your site.

Keep an eye on how long visitors spend on each page. Then you can see which pages hold their interest, and which need to be modified. Watch for keyword searches, as well, to keep tabs on what the majority of your visitors are looking for. Watch your PageRank over time. Make sure that your trust and relevance are on the rise, and not the decline. Check your link popularity, as the more popular your links are, the greater opportunity you have for visitors to see and come to your web site. Enter your keywords into Google and other search engines to check the positioning in the results. This gives you a better idea as to how to optimize your site.

Finally, remember to test the results of every change that you make. If your changes aren't producing positive results, abandon the technique and try something else. A free tool like Google Analytics is a good place to start, and it was upgraded recently with a whole set of new and useful features (December 2007). Others include IndexTools, ClickTracks, WebSideStory, Haveamint, and Omniture.

Google Webmaster Console

We discussed Google's Webmaster Console briefly in Chapter 7. It's an invaluable resource for webmasters. The console can help web site owners see exactly what on their site the Google indexing program can index, and what the program has trouble with. You can also learn which searches drive traffic to your site, and see exactly how users arrive there.

Google is always updating the console to provide new tools to webmasters. You can now view the internal and external links to your web site in detail. This helps you monitor your linking strategy. You can easily remove URLs from the index, show how many people are subscribed to your web site's feeds, and be provided with authenticated communication with site owners. The console includes a personal Google message center, with which you can receive personalized information, such as feedback or warnings, from the search engine.

To use Webmaster Console, you need to create a free Google account. Then have your webmaster follow the directions provided to place a small HTML file on your site, so that Google can confirm that you own the site before it reveals any statistics.

Site Explorer

The Yahoo! Site Explorer is a tool that lets you access the information Yahoo! has about your web site's online presence. You can see which sites and subpages are indexed by Yahoo! Search, track sites that link to your web page, and view the most popular pages from yours, or any, site. Like Google's Webmaster Console, this can be a great help to webmasters.

Site Explorer allows you to see information about another site so you can track those with whom you might want to associate. You have the option to have Yahoo! authenticate your web site, to allow other sites to see yours. You can also track feeds, use sitemaps, and delete URLs. The search engine offers a Site Explorer Badge, which validates your site's popularity and usefulness to visitors.

These are all very useful tools, not only in driving traffic to your web site, but in testing and monitoring exactly what that traffic does. Increasing traffic is one of the most important goals in improving your web site. Without visitors to your web site, you have no sales. In essence, increasing traffic and providing a good user experience, easy navigation, and relevant, compelling content helps your web site do the job you did all the hard work for.

Janet put together a press release schedule for the remainder of the year. She decided to take advantage of speaking engagements and seasonal trends to bring some publicity to her site. She mapped out topics and dates and hired a ghostwriter to do the releases. She also posted each release in the "press room" of her site. After the first release, she saw instant traffic. After three releases, Janet saw a large increase in her web site traffic. With little effort she was turning things around. She couldn't wait to implement the next tactic on her list—PPC advertising.

CHAPTER 11

Conversion

Nothing moves unless something is sold. That's the key to any and all businesses, online or off. That means you need a solid sales process and track every aspect of it.

It's fairly obvious that when you have done the work of selling the message, you need to be able to deliver when people come looking for you. If your internal processes break down it won't matter if you have a great service or product, because you won't be able to deliver or scale up, when and if you grow.

Use the following sales process when growing a business (online or offline):

- Set your sales goals.
- Map the sales process.
- Set objectives for key value points.
- Measure key value points.
- Identify critical vulnerabilities.

- Select your focus of effort.
- Decide on and take action on main effort.

You may notice that the process above ties back to identifying your market, researching the market and competition, and analyzing your place in it.

Measuring is an important part of your sales and marketing efforts. Measure those things that you can change, such as your message, your delivery method, and your media.

You can only measure things that move up or down, such as:

- Delivery rates
- Open rates
- Unique clicks/visitors
- Opt-ins
- Sales
- Up-sells
- Cross-sells

Let's assume you're doing an e-mail marketing campaign. If you send 10,000 e-mails, how many are being delivered? And, if the open rates are "good," is it really good? How many received it, or how many opened it? So, a strategic question would be: Should I increase "delivery rates" or "open rates"? If you tune the "open rate" and then increase the delivery rates, you will make more money just hours after sending.

Boost the numbers of e-mails being reviewed, and you're on your way. However, it's viewing everything, not just one or two metrics.

It's important to develop programs with a holistic view in mind. When you measure every single customer action you improve your value and your bottom line. Likewise, you must continuously review and improve your internal processes with an eye on growth. Will the same processes work when you go from ten customers to 500? How about when you reach 10,000 customers?

Another aspect of conversion is the psychological issue. Many people may feel uncomfortable or guilty "taking customers' money." You're not taking something, you are giving them something. When you offer a product or service that has value (meets a need, preference, or desire), your customer is simply exchanging money for access to that value.

Finally, you convert customers when you continually look to improve the experience from the customer perspective. Don't continue doing something because it works, but ask, "How can I make it better?" Tracking and measuring does not only apply to what your customers do, but what you do that facilitates the relationship.

CONVERSION CASE STUDIES

To illustrate advanced conversion techniques, I asked another expert to provide real-life examples of pay-per-click and affiliate marketing programs applied and the results. Below, you will see answers to the questions posed about projects, goals, challenges, and results. The second case shows you how to set up a simple A/B test for pages you select.

Case Study #1: ComputerRecover

Web site: www.computerrecover.com

Description: Landing Page Optimization—PPC

Contact: Nils Rognerud. For personal contact, go to www.rognerud.com

Goals and Challenges

1. **Can you define your goals?** The original landing page was converting 25.4 percent of visitors to the download page for the free trial software. I knew this rate could be improved with landing page optimization, but I did not know by how much.
2. What concerns did you face? When you optimize individual elements (color, text, fonts, headlines, images, etc.) within a web page, the possible combinations run into the thousands. For most web sites it's impossible to test all possible combinations of page elements, since there isn't enough traffic to test all the possible landing pages.

Approach

3. What did you do? Taguchi optimization (from a Japanese mathematician) is an efficient optimization algorithm to find the best combination of many elements. I used this software technology to improve the landing page conversion rate.
4. What surprises did you see? After the testing was complete, I was surprised to see that deleting two small text sections on the landing page improved the conversion rate from 25.4 to 41.8 percent. That's a huge improvement.
5. How long? By using various tools (a Taguchi tool installed on my own server, plus Google's AdWords Optimizer) it took less than a week to find the best landing page that produced the highest conversion rate. The Taguchi software only needed about 50 conversions to make recommendations for the optimum landing page. To test all possible combinations of the landing pages would take many months with medium- or low-traffic web sites. Taguchi is a great tool to quickly locate the best landing pages.

Final Results

Before. The original landing was converting 25.4 percent of visitors to the download page for the free trial software.

After. Deleting two small text sections on the landing page improved the conversion rate from 25.4 to 41.8 percent. That's a 64.5 percent improvement!

Here is an actual screen shot of the stats:

Combination	Estimated Conversion Rate Range [?]	Chance to Beat Orig. [?]	Chance to Beat All [?]	Observed Improvement [?]	Conversions / Visitors [?]
Original	25.4% ± 5.3%	—	0.00%	—	29 / 114
Combination 26	41.8% ± 6.4%	99.4%	45.2%	64.5%	41 / 98
Combination 4	38.2% ± 5.9%	98.0%	15.3%	50.1%	42 / 110
Combination 20	37.5% ± 5.9%	97.5%	12.1%	47.4%	42 / 112
Combination 6	36.2% ± 5.5%	96.6%	6.32%	42.4%	46 / 127
Combination 8	35.2% ± 6.0%	94.3%	5.23%	38.5%	37 / 105
Combination 22	34.8% ± 5.7%	9	Improvement!	36.7%	40 / 115
Combination 28	34.4% ± 5.3%	9		35.0%	45 / 131
Combination 12	34.2% ± 5.7%	92.6%	2.88%	34.5%	39 / 114
Combination 21	33.3% ± 5.7%	90.3%	2.02%	31.0%	37 / 111
Combination 16	33.0% ± 6.0%	88.7%	2.01%	29.7%	33 / 100
Combination 5	31.1% ± 6.3%	81.3%	0.91%	22.3%	28 / 90
Combination 30	31.0% ± 5.9%	81.5%	0.73%	21.9%	31 / 100
Combination 2	30.6% ± 5.3%	81.4%	0.29%	20.5%	38 / 124
Combination 24	30.0% ± 5.6%	77.6%	0.28%	17.9%	33 / 110
Combination 14	29.7% ± 5.2%	77.0%	0.13%	16.7%	38 / 128

Figure 11-1. ComputerRecover Statistics

Figure 11-2 shows part of the landing page with the deleted page element that improved conversion rates by 64.5 percent.

Lessons Learned, Recommendations

Taguchi technology will not design the web page(s) for you. However, it will test various combinations of colors, texts, fonts, images, links, etc., on your existing web pages.

For landing page optimization to work, you must include a tracking script (sometimes called a *pixel*) that enables the Taguchi software to track and measure the conversions in real time. Many affiliate networks, such as Clickbank, RegNow, Element5, Commission Junction, and the like, don't allow affiliates to include tracking scripts on their final shopping cart web pages. I hope that in the future these affiliate networks will allow tracking scripts to be included. It will benefit all parties, with better ads for the consumer and higher conversion rates for affiliates and affiliate networks.

No Logo at Top

Other things that I noticed—some are common sense, but others are totally unexplainable—that made a big difference in *improved* conversion rates: no company logo at the top.

This little tip may not be too popular with brand name advertisers, but it really works wonders with most little-known web sites. Figure 11-3 shows an example of the header of a web page before optimization (*lower* conversion rate). Figure 11-4 shows the top of the web page after optimization (*higher* conversion rate).

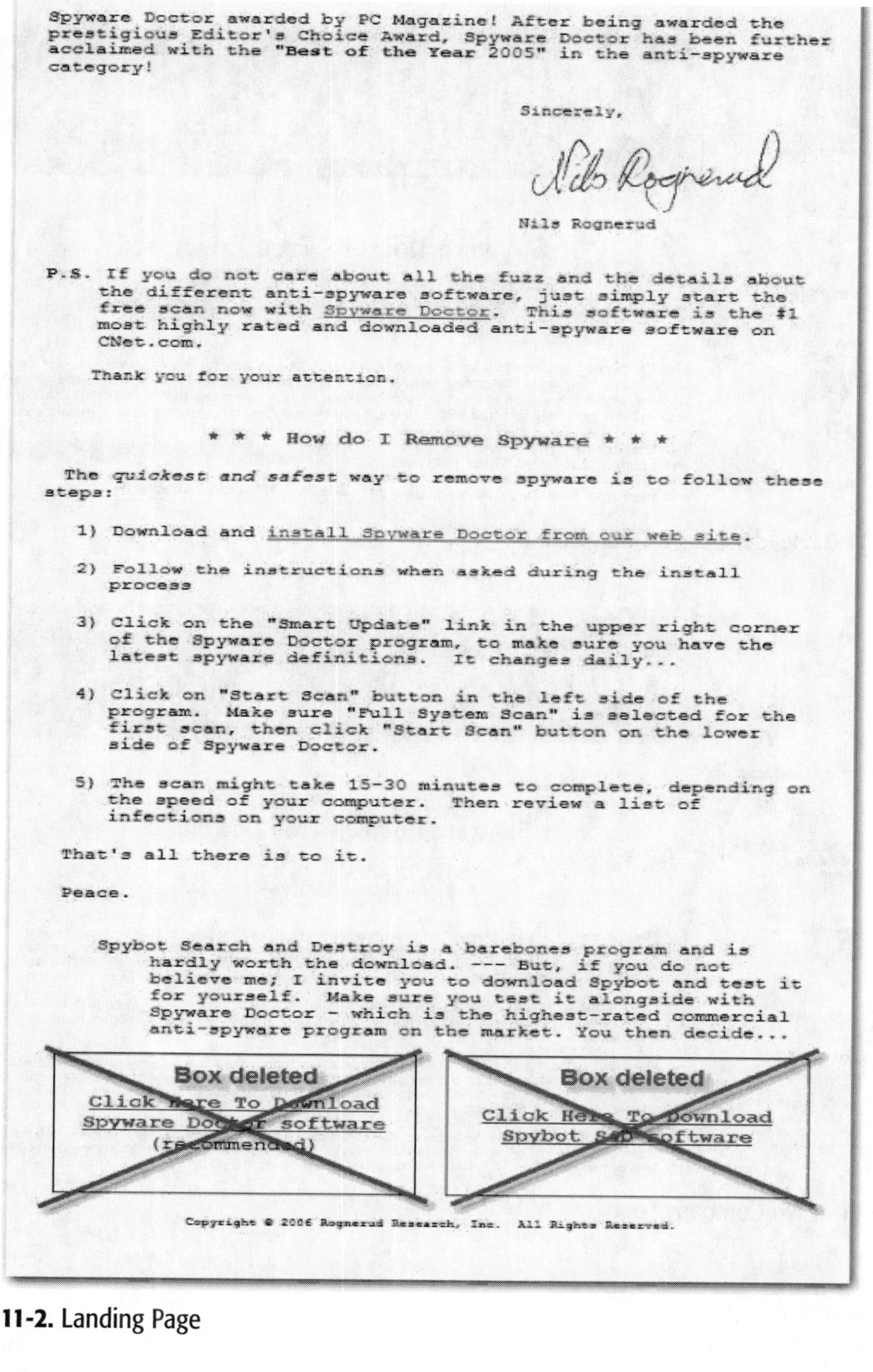

Spyware Doctor awarded by PC Magazine! After being awarded the prestigious Editor's Choice Award, Spyware Doctor has been further acclaimed with the "Best of the Year 2005" in the anti-spyware category!

Sincerely,

Nils Rognerud

Nils Rognerud

P.S. If you do not care about all the fuzz and the details about the different anti-spyware software, just simply start the free scan now with Spyware Doctor. This software is the #1 most highly rated and downloaded anti-spyware software on CNet.com.

Thank you for your attention.

* * * How do I Remove Spyware * * *

The *quickest and safest* way to remove spyware is to follow these steps:

1) Download and install Spyware Doctor from our web site.

2) Follow the instructions when asked during the install process

3) Click on the "Smart Update" link in the upper right corner of the Spyware Doctor program, to make sure you have the latest spyware definitions. It changes daily...

4) Click on "Start Scan" button in the left side of the program. Make sure "Full System Scan" is selected for the first scan, then click "Start Scan" button on the lower side of Spyware Doctor.

5) The scan might take 15-30 minutes to complete, depending on the speed of your computer. Then review a list of infections on your computer.

That's all there is to it.

Peace.

Spybot Search and Destroy is a barebones program and is hardly worth the download. --- But, if you do not believe me; I invite you to download Spybot and test it for yourself. Make sure you test it alongside with Spyware Doctor - which is the highest-rated commercial anti-spyware program on the market. You then decide...

Box deleted
Click Here To Download Spyware Doctor software (recommended)

Box deleted
Click Here To Download Spybot S&D software

Copyright © 2006 Rognerud Research, Inc. All Rights Reserved.

Figure 11-2. Landing Page

Figure 11-3. Header before Optimization

Figure 11-4. No Company Logo

White Space at Top

Another optimization I could not explain is that often a little bit of white space on top of the landing page increased conversion rates by up to 20 percent. That's such a small change: only a blank line at the top of your landing page could increase your sales by 20 percent.

This little simple tip is enough to pay for this book many times over. But, remember to test before you implement any of these ideas (Figure 11-5).

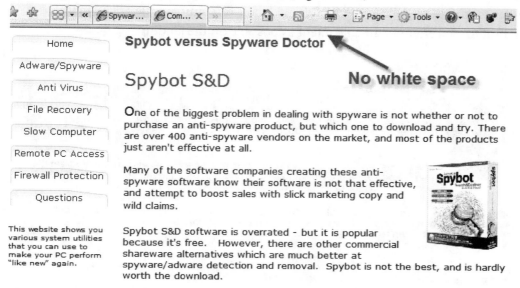

Figure 11-5. No White Space

Figure 11-6 shows the landing page with a white space and a grey (not black) line. It converts much *higher*:

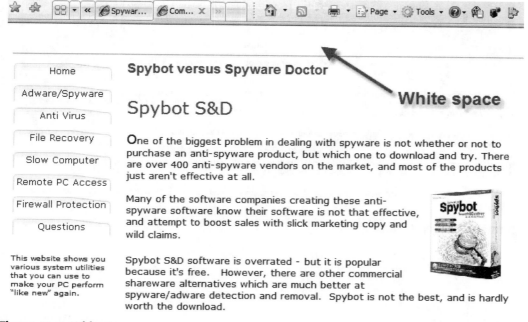

Figure 11-6. White Space

Larger Buttons for Clicking

Larger buttons for clicking and taking the next step in the sales process is perhaps easy to understand, but web developers often overlook this simple little trick—perhaps in an attempt to squeeze in as much content as possible on the landing page.

Spyware Doctor

 **Too small**

Spyware Doctor offers solid protection against spyware and a number of additional immunization features to block common security holes. Spyware Doctor installs easily and without any problems, and it is the largest commercial anti-spyware product in the world.

Try it now

Download:
Spyware Doctor - Free
Download

Spyware Doctor also lets you rollback any changes it makes, just in case the spyware was required by an otherwise useful program (Real Player and Kazaa are typical examples of programs that embed spyware on your PC and won't run without it).my words...

Spyware Doctor comes with a scheduler, but perhaps we would prefer it if scheduling was set up automatically when the program is installed. You have to remember to go in to the "OnGuard" settings and scroll down to find the scheduler buried way down at the bottom. The scheduler should be much more easy to find.

Spyware Doctor product also includes "OnGuard" memory agents which block common security holes, such as ActiveX, phishing sites, pop-ups, browser hijackers, and more.

Figure 11-7. Too Small Buttons

Spyware Doctor

 Better

FREE DOWNLOADS

Spyware Doctor offers solid protection against spyware and a number of additional immunization features to block common security holes. Spyware Doctor installs easily and without any problems, and it is the largest commercial anti-spyware product in the world.

Spyware Doctor - Free
Download!

Spyware Doctor also lets you rollback any changes it makes, just in case the spyware was required by an otherwise useful program (Real Player and Kazaa are typical examples of programs that embed spyware on your PC and won't run without it).my words...

Spyware Doctor

Spyware Doctor comes with a scheduler, but perhaps we would prefer it if scheduling was set up automatically when the program is installed. You have to remember to go in to the "OnGuard" settings and scroll down to find the scheduler buried way down at the bottom. The scheduler should be much more easy to find.

Spyware Doctor product also includes "OnGuard" memory agents which block common security holes, such as ActiveX, phishing sites, pop-ups, browser hijackers, and more.

PC Tools Spyware Doctor is an effective product that provides superior spyware removal capabilities and a great user interface, but there are a few minor problems with usability (such as the scheduler being very hard to find).

Overall, this anti-spyware software is highest-rated product on the market, and you can not go wrong with it! Mark my words...

Figure 11-8. Larger Buttons

Spyware Doctor

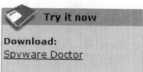

Spyware Doctor offers solid protection against spyware and a number of additional immunization features to block common security holes. Spyware Doctor installs easily and without any problems, and it is the largest commercial anti-spyware product in the world.

Spyware Doctor also lets you rollback any changes it makes, just in case the spyware was required by an otherwise useful program (Real Player and Kazaa are typical examples of programs that embed spyware on your PC and won't run without it). my words...

Spyware Doctor comes with a scheduler, but perhaps we would prefer it if scheduling was set up automatically when the program is installed. You have to remember to go in to the "OnGuard" settings and scroll down to find the scheduler buried way down at the bottom. The scheduler should be much more easy to find.

Spyware Doctor product also includes "OnGuard" memory agents which block common security holes, such as ActiveX, phishing sites, pop-ups, browser hijackers, and more.

Figure 11-9. Best Type of Button

Include Google and Yahoo! Ads

One of the strangest things that I noticed in landing page optimization is that Google ads (AdSense)—and other advertising—actually increased the conversion rates *and* sales of the landing pages. It's generally thought that web sites selling or promoting a product should never display competitors' ads, but I found this not to be true.

This result is *totally* counterintuitive, but I didn't argue with the testing numbers, which were clear. Including ads on the web site also generates a secondary source of income from visitors who click on the ads. Remember that it's normal for 98 percent of visitors to most landing pages to leave without taking action. Why not earn a few cents by letting them leave with an AdSense or Yahoo! ad click? But even without the income from the ads, the conversion rates and sales still go up by using this technique.

Figure 11-10 shows an example section without ads (*lower* conversion and dollar sales). Figure 11-11 shows an example of a web page section with higher conversion rates and higher total dollar sales. It includes ads from Yahoo!. As usual, test on your specific site before implementing this idea.

The Competition: Spyware Doctor

Spyware Doctor offers solid protection against spyware and a number of additional immunization features to block common security holes. Spyware Doctor installs easily and without any problems, and it is the largest commercial anti-spyware product in the world.

Spyware Doctor also lets you rollback any changes it makes, just in case the spyware was required by an otherwise useful program (Real Player and Kazaa are typical examples of programs that embed spyware on your PC and won't run without it).my words...

Spyware Doctor comes with a scheduler, but perhaps we would prefer it if scheduling was set up automatically when the program is installed. You have to remember to go in to the "OnGuard" settings and scroll down to find the scheduler buried way down at the bottom. The scheduler should be much more easy to find.

Spyware Doctor product also includes "OnGuard" memory agents which block common security holes, such as ActiveX, phishing sites, pop-ups, browser hijackers, and more.

Figure 11-10. Without Ads

The Competition: Spyware Doctor

Spyware Doctor offers solid protection against spyware and a number of additional immunization features to block common security holes. Spyware Doctor installs easily and without any problems, and it is the largest commercial anti-spyware product in the world.

Spyware Doctor also lets you rollback any changes it makes, just in case the spyware was required by an otherwise useful program (Real Player and Kazaa are typical examples of programs that embed spyware on your PC and won't run without it).

Spyware Doctor comes with a scheduler, but perhaps we would prefer it if scheduling was set up automatically when the program is installed. You have to remember to go in to the "OnGuard" settings and scroll down to find the scheduler buried way down at the bottom. The scheduler should be much more easy to find.

Spyware Doctor product also includes "OnGuard" memory agents which block common security holes, such as ActiveX, phishing sites, pop-ups, browser hijackers, and more.

Ads by Yahoo!

House Payments Fall Again
$180,000 Mortgage for $999/mo. See Rates - No Credit Check Required.
www.LowerMyBills.com

Like Games? Play Now Free - RealArcade
RealArcade gives you 500+ games to try free. Start playing now.
realarcade.com

Compare Mortgage Quotes
Up to 5 Free Quotes with 1 Form. Refi or Home Equity. Intro Terms.
www.NexTag.com/mortgages

Figure 11-11. Higher Conversion

Boost Conversions Today: Use Effective Google Web Optimizer A/B Page Tests

Now that you've seen conversion results from a live case study, you may be asking how do I implement these? What if I don't have any programming experience? What if I want to start at a much simpler level? The next few pages will be your short guide to web site optimization techniques using Google's Web Optimizer, specifically A/B Page testing, which is explained below.

The web optimizer is free, and it is Google's A/B and multi-variate testing tool. This tool allows you to continually test variations of your site to set optimial configurations for your landing pages and boost your conversions to more business! You can analyze the findings using graphs, charts, and lists with further opportunity for analysis via data exports to Excel and other file formats.

Before we begin, let's review landing page optimization. As defined by wikipedia,

> Landing page optimization is the process of improving visitors' perceptions of a web site by improving content and appeareance to make them more appealing to target audiences, as measured by target goals such as conversion rates.
>
> http://en.wikipedia.org/wiki/Landing_page_optimization

It should be obvious by now, but testing your site and specific pages is very important, and the rule is "Assume nothing. Test Everything." You have seen that the best internet marketers test their landing pages, from top level designs to user behavior/workflow (funnel). They may have the "secret" knowledge and best practices, but the testing of page designs/layouts in an A/B manner, as well as components or sections within a page or set of pages, is critical for optimal conversion. This is the true secret! No one can ultimately know this unless there is a test.

As you've seen, traffic is just one component of the magic that needs to happen online for increased business profits. If you are running PPC ads, you should start by testing those ads via creative adtext, split test them, title changes, and more. So, it really starts right after the user enters the search query. The path from query to conversion can be lengthy and possibly complex (e-commerce shopping cart and navigation) or shorter, or simpler, as in this illustration:

> **TIP:** See http://services.google.com/websiteoptimizer/case_studies.html to learn more about how some companies went from 20% to over 200% (!) in increased conversions by using the GWO (Google Web Optimizer) tool.

1. User enters a search query
2. User clicks (from organic results or paid search)
3. Lands on a page (assumed relevancy)
4. Enters name and e-mail address and receives or downloads a white paper,
5. Transaction completed

If you don't optimize, you could be leaving money on the table, and you always need to focus on the most desired action (MDA) for your page, with the least amount of distractions—to make it easier for your potential customer to take action. We'll use the above navigational path in our examples below.

What Pages Should You Select?

If you have click stream history, you should select pages for the tests that have a high bounce rate or the pages that have low conversion rates. Some pages may have a high exit rates and short time periods spent on them. And, you may have ideas for various pages but cannot decide on which ones to use. Those can be great starting points as well.

What Do You Need to Start?

- Google AdWords account. You should have one by now, if you read this book. If not, go to http://adwords.google.com and follow the instructions.
- Google Analytics account. Sign up for Analytics using the AdWords account you signed up with. This will allow the tight integration you need, including automatic tagging of destination URLs and cost data for important conversion metrics. Once Analytics is set up, you must copy the Analytics JavaScript code to the pages you want to track. I recommend placing them in a template and have it available on all the pages on your site. There are unique situations that may need special treatments. These can be related to dynamically generated pages, sites with frames, Google checkout, ecommerce sites, and content management systems. For most cases, Google Analytics works as described.
- Access to HTML code on the landing page(s). You need this for simple script inserts.
- Basic knowledge of HTML and Javascript. It's not hard; you can learn quickly.
- Once you log in to the AdWords system, you will have access to Google Website Optimizer (GWO), as seen in Figure 11-12.

Figure 11-12. Accessing Google Website Optimizer

What Is A/B Testing, and What Additional Testing Can You Do?

There are a couple of ways you can test your landing pages or sites. Specifically, they are:

- A/B Testing (the focus for this quick guide)—good for testing layout changes at the site level. You can test colors, fonts and more. Last year, I worked with a client who couldn't decide what page layout was best for a new SEO campaign, so we tested two versions using the A/B model to discover the winning page, and found what page the visitors preferred.
- Multi-Variate Testing (origins found at http://en.wikipedia.org/wiki/Multivariate_statistics)—great for testing inline or sectional items, like buttons, web copy, headers, subheaders and more. The GWO engine runs combinations or variations of all

of these to discover the most appealing page. For example, you'll be able to analyze combinations of factors for the winning page and/or interaction between specific factors.

How Long Will It Take for Results to Show?

For the tests, you should have a good amount of traffic. If you have no traffic, you can read this book and take actions to drive higher numbers to your test pages. The tests will take longer if you have less traffic, and if you have created many multi-

> **TIP:** Learn about fractional versus full factorial testing at http://adwords.google.com/support/bin/answer.py?hl=en&answer=74818.

variate combinations within sections on a page, it will take an even longer time. You can also choose to designate certain portions of traffic to the experiment, which is easy to do with PPC campaigns. When you assign a larger percent of traffic (in combination with existing organic search, for example), the experiment will be shorter.

Selecting and Setting Experiment Type

You must be sure to have logged into Google AdWords, and follow the instructions as shown in Figure 11-13.

Decide on which test to run and see references above as to what will make most sense to you. In this example, we will select the simple A/B test experiment (Figure 11-14).

> **TIP:** To plan for how long the tests will take, review the Google Website Optimization Duration Calculator at https://www.google.com/analytics/siteopt/siteopt/help/calculator.html. Expected improvement is really just a best guess, but should help guide you through the process.

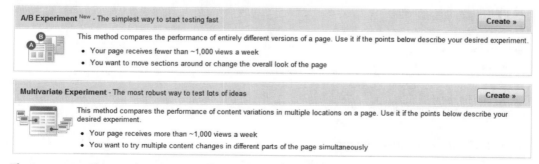

What type of experiment would you like to create?

Not sure which type of experiment is right for you? Learn more about Website Optimizer experiments

A/B Experiment New - The simplest way to start testing fast   Create »

This method compares the performance of entirely different versions of a page. Use it if the points below describe your desired experiment.
- Your page receives fewer than ~1,000 views a week
- You want to move sections around or change the overall look of the page

Multivariate Experiment - The most robust way to test lots of ideas   Create »

This method compares the performance of content variations in multiple locations on a page. Use it if the points below describe your desired experiment.
- Your page receives more than ~1,000 views a week
- You want to try multiple content changes in different parts of the page simultaneously

Figure 11-13. Choose the experiment for Google Web Optimizer

A/B Experiment Checklist

Before you start, make sure you complete the following:

1 **Choose the page you would like to test**
Examples of potential test pages could be your homepage or a product detail page.

2 **Create alternate versions of your test page**
Create and publish different versions of your test page at unique URLs so that Website Optimizer can randomly display different versions to your users. These URLs could be bookmarked by your users, so after your experiment finishes, you may want to keep these URLs valid.

3 **Identify your conversion page**
This is an existing page on your website which users reach after they've completed a successful conversion. For example, this might be the page displayed after a user completes a purchase, signs up for a newsletter, or fills out a contact form.

☐ I've completed the steps above and I'm ready to start setting up my experiment.

Figure 11-14. A/B Experiment Type

At this stage, you must choose what page you want to test. Once you've decided, make sure to click the checkbox, since that will enable a continue button, or you will not be able to proceed (Figure 11-15).

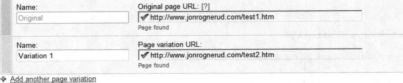

A/B experiment set-up: Name your experiment and identify pages

1 **Name your experiment**
The experiment name will help you to distinguish this experiment from others; your users won't see this name.

Experiment name:
Search Widget Page Test #1
Example: My homepage test #1

2 **Identify the pages you want to test**
Add as many variations as you like, naming them so you can easily distinguish them in your reports. At least two (including the original) are required. These URLs could be bookmarked by your users, so after your experiment finishes, you may want to keep these URLs valid. Learn more

Name: Original
Original page URL: [?]
✔ http://www.jonrognerud.com/test1.htm
Page found

Name: Variation 1
Page variation URL:
✔ http://www.jonrognerud.com/test2.htm
Page found

✚ Add another page variation

3 **Identify your conversion page**
This is an existing page which users reach after completing a successful conversion. For example, this might be the page displayed after a user completes a purchase, signs up for a newsletter, or fills out a contact form. Learn more

Conversion page URL:
✔ http://www.jonrognerud.com/thankyou.htm
Page found

Figure 11-15. A/B Experiment Setup

Your pages should have been copied to the server, including the thank-you page, which will capture success metrics for the conversion. Click "Continue" to proceed to the installation and validation of JavaScript tags (Figure 11-16).

A/B Experiment Set-up: Install and Validate JavaScript Tags

Now you need to add the Website Optimizer JavaScript tags to your pages' source code. <u>Learn more</u>

Who will install and validate the JavaScript tags?

○ **My web team will install and validate JavaScript tags**
Google will provide a link to the installation and validation instructions for you to send to your team. You'll be able to check on the status by returning to this page.

○ **I will install and validate the JavaScript tags**
You should be comfortable with basic HTML editing, have access to your web pages, and be able to upload the tagged pages to your server.

Figure 11-16. A/B Setup of JavaScript Code

You have a choice here. If you are not familiar with HTML and not comfortable dealing with code, you can choose to have your webmaster install the code, but I prefer to do it myself. If you have access to your server, it's easy to do, and GWO helps with final validation. Try it yourself!

Select "I will install and validate the JavaScript tags" and click the "continue" button (Figure 11-17, next page).

This step validates your scripts on these pages. You need to open the three pages (test1.htm, test2.htm, and thankyou.htm) in your favorite HTML editor and apply the scripts as indicated. I have done this, and you can see the results on the web at the page locations above. You should have Google Analytics code already applied. Place GWO code after the Google Analytics code on the page.

> **TIP:** If you need a break during GWO setup, you have that option. Choose "Save progress and finish later."

Here's an example of the results you get if you try to check pages by clicking the "Validate Pages" button before code is applied to the pages shown in Figure 11-18.

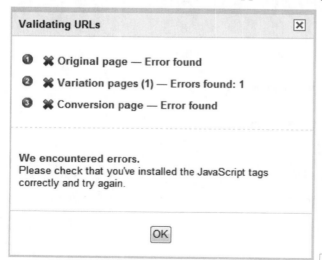

Figure 11-18. Validation Problem

I copied the code as instructed above, and sent the three files to the server. I clicked the "Validate Pages" button again, and I got the results I was looking for (Figure 11-19).

After the "Continue" button, I now see that I'm ready to start the experiment (Figure 11-20, page 202).

However, I recommend that you preview the experiment first. The link in the Figure 11-21 (page 202) will reveal the A/B

❶ Original page: add control and tracking scripts

○ Original: 🔲 http://www.jonrognerud.com/test1.htm

Add the control script to your original page

Paste the following **at the beginning** of your original page's source code.

```
<script>
function utmx_section(){}function utmx(){}
(function(){var k='1911327927
',d=document,l=d.location,c=d.cookie;function f(n){
```

Add the tracking script to your original page

Paste the following **at the end** of your original page's source code.

```
<script>
if(typeof(urchinTracker)!='function')document.write('<sc'+'ript
src="'+
'http'+(document.location.protocol=='https:'?'s://ssl':'://www')+
```

❷ Variation pages: add tracking script to each page

○ Variation 1: 🔲 http://www.jonrognerud.com/test2.htm

Add tracking script to each page

Paste the following **at the very end of all (1) of your variation pages'** source code.

```
<script>
if(typeof(urchinTracker)!='function')document.write('<sc'+'ript
'http'+(document.location.protocol=='https:'?'s://ssl':'://www')+
'.google-analytics.com/urchin.js'+'"></sc'+'ript>')
```

❸ Conversion page: add tracking script

○ Conversion page: 🔲 http://www.jonrognerud.com/thankyou.htm

Add the tracking script to your conversion page

Paste the following **at the very end** of your conversion page's source code.

```
<script>
if(typeof(urchinTracker)!='function')document.write('<sc'+'ript
src="'+
'http'+(document.location.protocol=='https:'?'s://ssl':'://www')+
```

Figure 11-17. JavaScript Tags and validation

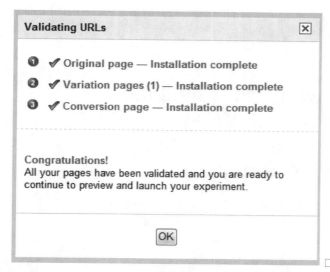

Figure 11-19. Validation Success, A/B Test

test screens, and you can see the two versions by stepping through them in this screen. The system will alternate between these two versions once it's live.

Please be aware that the differences between the two versions are the picture reference and the header and subhead. The first version has a red header and black subhead. The second variation has a blue header and red subhead. (The colors don't show up in the book, but you can see them online).

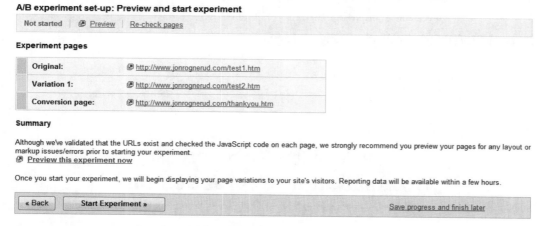

Figure 11-20. A/B Test Setup, Ready to Start the Experiment

You are now ready to begin the actual experiment. So now click the start button.

Congratulations! You're off and running with your first A/B page test, and you can see the confirmation in the experiment pages list below. When visitors sign up to download the example search widget, the "thankyou" page serves as a download page and a confirmation of transaction success. The saved data will pinpoint the winning page over time in the GWO reports (Figure 11-23).

You can click the "View Report" link above to check for data points from GWO and Analytics data capture, but don't expect results immediately. It will take some time, and

Figure 11-21. A/B Preview Window, Original Page

**Before It's Too Late!
Download the *Secret Search
Widget* that in 24 hours will
outrank your competition in
Google.**

**Google wants this top search marketing
engineer to immediately halt development of the
widget, or else...**

Your Lead paragraph Goes Here. The purpose of the lead
paragraph is to **get someone involved** in reading more of
the page.

PICTURE OF THE
SEARCH
MARKETER

Short, **easy to read paragraphs** are usually better and will
be read more often than longer, unscannable paragraphs that go on and on forever. Also,
do your best to write in a **conversational and informal** way.

Figure 11-22. A/B Preview Window, Variation Page

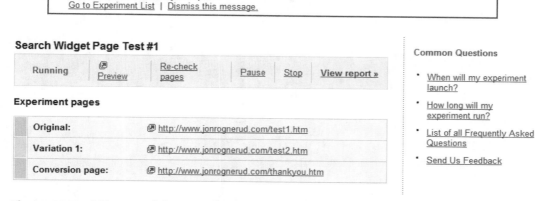

Figure 11-23. A/B successful Start and "Live" Run

depending on traffic flow and Google database update frequency. You may not see anything until the next day. Relax, listen to some music, and the internet will be there for you tomorrow.

Additional Resources for Analytics and Google Web Optimizer

- www.roirevolution.com/blog
- www.kaushik.net/avinash
- www.webanalyticsassociation.org
- http://services.google.com/websiteoptimizer

TIP: For more information, see the member site at www.jonrognerud.com/amember under "conversions," and to learn more about multivariate testing solutions.

CLOSING

I hope that by now you're as excited as I am about what effective search marketing can do for your business. As you begin to apply the principles and strategies you learned in this book, you are certain to have questions. Review the CD that comes with the book, and visit the complimentary member site (www.jonrognerud.com/amember) for help and resources. There you'll find video demonstrations, articles, how-tos and much more.

Glossary

A

200 Status OK. The file request was successful. For example, a page or image was found and loaded properly in a browser. Some poorly developed content management systems return 200 status codes even when a file doesn't exist.

301 Moved Permanently. The file has been moved permanently to another location. The preferred method of redirecting for most pages or web sites.

404 Not Found. The server was unable to locate URL.

absolute link A link that specifies the website link in full rather than an abbreviated version.

above the fold The portion of a web page that's viewable without scrolling.

ad blocking The blocking of web advertisements, typically the image in graphical web advertisements.

ad click rate Sometimes referred to as *click-through*, the percentage of ad views that resulted in an ad click.

ad clicks Number of times users click on an ad banner.

ad network An aggregator or broker of advertising inventory from many sites. 24/7 Media is an ad network.

AdSense Contextual advertising network from Google. Shares profits with Google.

ad space The space on a web page available for advertisements

ad views (impressions) Number of times an ad banner is downloaded and seen by visitors.

AdWords Google advertising network. Uses keywords and cost per click.

advertising network A network representing many web sites in selling advertising. Allows ad buyers to easily reach broad audiences through run-of-category and run-of-network buys.

address A unique identifier for a computer or site online, usually a URL for a web site or marked with an @ for an e-mail address. It's how your computer finds a location on the information highway.

add URL (see *search engine submission*)

affiliate The publisher/salesperson in an affiliate marketing relationship.

affiliate directory A categorized listing of affiliate programs.

affiliate forum An online community where visitors can read and post topics related to affiliate marketing.

affiliate fraud Bogus activity generated by an affiliate in an attempt to generate illegitimate, unearned revenue.

affiliate marketing Revenue sharing between online advertisers/merchants and online publishers/salespeople. Compensation is based on performance measures, typically in the form of sales, clicks, registrations, or a hybrid model.

affiliate merchant The advertiser in an affiliate marketing relationship.

affiliate network A value-added intermediary providing services, including aggregation, for affiliate merchants and affiliates.

affiliate software Software that, at a minimum, provides tracking and reporting of commission-triggering actions (sales, registrations, or clicks) from affiliate links.

age Some social networks or search systems may take site age, page age, user account age, and related historical data into account when determining how much to trust that person, web site, or document. Some specialty search engines, like blog search engines, may also boost the relevancy of new documents. When "Age" is used in context of search engines, web sites and pages, "Age" is correct. It's referred to here as an "importance factor" and defines what Age means in the context.

AJAX Method of uploading information without a web page reload.

AltaVista Yahoo!-owned search engine.

AllTheWeb Yahoo!-owned search engine.

ALT text HTML attribute that provides alternative text when non-textual elements, typically images, cannot be displayed.

Analytics Software that allows users to track page views, user paths, and conversion statistics based on interpreting log files or through a JavaScript tracking code on the user's site.

anchor A word, phrase, or graphic image in hypertext. It's the object that's highlighted, underlined, or "clickable" which links to another site.

anchor text Text associated with a hyperlink.

animated GIF A graphic in the GIF89a file format that creates the effect of animation by rotating through a series of static images.

Apache The most common web server (or HTTP server) software on the internet. An open-source application originally created from a series of changes ("patches") made to a web server. Designed as a set of modules to enable administrators to choose which features they want to use and to make it easy to add features to meet specific needs, including handling protocols other than the web-standard HTTP.

applet An application program written in Java that allows viewing simple animation on web pages.

ARPANet (Advanced Research Projects Agency Network) The precursor to the internet. Developed in the late 60s and early 70s by the U.S. Dept. of Defense as an experiment in wide-area-networking to connect computers that were running different systems, allowing users at one location to use computing resources at another location.

ASCII (American Standard Code for Information Interchange) The de facto worldwide standard for the code numbers used by computers to represent all upper- and lower-case Latin letters, numbers, punctuation, etc. There are 128 standard ASCII codes, each of which can be represented by a seven-digit binary number: 0000000 through 1111111.

Ask Search engine owned by InterActive Corp.

ASP (application service provider) An organization (usually a business) that runs one or more applications on their own servers and provides (usually for a fee) access to others.

authority The ability of a page or domain to rank well in search engines. Five factors associated with site and page authority are link equity, site age, traffic trends, site history, and publishing unique original-quality content.

B

B2B Business that sells products or provides services to other businesses.

B2C Business that sells products or provides services to end-user consumers.

backbone A high-speed line or series of connections that forms a large pathway within a network. The term is relative to the size of network it's serving. A backbone in a small network would probably be much smaller than many non-backbone lines in a large network.

bad neighborhood A web page that has been penalized by a search engine (most notably Google) for using shady SEO tactics, such as hidden text or link farms.

bandwidth How much data can be sent through a connection. Usually measured in bits-per-second (bps).

banner ad A graphical web advertising unit, typically measuring 468 pixels wide and 60 pixels tall. Usually "hot-linked" to the advertiser's site.

banner blindness The tendency of web visitors to ignore banner ads, even when they contain information visitors are actively looking for.

banner exchange Network where participating sites display banner ads in exchange for credits which are converted (using a predetermined exchange rate) into ads to be displayed on other sites.

baud The rate at which bits can be sent or received per second. The number of times per second that the carrier signal shifts value; for example, a 1,200 bit-per-second modem actually runs at 300 baud, but it moves 4 bits per baud (4x300 = 1,200 bits per second).

behavioral targeting Ad targeting based on past recent experience or implied intent. For example, if I recently searched for mortgages before reading a book review, the book review page may still show me mortgage ads.

binary Information consisting entirely of 1s and 0s. Commonly refers to files that are not simply text files, e.g., images.

black hat SEO Deceptive marketing techniques. Search engines set up guidelines that help them extract billions of dollars of ad revenue from the work of publishers and the attention of searchers. The search guidelines are not a static set of rules, and things that may be considered legitimate one day may be considered deceptive the next. Search engines are not without flaws in their business models, but it's not unethical or illegal to test search algorithms to understand how search engines work.

blog A frequent, chronological publication of personal thoughts and web links (shortened version of web log).

blogroll Link list on a blog, usually linking to other blogs owned by the same company or friends of that blogger.

bookmark Link stored in a web browser for future use. An easy way to return to a web site of interest.

bounce What happens when e-mail is returned as undeliverable.

brand A name, term, design, symbol, or other feature that identifies one seller's goods or services as distinct from those of other sellers. The legal term for brand is *trademark*. A brand may identify one item, a family of items, or all items of that seller. If used for the firm as a whole, the preferred term is *trade name*.

broken link A non-functioning link.

browser An application used to view information from the internet. It provides a user-friendly interface for navigating through and accessing the vast amount of information on the internet.

browser caching To speed surfing, browsers store recently used pages on a user's disk. If a site is revisited, browsers display pages from the disk instead of requesting them from the server. As a result, servers under-count the number of times a page is viewed.

browsing A term that refers to exploring an online area, usually on the world wide web.

buttons Objects that, when clicked once, cause something to happen.

button ad A graphical advertising unit, smaller than a banner ad.

button exchange Network where participating sites display button ads in exchange for credits that are converted (using a predetermined exchange rate) into ads to be displayed on other sites.

C

cache A storage area for frequently accessed information. Retrieval of the information is faster from the cache than the originating source. Types of caches include RAM cache, secondary cache, disk cache, and cache memory.

cascading style sheet (CSS) A standard for specifying the appearance of text and other elements. Typically used to provide a single "library" of styles that are used over and over throughout a number of related documents, as in a web site. A CSS file might specify that all numbered lists appear in italics. By changing that specification, the look of a number of documents can be easily changed.

click The opportunity for a user to be transferred to a location by clicking on an ad, as recorded by the server.

click-through rate (CTR) The average number of click-throughs per 100 ad impressions, expressed as a percentage.

client A program, computer, or process that makes information requests to another computer, process, or program.

cloaking Displaying different content to search engines and searchers. Depending on the intent of the display discrepancy and the strength of the brand of the person/company cloaking, it may be considered reasonable or it may get a site banned from a search engine.

conversion rate The percentage of visitors who take a desired action.

co-citation In topical authority-based search algorithms, links that appear near one another on a page may be deemed related. In algorithms like latent semantic indexing, words that appear near one another often are frequently deemed to be related.

CGI (common gateway interface) Interface software between a web server and other machines or software running on that server. Many CGI programs are used to add interactivity to a web site.

concept search A search that attempts to conceptually match results with the query, not necessarily with those words.

conceptual links Links that search engines attempt to understand beyond the words in them.

content The information located on a web page. Includes text, images, and other information that a webmaster places on the page.

content management system (CMS) Tool that enables easy update and addition of information to a web site.

contextual advertising Ad programs that generate relevant ads based on the content of a web page.

conversion Accomplishment of a desired goal, such as viewing an online ad.

cookie A file on a computer that records information, such as sites visited by a user on the world wide web.

cost-per-action (CPA) Online advertising payment model in which payment is based solely on qualifying actions, such as sales or registrations.

cost per click (CPC) The cost or cost-equivalent paid per click-through.

cost per lead (CPL) The cost or lead paid for each lead referred to an affiliate site.

CPM cost per thousand impressions Defines the cost an advertiser pays for 1,000 impressions of an advertisement, such as a banner ad, text ad, or other promotion. An impression is counted each time an advertisement is shown. If an ad appears on a web page 1000 times and it costs $1, then the CPM would be $1.

CPT (cost per transaction) An alternative to the traditional cost-per-click or cost-per-thousand pricing models, where an advertiser would pay per actual sale/transaction.

CPTM (cost per targeted thousand impressions) Implies that the audience one is trying to reach is defined by particular demographics or other specific characteristics, such as male skiers age 20-30. The difference between CPM and CPTM is that CPM is for gross impressions, while CPTM is for targeted impressions.

CPU (central processing unit) The main "brain" of the computer, where information is processed and calculations are done.

coverage The percentage of a population group covered by the internet.

crawl Same as spidering: search engines crawl links/pages and collect information about each page along the way.

crawl depth How deeply a web site is crawled and indexed.

crawl frequency How frequently a web site is crawled

crawler A software program that web sites use to index pages throughout a site or several web sites on the internet.

creative The technology used to create or develop an ad unit. The most common creative technology for banners is GIF or JPEG images. Other creative technologies include Java, HTML, or streaming audio or video. Commonly referred to as *rich media banners*.

cross linking When the owners of two or more web sites interlink the sites so as to boost their search engine rankings. If detected, cross linking often results in a search engine penalty.

customer acquisition cost The cost associated with acquiring a new customer.

cyberspace Term originated by William Gibson in his novel *Neuromancer*. Used to describe the whole range of information resources available through computer networks.

D

del.icio.us Social bookmarking web site.

de-listing Temporarily or permanently becoming de-indexed from a directory or search engine.

deep linking Linking to a web page other than a site's home page.

demographics Statistical data or characteristics that define segments of a population.

description meta tag Describes the content of the web page in which it's found. Used by some search engines for keyword density purposes.

description tag An HTML tag used by web page authors to provide a description for search engine listings.

digg Social news site where users vote on which stories get the most exposure and become the most popular.

direct response The school of advertising that says, "The internet is an interactive medium. If the consumer interacts with our marketing efforts, we've done our job." Unfortunately for agencies, there's nowhere to hide with interactive campaigns, as they produce precise success or failure measurements. Same as Direct Marketing; relates to promotions or requests from advertiser by responding directly via e-mail, phone, or other means.

DMOZ (Open Directory Project) The largest human-edited directory of web sites. Owned by AOL, and primarily run by volunteer editors.

DNS (domain name system) The system that translates internet domain names into IP numbers. A "DNS server" is a server that performs this kind of translation.

domain name The unique name that identifies an internet site. Domain names always have two or more parts, separated by dots. The left side is the most specific, and the part on the right is the most general. A given machine may have more than one domain name but a given domain name points to only one machine.

doorway domain A domain used to rank well in search engines for particular keywords, serving as an entry point through which visitors pass to the main domain.

doorway page A page made specifically to rank well in search engines for particular keywords, serving as an entry point through which visitors pass to the main content. When used in bulk they are considered to be search engine spam.

duplicate content Two or more web pages that contain substantially the same content.

dynamic content A dynamic page web page that is often generated from database information based on queries initiated by users.

dynamic IP address An IP address that changes every time a computer logs on to the internet. See also *static IP address*. AOL users show different IP numbers every time they log on, for example.

dynamic language Programming language such as PHP or ASP that builds web pages on the fly.

E

earnings per click Many contextual advertising publishers estimate their potential earnings based on how much they make from each click.

editorial link Search engines count links as votes of quality. Using an algorithm similar to TrustRank, some search engines may place more trust in well-known sites with strong editorial guidelines.

e-mail, electronic mail Text files sent from one person to another.

e-mailing The sending of e-mail or text files from one person to another.

e-mail marketing The promotion of products or services via e-mail.

e-mail spam Unwanted, unsolicited e-mail.

emphasis An HTML tag used to emphasize text.

entry page The page from which a user enters a site.

ethical SEO Search engines like to paint SEO services that manipulate their relevancy algorithms as being unethical. Many feel that "ethics" for search engines is not a valid term, since search engines are all software and machines, and cannot hurt humans per se. Ethical SEO refers to a term and related optimization techniques that owners of search engines (i.e. Google) consider OK (compare to "Black Hat SEO"). It's search engine optimization that does not use trickery or tactics that are frowned on by the search engines.

exclusivity Contract term in which one party grants another party sole rights with regard to a particular business function.

expert document Quality page that links to many non-affiliated topical resources.

external link Link that references another domain.

extranet Extranet refers to a group of web sites belonging to independent entities that are combined together in order to share information. For example, an organization may grant limited access to its internal network - to customers, or suppliers. This is in contrast to an intranet, which is a private site that is only accessible for employees of an entity.

ezine An electronic magazine, whether delivered via a web site or an e-mail newsletter.

ezine directory Directory of electronic magazines, typically of the e-mail variety.

F

filter A software routine that examines web pages during a robot's search for search engine spam. If the filter detects spam on the page, a ranking penalty is assessed.

firewall A combination of hardware and software that separates a network into two or more parts for security purposes.

FTP (file transfer protocol) A common method of moving files between two internet sites.

FFA Free-for-all links list: a web page that contains a collection of indiscriminate and often unrelated links. FFA pages do not qualify the links or the quality but allow you to simply add your URL. These pages are used to artificially boost link popularity and are considered spam by the major search engines.

Flash Multimedia technology developed by Macromedia to allow a lot of interactivity to fit in a relatively small file size.

frame A technique to display multiple smaller pages on a single display. Created by Netscape.

G

gateway A link from one computer system to a different computer system.

GIF (graphic interchange format) A graphics format that can be displayed on most web browsers. A common compression format used to transfer graphics files between different computers. Most "pictures" online are GIF files. They display in 256 colors and have built-in compression. GIF images are the most common form of banner creative.

Google Base Free database of semantically structured information.

Google bombing Making a prank rank well for a specific search query by pointing hundreds or thousands of links at it with the keywords in the anchor text.

Google bowling Knocking a competitor out of the search results by pointing hundreds or thousands of low-trust, low-quality links at its web site.

Google Checkout Google payment service that helps Google better understand merchant conversion rates and the value of different keywords and markets.

Google dance Google used to update its index about once a month. Those updates were named Google dances. Google has since shifted to a constantly updating index.

Google keyword tool Tool provided by Google to estimate the competition for a keyword, recommend related keywords, and tell the user what keywords Google thinks are relevant to a site or a page on your site.

Google OneBox Portion of the search results page above the organic search results which Google sometimes uses to display vertical search results from Google News, Google Base, and other Google-owned vertical search services.

Google sitemap Program that webmasters use to help Google index their contents.

Google sitelink On some search results where Google thinks one result is more relevant than other results (like navigational or brand-related searches), it may list numerous deep links to that site at the top of the search results.

Google supplemental index Index where pages with lower trust scores are stored. Pages may be placed in Google's supplemental index if they consist largely of duplicate content, if the URLs are excessively complex in nature, or if the site that hosts them lacks significant trust.

Google toolbar A downloadable toolbar for Internet Explorer that allows a user to do a Google search without visiting the Google web site. The toolbar also displays the Google PageRank (PR) of the page currently displayed in the browser. Also includes a pop-up blocker.

Google Traffic Estimator Tool that estimates bid prices and how many Google searchers will click on an ad for a particular keyword.

Google Trends Tool that allows a user to see how Google searches volumes for a particular keyword change over time.

Google Website Optimizer Free multivariable testing platform used to help AdWords advertisers improve their conversion rates.

Google.com The leading search engine on the internet. When people speak of search engine optimization (SEO), they're often referring to Google.

Googlebot The crawler that Google uses on a daily basis to find and index new web pages.

guerrilla marketing Unconventional marketing intended to get maximum results from minimal resources.

H

hacker Originally described a computer enthusiast who pushed a system to its highest performance through clever programming. Term has since been used to identify computer enthusiasts who use their abilities to enhance and better computer systems; these hackers are referred to as *white hat*. Term also describes those who alter computer systems in a negative way; known as *black hat*.

header tags HTML tags that outline a web page or draw attention to important information. Keywords located inside header tags provide a rankings boost in the search engines. For example:
<>This is a tag.</>
<h2>This is an H2 tag.</h2>

hidden text, hidden link Using a text font the same color as the background color, rendering the text or link invisible or very difficult to read.

host Any computer on a network that's a repository for services available to other computers on the network. It's ommon to have one host machine provide several services, such as SMTP (e-mail) and HTTP (web).

HTML (hypertext markup language) The coding language used to create hypertext documents for use on the world wide web. HTML looks like old typesetting code, where the user surrounds a block of text with codes to indicate how it should appear. HTML files are meant to be viewed using a web browser.

.htaccess Apache directory-level configuration file used to password protect or redirect files.

HTTP (hypertext transfer protocol) The protocol for moving hypertext files across the internet. Requires an HTTP client program on one end, and an HTTP server program (such as Apache) on the other end. HTTP is the most important protocol used in the world wide web.

hypertext Generally, any text that contains links to other documents, words, or phrases in the document that can be chosen by a reader and that cause another document to be retrieved and displayed.

I

image map Placing separate hyperlinks on different areas of the same image.

impression, ad impression, page impression A single instance of an online ad being displayed.

index Collection of data used as a bank to find a match to a user-fed query. The largest search engines have billions of documents in their catalogs.

indexing After a search engine has crawled the web, it ranks URLs found using various criteria and places them in the database, or index.

information architecture Designing, categorizing, organizing and structuring content in a useful and meaningful way.

internet A connection of two or more networks. Also the vast collection of interconnected networks that are connected using the TCP/IP protocols. Evolved from the ARPANET of the late '60s and early '70s.

internet marketing Online marketing strategies to help a web site improve its ranking in search engines. Also refers to marketing strategies that include web site optimization, displaying ads or links throughout the internet with the common goal of improving the quantity and quality of visitors to a web site.

internet marketing company A company that provides internet marketing and often search engine marketing for its clients.

intranet A private network of a company or organization that uses the same kinds of software found on the public internet, but is only for internal use. Compare with *extranet*.

IP number Internet protocol number sometimes called a "dotted quad." A unique number consisting of four parts separated by dots, e.g., 165.113.245.2

IP delivery See *cloaking*.

IP spoofing Returning an IP address different from the one actually assigned to the destination web site. Often done with redirects. Unethical practice and a criminal offense under certain circumstances.

J

Java A network-friendly programming language invented by Sun Microsystems.

JavaScript A programming language mostly used in web pages, usually to add features that make the web page more interactive. When JavaScript is included in an HTML file it relies on the browser to interpret the JavaScript. When JavaScript is combined with cascading style sheets and HTML (4.0 and later) the result is often called DHTML.

K

keyword A word used in performing a search. Used to focus a search by categorizing web sites and locating specific topics.

keyword density Keywords as a percentage of text words that can be indexed.

keyword marketing Putting a message in front of people who are searching using particular keywords and keyword phrases.

keyword research The search for keywords related to a web site, and the analysis of which ones yield the highest return on investment.

keyword stuffing Writing copy that uses excessive instances of the core keyword.

keywords tag Meta tag used to define the primary keywords of a web page.

L

LAN (local area network) A computer network limited to the immediate area, usually the same building or floor of a building.

landing page The page on which a visitor arrives after clicking on a link or ad.

link URL placed within a web page so that when it's clicked on the browser is served with a different web page, often on a completely different web site. Also a citation from one web document to another web document or another position in the same document.

link anchor text The clickable part of the link structure. Using keywords in the link anchor text of inbound links helps the search engine rank for those keywords.

link baiting Targeting, creating, and formatting content or information in a way that encourages the target audience to point high-quality links at a site.

link building The process of building links. Can be inbound or outbound.

link bursts A rapid increase in the quantity of links pointing at a web site.

link checker Tool used to check for broken hyperlinks.

link churn Refers to the rate at which a site loses links.

link equity A measure of the strength of a site based on inbound link popularity and the authority and quality of the sites providing the links.

link farm One or a group of web sites that link to other sites without regard to content or relevancy. Free For All pages are examples of link farms.

link hoarding Keeping all of a link's popularity by not doing outbound links or only linking out using JavaScript or redirects.

link popularity A measure of the quantity and quality of inbound links pointing to a particular web site. Used by search engines to position web pages in search engines indexes.

link rot When web pages previously accessible at a particular URL are no longer reachable at that URL due to movement or deletion of the page.

linking Placing a link to another web page (usually on another web site).

Linux A widely used open-source Unix-like operating system. First released by its inventor Linus Torvalds in 1991. The inner workings of Linux are open and available for anyone to examine and change as long as they make their changes available to the public.

Live.com Search platform provided by Microsoft.

log file A record of the activity on a web server that tracks network connections.

login The identification or name used to access a computer, network, or site.

long domain name Domain names longer than the original 26 characters, up to a up to a theoretical limit of 67 characters.

LSI (latent semantic indexing) A way for search systems to mathematically understand and represent language based on the similarity of pages and keyword co-occurence. A relevant result may not even have the search term in it. It may be returned only because it contains many similar words to those appearing in relevant pages which contain the search words.

M

mailing list An automatically distributed e-mail message on a particular topic going to certain individuals. Users can subscribe or unsubscribe to a mailing list by sending a message via e-mail.

manual submission Adding a URL to the search engines one at a time.

marketing plan The part of the business plan outlining the marketing strategy for a product or service.

meta description Typically a sentence or two that describes the content of the page.

meta keywords A tag that used to highlight keywords and keyword phrases that the page is targeting.

meta search A search engine that pulls top-ranked results from multiple other search engines and rearranges them into a new result set.

meta search engine A web site that takes a search query and sends it to several search engines and directories, then summarizes the results in a logical manner for review.

meta tag A specific type of HTML tag that contains information not normally displayed to the user. Meta tags can be seen in a page by viewing the page's source code.

Microsoft Maker of the popular Windows operating system and internet Explorer browser.

mindshare A measure of the number of people who think of a specific product when thinking of products in a category.

mirror sites Identical, but separate web sites on different domains. Commonly used legitimately by large web sites to share heavy server loads, and by search engine spammers to generate more search engine referrals and revenue.

N

natural language processing Algorithms that try to understand the true intent of a search query rather than only matching results to keywords.

navigation That which facilitates movement from one web page to another web page.

netizen Derived from *citizen*, referring to a citizen of the internet, or someone who uses networked resources. The term connotes civic responsibility and participation.

niche A topic or subject that a web site is focused on.

nofollow Attribute used to prevent a link from passing link authority. Commonly used on sites with user-generated content, like blog comments.

not relevant A result generally unhelpful to the user but still connected, however remotely, with the query.

O

off topic Unrelated to the query.

one-way link A hyperlink that points to a web site without a reciprocal link; thus the link goes in only one direction.

online business community Social network for business users to promote and find businesses.

online marketing Form of web site promotion completed online as opposed to offline.

opt-in e-mail E-mail requested by the recipient.

opt-out A type of program that assumes inclusion unless stated otherwise. Opt out also means to remove oneself from an opt-out program.

organic search results Results that consist of paid ads and unpaid listings.

outbound link Link from one web page to another.

P

page jacking Theft of a page from the original site and publication of a copy (or near-copy) at another site.

PageRank (PR) A proprietary numerical score assigned by Google to every web page in its index. PR for each page is calculated by Google using an algorithm based on the number and quality (as determined by Google) of the inbound links to the page.

page view Request to load a single HTML page.

paid inclusion Some directories that accept a URL into their database only if paid a fee.

paid link Link purchased for advertising

pay for performance Payment structure where affiliated sales workers are paid a commission for getting consumers to perform certain acts.

pay per click (PPC) Online advertising payment model in which payment is based solely on qualifying click-throughs.

pay-per-click search engine (PPCSE) Search engine where results are ranked according to the bid amount. Advertisers are charged only when a searcher clicks on the search listing.

pay per lead (PPL) Online advertising payment model in which payment is based solely on qualifying leads.

pay per sale (PPS) Online advertising payment model in which payment is based solely on qualifying sales.

PHP (hypertext preprocessor) Programming language used mainly to create software that's part of a web site. The PHP language is designed to be intermingled with the HTML that's used to create web pages. Unlike HTML, PHP code is read and processed by the web server software.

pop-under ad Ad that displays in a new browser window behind the current browser window.

pop-up ad Ad that displays in a new browser window.

portal A site that offers many commonly used services. Serves as a starting point and frequent gateway to the web.

PPP (point-to-point protocol) Language that enables a computer to use telephone lines and a modem to connect to the internet. Gradually replacing SLIP as the preferred means of connection.

protocol Usually refers to a set of rules that define the format for communication between systems.

Q

quality content Linkworthy content.

quality link Search engines count a link a vote of trust.

query A request for information, usually to a search engine.

R

rank An ad's standing in comparison to other ads, based on the graphical click-through rate. Rank provides advertisers with information on an ad's performance across sites.

rate card Document detailing prices for ad placement options.

reciprocal link Link exchanged between two sites.

reciprocal link Link to a web site placed on another site in exchange for a link back to the original web site.

redirect A tactic sometimes used to send a user to a page different other than the one found in the SERPS.

referrer, referring URL The URL of the web page where a visitor clicked a link to come to another site.

registrar A company that registers domain names.

relevancy The degree to which the content on a web page that's returned in a list of search results (SERPS) matches the topic of the information that the user was searching for.

relative link A link that shows the relationship of the current URL to the URL of the page being linked to.

rich media New media that offers an enhanced experience relative to older, mainstream formats.

robot A program used by a search engine to crawl the web to find, rank and index new web pages.

robots.txt A special file commonly used to exclude some or all robots from crawling certain files or directories on a web site.

ROAS Stands for Return On Advertising Spending and represents the dollars earned per dollars spent on the corresponding advertising. To determine ROAS, divide revenue derived from the ad source by the cost of that ad source. Values less than one indicate that less revenue is generated than is spent on the advertising.

ROI (return on investment) ROI is trying to find out what the end of result of the expenditure is, and what positive or negative results will exist. In advertising the ROI metric assesses what the advertiser received for the cost of the advertisement (see *ROAS*).

RSS, rich site summary, RDF site summary, real simple syndication A commonly used protocol for syndication and sharing of content. Originally developed to facilitate the syndication of news articles, now widely used for syndication and other kinds of content-sharing.

run of network (RON) Ad-buying option in which ad placements may appear on any pages on sites within an ad network.

run of site (ROS) Ad-buying option in which ad placements may appear on any page of the target site.

S

search engine A program that searches and indexes documents, then tries to match documents relevant to the user's search requests.

search engine marketing The act of marketing a web site via search engines, whether this be improving rank in organic listings, purchasing paid listings, or a combination of these and other search engine-related activities.

search engine optimization The process of choosing targeted keyword phrases related to a site. Ensuring the site places well when those keyword phrases are part of a web search.

search engine spam Excessive manipulation to influence search engine rankings, often for pages that contain little or no relevant content.

search engine submission Supplying a URL to a search engine in an attempt to make a search engine aware of a site or page.

search spy A perpetually refreshing page that provides a real-time view of actual web searches.

self-serve advertising Advertising that can be purchased without the assistance of a sales representative.

SEO See *search engine optimization.*

SERP (search engine results page) A search engine results page, or SERP, is the listing of web pages returned by a search engine in response to a keyword query. The results normally include a list of web pages with titles, a link to the page, and a short description showing where the keywords have matched content within the page.

server A computer or software package that provides a specific kind of service to client software running on other computers. The term can refer to a particular piece of software, such as a WWW server, or to the machine on which the software is running.

servlet Small computer program designed to add capabilities to a larger piece of server software.

siphoning Techniques used to steal another web site's traffic, including the use of spyware or cybersquatting.

site map Page that can be used to give search engines a secondary route to navigate through a site.

social media Web sites that allow users to create the valuable content.

social network A community web site that lets users create profiles and find friends. Often a social network allows users to find other users based on interest, location, or name searches.

spam Inappropriate commercial e-mail message of extremely low value.

spam, spamming An inappropriate attempt to use a mailing list, USENET, or another networked communications facility as if it were a broadcast medium (which it is not) by sending the same message to a large number of people who didn't ask for it.

spider Software that web sites use to index pages throughout a site or several web sites on the internet.

splash page A branding page before the home page of a web site.

splog Spam blog, typically consisting of stolen or automated low-quality content.

sponsorship Advertising that seeks to establish a deeper association and integration between an advertiser and a publisher, often involving coordinated beyond-the-banner placements.

spyware Software secretly installed on a user's computer that monitors computer use in some way without the user's knowledge or consent.

SQL (structured query language) A specialized language for sending queries to databases.

SSI (server side includes) A way to call portions of a page in from another page. SSI makes it easier to update web sites.

SSL (secure socket layer) A protocol designed by Netscape Communications to enable encrypted, authenticated communications across the internet.

static content Content that changes infrequently. May refer to content that has no social elements and doesn't use dynamic programming languages.

static IP address An IP address permanently assigned to a computer.

static rotation Ads rotate based on the entry of users into a screen. Regardless of the amount of time a user spends with a screen, ads remain on the screen for the entire time and don't change.

stemming Using the stem of a word to satisfy search relevancy requirements.

stickiness The amount of time spent at a site over a given time period.

super affiliate Affiliate able to generate a significant percentage of an affiliate program's activity.

T

tag A noun or verb. As a noun, it's a basic element of the languages used to create web pages (HTML) and similar languages such as XML. Another, more recent meaning of tag is related to reader-created tags where blogs and other content (such as photos or music) may be "tagged," which means to assign a keyword.

targeted marketing Banners or other promotions aimed, on the basis of demographic analysis, at one specific subsection of the market.

TCP (transmission control protocol) Works with IP to ensure that packets travel safely on the internet. The method by which most internet activity takes place.

text ad Ad using text-based hyperlinks.

text link exchange Network where participating sites display text ads in exchange for credits that are converted (using a predetermined exchange rate) into ads to be displayed on other sites.

throughput The amount of data transmitted through internet connectors in response to a given request.

title tag HTML tag used to define the text in the top line of a web browser. Used by many search engines as the title of search listings.

TCP/IP (transmission control protocol/internet protocol) A suite of protocols that defines the internet. Originally designed for the UNIX operating system, TCP/IP software is now included with every major kind of computer operating system. To be on the internet, your computer must have TCP/IP software.

U

under delivery Delivery of fewer impressions, visitors, or conversions than contracted for a specified period of time.

unique visitors, unique users Users who have visited a web site (or network) at least once in a during a fixed time.

Unix Computer operating system. Designed to be used by many users at the same time and has TCP/IP built in. The most common operating system for servers on the internet.

URI (uniform resource identifier) Address for a resource on the internet. The first part of a URI is called the "scheme." The best known scheme is http, but there are many others. Each URI scheme has its own format for how a URI should appear.

URL (uniform resource locator) Synonymous with URI. URI has replaced URL in technical specifications.

URN (uniform resource name) A URI that is supposed to be available for a long time. For an address to be a URN, an institution must commit to keep the resource available at that address.

V

vertical banner Banner ad measuring 120 pixels wide by 240 pixels tall.

viral marketing Marketing phenomenon that facilitates and encourages people to pass along a marketing message.

volunteer directory A web directory staffed primarily by unpaid volunteer editors. The most popular volunteer directory to date is DMOZ.

W

web browser A software application that allows for browsing of the world wide web.

web design The selection and coordination of available components to create the layout and structure of a web page.

web directory Organized, categorized listing of web sites.

web hosting The business of providing the storage, connectivity, and services needed to serve files for a web site.

web site traffic The number of visitors and visits a web site receives.

web site usability The ease with which visitors are able to use a web site.

whois A utility that returns ownership information about second-level domains.

X

XHTML (extensible hypertext markup language) HTML expressed as valid XML. Intended to be used in the same places you would use HTML (creating web pages) but is more strictly defined, which makes it easier to create software that can read it, edit it, check it for errors, etc. XHTML is expected to replace HTML.

XML (extensible markup language) Widely used system for defining data formats. Provides a rich system to define complex documents and data structures such as invoices, molecular data, news feeds, glossaries, inventory descriptions, real estate properties, etc.

Additional Resources

Adwords

www.google.com/adwords/learningcenter—The Adwords Learning Center

www.mikes-marketing-tools.com/adwords-wrapper.html—Power tools for adwords wrapping

http://adwords.blogspot.com—Default resources for all things Adwords

www.ewhisper.net

Analytics

www.clickdensity.com—Useability toolkits

www.crazyegg.com—Similar to clickdensity, my preferred one

www.clicktale.com—Record user behaviors

www.clicktracks.com—Popular analytics software

www.haveamint.com—New analytics tracking software

www.google.com/analytics—Free software from Google

analytics.blogspot.com—Resources for analytics from Google

www.indextools.com

www.webanalyticsdemystified.com

www.getclicky.com

www.websidestory.com

www.omniture.com

Articles and Articles Management, Writer Resources

www.goarticles.com—Very popular, good resource

www.ezinearticles.com—Also very popular, recommended

www.escriptionist.com—Create articles from anything digital and more

www.elance.com—Get writers for a cost, popular

www.guru.com—Another resource to create written materials by other people

www.rentacoder.com—Developers at your fingertips

Audio and Video Tools

http://audacity.sourceforge.net/about/?lang=en—Audio editor for windows

www.audioacrobat.com—Create audio and video easily

Auto Responders

www.aweber.com—I use this, many good ones in this category

www.verticalresponse.com

www.constantcontact.comindex.jsp

www.getresponse.com

Black Hat SEO

www.davidnaylor.co.uk

www.syndk8.net

www.blackhatseo.com—Many resources here

Blogs General

www.copyblogger.com

www.problogger.net

http://blogoscoped.com

www.mattcutts.comblog

www.blogpulse.comindex.html

www.technorati.com

www.techmeme.com

http://valleywag.com

www.searchengineland.com

www.sphinn.com

www.seobook.com

www.seomoz.org

Competitive Research

www.compete.com

http://googspy.com

www.spyfu.com

www.quantcast.com

www.statsaholic.com

Conversion

www.google.comanalytics/conversionuniversity.html—Top resources from Google

www.hypertracker.com—Tracking software

http://browsershots.org—Test in browsers—maximize for compatibility and usability

www.conversionruler.com

Copywriting

www.copyblogger.comseo—Copywriting

www.hoskinson.net/ultimate.research.assistant—Mining topics data on the Internet

www.contentrover.com

http://creativecommons.org

www.copyscape.com—Check for duplicate content

CSS

www.alvit.de/css-showcase/css-navigation-techniques-showcase.php

www.w3schools.comcss/default.asp

Directories

www.strongestlinks.comdirectories.php

http://info.vilesilencer.commain.php?rock=seo-friendly.php

www.best-web-directories.comdirectories-under-review.html—Any spammy directories

Domain Stuff

www.dnforum.com

www.namecheap.com

www.leasethis.com—Top domain renting

www.namepros.com

www.parked.com

www.godaddy.com

www.hostgator.comdomains

www.regselect.com

www.dnsstuff.com

http://livehttpheaders.mozdev.org—Browser tool specific

Forums

www.cre8asiteforums.com

www.highrankings.comforum

www.isedb.com

http://forums.searchenginewatch.com

http://smallbusinessbrief.comforum

http://forums.spider-food.net

www.searchengineforums.com

www.warriorforum.comforum—Top internet marketers found here

http://forums.digitalpoint.com

www.webmasterworld.com

Google Resources and More

http://books.google.com

www.google.comcodesearch

http://catalogs.google.com

http://labs.google.com

http://labs.google.comsets

http://google.blogspace.com

www.google.comwebmasters/

www.google.combase/help/sellongoogle.html

Graphics–Photos

www.bannersmall.com—Cheap banners, logos and more

www.phototricity.comindex.php—Affordable stock photos for a buck or so

www.powstock.com

www.istockphoto.com

www.sxc.hu/–international

www.veer.com

www.tonystone.com–now gettyimages

Keyword Research

www.definr.com

http://dictionary.reference.com

www.digitalpoint.comtools/suggestion/

www.digitalpoint.comtools/keywords/

www.goodkeywords.com

https://adwords.google.comselect/KeywordToolExternal

www.google.comwebhp?complete=1&hl=en—Google Suggest

www.hittail.com

www.keyworddiscovery.com

www.wordtracker.com

www.metaglossary.com

http://adlab.msn.comForecastV2/KeywordTrendsWeb.aspx

www.epinions.com—Find out what people are talking about, research keywords

www.spyfu.com

www.scrutinizethis.com

http://thesaurus.reference.com

http://tools.seobook.comkeyword-tools

www.wordspy.com

www.wordze.com

www.google.comtrends/hottrends

Links

www.backlinkwatch.com

www.textlinkbrokers.comlink-buying-guide.html

www.commenthunt.com

www.brandon-hopkins.com66-ways-to-build-links-in-2007

http://hubpages.com

www.marketleap.com

www.linkbuildingblog.com

www.alliance-link.com

www.stuntdubl.comcategory/link-development

www.toprankblog.comcategory/seo/link-building

www.wolf-howl.comcategory/link-development

www.linkexplore.com

www.soloseo.comtools/linksearch.html

www.linkconnector.com

www.linkjuicy.com

www.linkworth.com

www.strongestlinks.comdirectories.php

www.text-link-ads.comlink_calculator.php

www.socialposter.com—Web 2.0 services

www.linkhounds.comhub-finder/hubfinder.php

www.linkadage.com

www.linkvendor.com

http://sitemaps.org—Sitemap to optimize onpage link profiles

Live Chat

www.boldchat.com

www.liveperson.com

www.phplivesupport.com

http://phpopenchat.org

Radio–Podcast

www.webpronews.com

www.seoradio.com

PPC

www.goclick.com

http://adwords.google.com

http://7search.com

http://perrymarshall.comgoogle

www.mammamediasolutions.com

www.miva.comus

http://adcenter.msn.com

http://searchmarketing.yahoo.com

www.ppseer.com

http://searchmarketing.yahoo.comcalculator/roas.php—Return on ad spend

http://searchmarketing.yahoo.comcalculator/roi.php

Press Release Management

www.prweb.com

www.marketwire.com

www.publicityinsider.comrelease.asp—How to write a press release

Ranking Factors—Search Engines

www.vaughns-1-pagers.cominternet/google-ranking-factors.htm

http://rankpulse.com

www.seomoz.org/article/search-ranking-factors—A great post

Reputation Management

www.marketingpilgrim.com2007/08/26-free-tools-for-buzz-monitoring.html

RSS

www.feedburner.com

http://en.wikipedia.org/wiki/Web_feeds

Tools

www.bad-neighborhood.comtext-link-tool.htm

www.internet-marketing-australia.comseo-explorer/seo-explorer-download.php

http://wufoo.com—Great form builder

www.polldaddy.com

www.googlerankings.com

www.hubspot.com

www.websitegrader.com

www.amember.com

www.webuildpages.comsearch

Video Tools / Web 2.0

www.jingproject.com

www.videolan.org

www.youtube.comrssls—Video and rss overview

www.tubemogul.com

www.techcrunch.com2007/11/22/the-secret-strategies-behind-many-viral-videos

Web 2.0

www.blinklist.com

http://del.icio.us

www.fanpop.com

www.friendster.com

www.go2web20.net

www.myspace.com

www.onlywire.com

http://reddit.com

www.ryze.com

www.secondlife.com

www.socialmediadaily.com

www.technorati.com

Web Site Design, Coding

www.edit.com

www.auditmypc.comfree-sitemap-generator.asp

www.chami.comhtml-kit/tour—Free editor

www.webreference.comdev/graphics/compress.html

www.techsmith.comscreen-capture.asp

www.sitesell.com

http://browsershots.org

http://typetester.maratz.com

www.webmastereyes.com

http://websitetips.comaccessibility/w3c

www.xsitepro.com

Web Tools

http://wordpress.org

www.webposition.com

www.contentcomposer.com

www.webceo.com

www.ibusinesspromoter.com

www.keywordelite.comindex1.htm

www.keywordsanalyzer.com

www.seoelite.comindex2.htm

www.windrosesoftware.com

Index